Contents

A Colour Guide to The Nursing Management of Wounds

Moya Morison, BSc, BA, MSc, RGN
Clinical Audit Coordinator
Stirling Royal Infirmary, UK

Wolfe Publishing Limited

Copyright © Moya Morison, 1992

Published by
Wolfe Publishing Limited
Brook House
2–16 Torrington Place
London WC1E 7LT

Printed by BPCC Hazells, Aylesbury, England

British Library Cataloguing in Publication Data
  Morison, Moya J.
  The nursing management of wounds
  (Clinical skills series)
  I. Title
  616.545

  ISBN 1 8700 6520 4

For full details of all Wolfe titles please write to
Wolfe Publishing Ltd, Brook House, 2–16 Torrington Place,
London WC1E 7LT, England.

Foreword

Although Moya Morison calls this book *A Colour Guide to The Nursing Management of Wounds*, I believe that practitioners of all disciplines would benefit from acquiring the knowledge and insights to wound care that the author obviously has. This is a most comprehensive and easy-to-use reference book for all those who deliver and manage clinical care in a wide variety of settings. The careful and rigorous literature search into the uses and abuses of antiseptic solutions for wounds will aid all those who wish to deliver responsible research-based practice, and shows how to influence our more backward colleagues of all disciplines. The emphasis on understanding the process of wound healing and, from this, being able to assess the stage at which the wound is, demonstrates how we all need this basic information before we can decide the correct treatment for the wound. Managers, too, will find the knowledge within this book vital if they are to deliver care that is cost-effective as well as of high quality. The information herein will enable the managerial process to facilitate practitioners in providing high-quality care by making sure that the high standards and tools are present; the greatest of these, of course, is knowledge.

The importance of recognising the cost implications of acquired infection becomes obvious to all when reading this chapter. The need for work in this field is more important than ever before. As the patient population is changing, there are more frail elderly and patients with compromised immune systems to cope with, as well as increased throughput and more resistant organisms to contend with. Wound care and all that goes with it should be high on everyone's agenda. All through the book the treatment plans are well researched, and it is the emphasis on prevention and the positive way the author deals with chronic wounds that is so welcome. Wounds are not discussed as an isolated aspect of care but as part of the whole. The importance of assessing and treating the whole person, as well as involving the patient in the care plan, means that intrinsic and extrinsic factors are considered together. This makes care much more effective, but also more satisfying to those giving the care.

Factors that affect pressure-sore prevention, avoiding amputations for diabetic foot ulcers, and ways of diagnosing potential leg ulcer formation are well addressed, making clear the potential we all have to improve the quality of life for so many people. Useful algorithms are given to aid the management of trauma and surgical wounds. The nurse's role in the management of wounds and the consequences of mismanagement are emphasised. The patient's psychosocial needs are never forgotten. The chapter on patient education and participation sees care as a partnership, whereby patients can be motivated to change their own behaviour. Each chapter has a comprehensive list of references and further reading, and the case studies are an interesting way of working out principles of wound management.

To increase the body of knowledge of wound care that practitioners have, of all disciplines, will have great influence in developing successful outcomes of care, as well as in improving the quality of care for so many people. All this needs is for practioners to absorb the contents of this book and apply the principles learned.

Miss P J Hibbs, OBE, BA, RGN, RHV, FRCN
Chief Nurse & Director of Quality Assurance,
City & Hackney Health Authority

Preface

My interest in wound care began when I was a student nurse. Training exposes students to many new experiences. The 'lay person' in me was shocked at the first sight and smell of a large infected pressure sore into which I could have placed my outstretched hand. The 'apprentice professional' in me wanted to know the principles behind treating the wound to alleviate such obvious suffering.

Any student nurse will tell you that there are many trained staff who do not like being asked questions! When, in the following year, I tentatively asked the more approachable staff for the rationale behind the dressings that they used, the replies helped me no nearer to establishing the principles that I was looking for. Reasons that I was given for choosing a dressing included: 'Sister likes it done this way', 'We had the dressing in the cupboard', 'It seemed to do the trick for Mrs Brown', and 'The representative came round last week and left us some samples to try'. Never during this time did any one of the representatives leave us any kind of form for evaluating the dressing's performance. How could we tell whether a wound was healing or regressing when a different nurse changed the dressing every day? If a wound did appear to be improving, was this because of, or in spite of, our best efforts?

In spite of the excellent advice that I would be buried under the weight of articles written on pressure sores, I chose this as the subject for my final year nursing degree dissertation. I very quickly learned that in spite of the large body of research on pressure sore prevention and treatment in the past 30 years, there seemed to be a very wide gulf between theory and practice. There was little evidence that the incidence of pressure sores in elderly and debilitated hospitalised patients had declined or that the treatment of pressure sores had become routinely based on sound scientific principles. Working on the dissertation gave me the marvellous opportunity to cull these principles from the vast body of available literature, and I developed a simple algorithm to help me to decide priorities in the local management of open wounds and the main treatment options. To my delight this was published as a wallchart, which I still see in treatment rooms and wards on my travels throughout the UK. I have updated the algorithm in this book (Chapter 3, *Figure 3.1*) to take account of the many new dressings that have come on the market since 1987, but the principles are largely unchanged.

This book has been written for health care professionals who, like me, want to have a rational, logical basis for wound management. The book includes chapters on related physiology and microbiology, patient assessment, cleansing agents, and dressings, as well as individual chapters or sections on the assessment and management of patients with particular types of wound. Strong emphasis is placed on accurate patient assessment, including: assessing local problems at the wound site, assessing the underlying cause of the wound and any pathophysiological factors that, if uncorrected, could delay healing, as well as assessing the possible consequences of the wound for the individual. A rational theoretical basis is given for deciding on the most appropriate treatment. The relationship between theory and practice is given at every stage, be it in the characteristics of compression bandages and how to apply them in the treatment of venous ulceration, in the properties of cleansing agents and dressings and the situations in which they are most beneficial, or in the principles behind the management of diabetic foot ulcers, or malignant, traumatic, or closed surgical wounds.

What this book is not, is a procedure manual. Each hospital or unit will have its own procedure manual and policies for aseptic dressing technique, the management of wound drains, and so on. The design of wound drains and dressings is changing very rapidly, and procedures should keep pace with these changes. Ritualistic adherence to procedures that were developed 40 years ago, in very different circumstances, blunts the nurse's problem-solving approach to handling today's wound-care products. However, the principles of asepsis and the prevention of avoidable infection do not change and it is these principles that are emphasised herein.

For similar reasons I have avoided giving rigid protocols for the management of local problems at the wound site, such as hard, black necrotic tissue or slough. The advantages and disadvantages of a range of current options are discussed, as is the importance of selecting a dressing regimen that suits the patient's wider needs. As new products appear on the market, these can be added as appropriate to the decision-making algorithm shown in *Figure 3.1*.

The responsibility for managing open wounds, especially chronic open wounds such as pressure sores and leg ulcers, is usually delegated to the nurse, whether in hospital or the community. The emphasis of this book is therefore on the nursing management of open wounds. The management of general surgical wounds is also given in some detail. It must be said that most surgeons take considerably more interest in the wounds that they have created than in chronic open wounds, and they will normally prescribe care of these wounds, often in considerable detail, up to and beyond the time of the patient's discharge from hospital. Surgeons differ widely in their surgical techniques, their use of prophylactic antibiotics and wound drains, and their preferences for particular wound dressings. A consensus on what constitutes 'good practice' can be difficult enough to arrive at within one hospital, or one department within one hospital, let alone throughout the UK, especially when it comes to the management of wounds in special sites and to the management of traumatic wounds, such as extensive burns. In any situation several different approaches may be equally valid, especially in the absence of carefully controlled comparisons of the effectiveness of different treatments. In the specialist fields of burns, plastic surgery, and so on, new techniques are continually being introduced. It is for all these reasons that I have decided not to enter into a detailed debate on the advantages and disadvantages of current practice in wound management in special sites, and have given, instead, specialist texts in the Further Reading sections. An understanding of the principles behind patient assessment, practical wound management, the observation for and prevention of infection, and factors affecting wound healing, as outlined in this book, will, nevertheless, help the nurse to be an effective team member in relation to wound care, even in a specialist setting.

Dedication

This book is dedicated to Graeme, Helen and Alastair, without whose tireless practical assistance and encouragement it would not have been possible.

Acknowledgements

This book has been made possible by the good will and encouragement of many people: my husband, Graeme, who proofread the material and assisted with the illustrations; my parents-in-law, Helen and Alastair, who spent many long hours typing the manuscript and its many revisions; my parents, Joy and Morris, who ensured that I received the education that has enabled me to embark on the project; the many staff of Stirling Royal Infirmary who reviewed the work informally and made many valuable comments; my tutors at Queen Margaret College who have broadened my perspectives on wound healing; and the patients from whom I learned so much. My sincere thanks.

I would also like to thank the following companies, organisations and individuals who supplied many of the illustrations used in this book:

Arjo-Mecanaids	*Colour Plate* **48**
Bache *et al., A Colour Atlas of Nursing Procedures in Accidents and Emergencies* (Wolfe Publishing Ltd)	*Colour Plates* **113–116**
Britcair	*Colour Plates* **1, 86**
Coloplast	*Colour Plates* **25, 26, 29, 87**
ConvaTec (UK)	*Colour Plates* **2, 4, 13, 39–43, 63, 85, 88, 99**
Dermatology Department, Slade Hospital, Oxford	*Colour Plates* **3, 23, 24, 61, 64, 77, 78**
Ethicon	*Figures 9.7, 9.11*
Huntleigh Health Care	*Colour Plates* **49, 51, 52, 57, 58**
Johnson and Johnson	*Colour Plates* **5–8, 19, 22, 94**
Kabi-Pharmacia	*Colour Plates* **15, 20, 21**
Lederle Laboratories	*Figure 3.2* *Colour Plates* **10–12**
Medi (UK)	*Colour Plates* **79, 80, 84**
Medical-Assist	*Colour Plates* **90, 91, 98**

Mediscus	*Colour Plate* **46**
Mills *et al., A Colour Atlas of Accidents and Emergencies* (Wolfe Publishing Ltd)	*Colour Plates* **9, 37, 38, 95, 97, 104, 105, 107–110, 120–122**
Molnlycke	*Colour Plate* **92**
Paraglide	*Colour Plates* **44, 47, 53**
Pegasus Airwave	*Colour Plate* **50**
Perstorp Pharma	*Colour Plates* **17, 18**
Raymar	*Colour Plates* **54, 55**
Ruckley C.V., *A Colour Atlas of Surgical Management of Venous Disease* (Wolfe Publishing Ltd)	*Colour Plates* **16, 62, 67, 81, 82**
Seton	*Colour Plates* **68–75, 112, 117–119**
Smith & Nephew	*Colour Plates* **14, 31, 34, 76, 93**
Spenco Medical (UK)	*Colour Plate* **56**
Steriseal	*Colour Plates* **30, 33, 36**
Stirling Royal Infirmary	*Colour Plates* **65, 66, 83**
Summit Medical	*Colour Plate* **89**
Support Systems International	*Colour Plates* **45, 59, 60**
Wellcome Foundation	*Colour Plates* **96, 101–103, 106**
3M Health Care	*Figure 9.6* *Colour Plates* **27, 28, 32, 35, 100, 111**
Mr Stan Dobranski, Bradford	*Colour Plate* **4**

1 The Physiology of Wound Healing

1.1 Introduction

The same basic biochemical and cellular processes are involved in the healing of all soft-tissue injuries, whether they are chronic ulcerative wounds, such as pressure sores and leg ulcers; traumatic wounds, such as lacerations, abrasions, and burns; or surgically made wounds.

The physiological processes can be divided into four main phases:

I *Acute inflammatory response to injury*: Involves haemostasis, the release of histamine and other mediators from damaged cells, and the migration of white blood cells (polymorphonuclear leucocytes and macrophages) to the damaged site.

II *Destructive phase*: Clearance of dead and devitalised tissue by polymorphs and macrophages.

III *Proliferative phase*: During which new blood vessels, supported by connective tissue, infiltrate the wound.

IV *Maturation phase*: Involves re-epithelialisation, wound contraction, and connective tissue reorganisation.

The main cellular and biochemical events in each phase are described in more detail in *Table 1.1*, which highlights the practical implications for wound management at each stage.

In reality, the phases of healing overlap and the duration of each phase and the time to complete healing depend on many factors, including the size and site of the wound, the patient's general physiological condition, and the helpfulness or otherwise of outside interventions aimed at promoting healing (*Figure 1.1*). These factors are discussed in more detail in Section 1.6.

1.2 Haemostasis

A number of mechanisms are involved in the natural arrest of bleeding (haemostasis). Damage to very large blood vessels often leads to fatal haemorrhage, unless the bleeding is stopped artificially by direct

Table 1.1 The physiology of wound healing and its implications for wound management

Phase and summary of physiological processes	Duration of phase	Implications for wound management
I ACUTE INFLAMMATORY RESPONSE TO INJURY *Haemostasis:* Temporary vasoconstriction of damaged blood vessels occurs while a platelet plug is formed and reinforced by fibrin fibres to form a clot. *Damaged tissue response:* Damaged tissue and mast cells release histamine and other mediators, causing vasodilation of surrounding intact blood vessels and increased blood supply to the area, which becomes red and warm. Permeability of blood capillaries increases and protein-rich fluid passes into the interstitial spaces, causing local oedema and perhaps loss of function over a joint. Polymorphonuclear leucocytes (polymorphs) and macrophages migrate out of the capillaries into the damaged area in response to chemotactic agents triggered by the injury.	0–3 days	This phase is an essential part of the healing process and no attempt should be made to damp it down, unless it occurs in a closed compartment where important structures may be compressed (e.g., burns to the neck). However, if it is prolonged by the continued presence of devitalised tissue, foreign bodies, excess slough, recurrent trauma, or by the injudicious use of topical wound preparations, such as antiseptics, antibiotics, or acid creams, healing is delayed and the wound's tensile strength remains low. The large number of cells attracted to the site compete for available nutrients. Too much inflammation can lead to excessive granulation in Phase III and to hypertrophic scarring. Discomfort due to oedema and throbbing at the wound site is also prolonged.
II DESTRUCTIVE PHASE *Clearance of dead or devitalised tissue and bacteria by* polymorphs and macrophages. The polymorphs engulf and destroy bacteria. High levels of polymorph activity are short lived and healing can proceed in their absence. However, healing ceases if the macrophages are deactivated. These cells are not only able to destroy bacteria and remove devitalised tissue and excess fibrin, but also they stimulate the formation of fibroblasts, which synthesise the structural protein collagen and produce a factor which stimulates angiogenesis (Phase III).	1–6 days	Polymorphs and macrophages are susceptible to a fall in temperature at the wound site, as can happen when a wet wound is left exposed, when their activity may fall to zero. Their activity can also be inhibited by chemical agents, by hypoxia, and by the build-up of metabolic wastes due to poor tissue perfusion.

III *PROLIFERATIVE PHASE* *Fibroblasts lay down ground substance and collagen fibres and new blood vessels start to infiltrate the wound.* As collagen is laid down there is a rapid increase in the tensile strength of the wound. Capillaries are formed by endothelial budding, a process called angiogenesis. The fibrin clot produced in Phase I is removed as the new capillaries provide the necessary enzymes. The signs of inflammation begin to subside. The tissue formed from the new capillary loops, supporting collagen and ground substance, is called granulation tissue because of its granular appearance. It is bright red.	3–24 days	The new capillary loops are numerous and very fragile and are easily damaged by rough handling, such as pulling off an adherent dressing. Vitamin C is essential for collagen synthesis. Without it, collagen synthesis ceases, the unsupported new blood capillaries break down and bleed, and wound healing ceases. Other systemic factors that delay healing at this stage include iron deficiency, hypoproteinaemia, and hypoxia. The proliferative phase proceeds more slowly with increasing age.
IV *MATURATION PHASE* *Epithelialisation, contraction, and connective tissue reorganisation:* In any injury involving skin loss, epithelial cells at the wound margins and from remnants of hair follicles, and sebaceous and sweat glands, divide and begin to migrate over the newly granulating tissue. Since they can only move over living tissue they pass under any eschar or drying dermis. When they meet other migrating epithelial cells, mitosis ceases, due to contact inhibition. Wound contraction is due to contractile myofibroblasts which help to bring the wound edges together. There is a progressive decrease in the vascularity of the scar tissue, which changes in appearance from dusky red to white. The collagen fibres are reorganised and the wound's tensile strength increases.	24–365 days	The wound is still very vulnerable to mechanical trauma (only 50% of the normal tensile strength of the skin is regained within the first three months). Epithelialisation occurs up to three times faster in a moist environment (under an occlusive or semipermeable dressing) than in a dry environment. Wound contraction is normally a helpful phenomenon, reducing the surface area of a wound and leaving a relatively small scar, but it proceeds poorly in certain areas, such as over the tibia, and can cause distortion of the features in facial injuries. Occasionally, fibrous tissue in the dermis becomes grossly hypertrophic, red, and raised, leading, in the extreme, to unsightly keloid scarring.

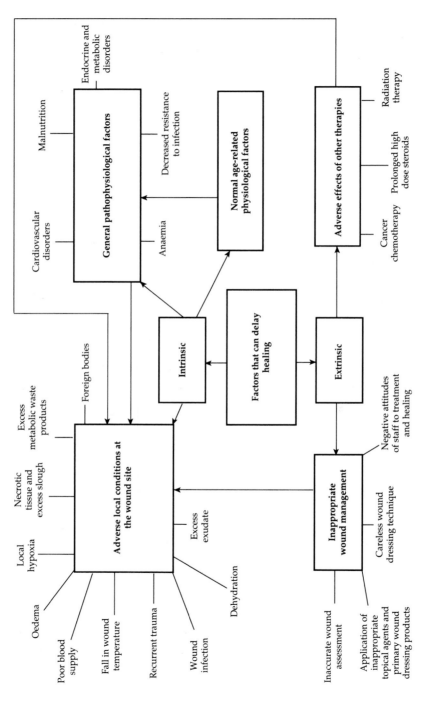

Figure 1.1. Factors that can cause delayed wound healing.

pressure, tourniquets, or ligatures. However, local trauma to arterioles and to smaller arteries severed transversely results in temporary constriction of the severed vessel ends. Platelets accumulate at the site of the damage and adhere to one another, forming a platelet plug. The blood vessels are lined with endothelial cells. However, damage to the vessel results in exposure of underlying collagen fibres. The contact of the platelets with the exposed collagen triggers the release of a number of platelet factors, including ADP, serotonin, and coagulation factor 3, which stimulate:

- Further platelet aggregation.
- Continued, but temporary, local vasoconstriction of the damaged vessel.
- A cascade of enzymatic reactions, which result in the platelet plug being reinforced with fibrin fibres (*Figure 1.2*).

The coagulation cascade (*Figure 1.2*) is, in fact, initiated in two ways: the intrinsic pathway just described, which is triggered by abnormalities in the blood vessel lining, and an extrinsic pathway triggered by tissue damage. The two pathways converge to activate factor X and the final common pathway results in the conversion of the inactive enzyme prothrombin into the active enzyme thrombin. It is thrombin that brings about the polymerisation of the soluble plasma protein fibrinogen into long strands of insoluble fibrin fibres, which reinforce the platelet plug.

The formation of fibrin requires calcium ions and the full complement of coagulation factors that lead to the activation of thrombin (*Figure 1.2*). Vitamin K is needed for the synthesis of some of these factors (II, VII, IX, and X) in the liver. Deficiency of vitamin K can lead to poor haemostasis. This is why vitamin K supplements may be given to patients thought to be deficient in the vitamin, prior to major surgery. Conversely, analogues of vitamin K, which competitively inhibit the synthesis of coagulation factors in the liver, can be used as antithrombotic drugs. A much faster, though short-acting agent, used in the prevention and treatment of unwanted thrombi, especially in the deep veins of the legs, is heparin. Its effect is to interfere with the coagulation cascade in several ways. Since its effects are shortlived, heparin must be given by regular injection (intravenous or subcutaneous) or by continuous infusion.

A coagulation factor may be deficient due to one of a number of inherited genetic defects, resulting in clotting defect disorders known collectively as haemophilia. The most common forms of haemophilia are due to deficiencies of factors VIII or IX. The genes involved are sex-linked recessive genes on the 'X' chromosome, which is why almost all haemophiliacs are males. The effects of a defective coagulation mechanism include the risk of major haemorrhage following even

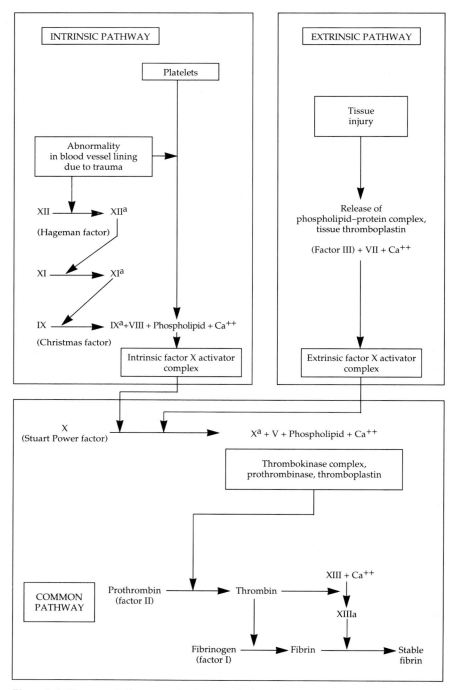

Figure 1.2. The coagulation cascade: the coagulation factors are given in roman numerals (superscript ^{a} indicates the factor has been converted into the active form). The stable insoluble fibrin fibres reinforce the platelet plug at the site of blood vessel injury.

minor trauma, including dentistry, and a tendency to internal bleeding from minor injuries, especially in the joints where blood vessels are continually being subjected to distortion.

Following normal haemostasis it is important not to disturb the blood clot formed. There is an adage: 'It takes two clots to make a haemorrhage, the clot on the vessel and the clot who knocks it off!' In an extreme case, prematurely dislodging a blood clot before fibroblasts have moved into the area and formed a permanent connective tissue seal can be fatal, as the following example illustrates. A major penetrating traumatic wound to the thorax may stabilise due to equalisation of the pressure in the damaged blood vessel as a result of accumulation of blood in the surrounding tissue spaces and a drop in systemic arterial pressure. By restoring blood volume and increasing blood pressure, an early blood transfusion can lead to detachment of the naturally formed haemostatic plug in the vessel, overcoming the local constriction of the blood vessel, and leading to fatal haemorrhage. Removing a knife or other penetrating object from a patient with a traumatic wound before the patient is in theatre can have similar fatal results. The active management of haemorrhage in both major and minor traumatic wounds is discussed in Chapter 11.

During surgery (Chapters 9 and 10), it is also normally necessary to manage haemorrhage artificially. Many methods are used, depending on the size of the blood vessels being divided and the vascularity of the organs involved. Methods include clamp and ligature of vessels, electrocoagulation, and occasionally the topical application of haemostatic agents in specialised sites.

The formation of a blood clot, reinforced by fibrin fibres, is an essential component of natural haemostasis, but fibrin formed within blood vessels is rapidly dissolved by a process called fibrinolysis. Fibrinolysis is essential to the maintenance of unimpeded blood flow throughout the body. A proteolytic enzyme called plasmin facilitates the conversion of insoluble fibrin fibres back to soluble fibrinogen. A whole range of factors can act as plasminogen activators:

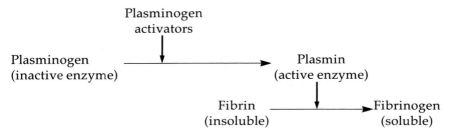

Therapeutically, the enzyme streptokinase can be given intravenously to patients with unwanted thromboses to facilitate the rapid dissolution of the clots.

1.3   Wounds that heal by primary intention

Where there is little tissue loss, as in a clean surgically made wound (Chapter 9), or a minor laceration whose edges are held together by skin tapes (Chapter 11), healing occurs by primary intention, that is by union of the two closely opposing wound edges (*Figure 1.3*). Very little granulation tissue is produced. Within 10–14 days, re-epithelialisation is normally complete, and usually only a thin scar remains, which rapidly fades from pink to white. However, it will take many months for the tissues to regain anything like their former tensile strength.

1.4   Wounds that heal by secondary intention

In open wounds, where there is significant tissue loss, healing is said to occur by *secondary intention*. Chronic open wounds, such as pressure sores (Chapter 6) and leg ulcers (Chapter 7), belong to this category, but so, too, do some surgically made wounds that are deliberately left open, such as newly drained abscesses or a laid-open pilonidal sinus (Chapter 10).

Granulation tissue, composed of new blood capillaries supported by connective tissue, develops in the base of the wound (*Figure 1.4*) and epithelial cells migrate towards the centre of the wound's surface from the margins, and from islands of epithelial tissue associated with hair follicles, sebaceous glands, and sweat glands. The surface area of the wound becomes smaller by a process known as contraction and the connective tissue is reorganised to give tissue that gains in strength with time.

At first the scar tissue is red and indurated. In time, the induration and redness usually lessen and eventually disappear to leave a soft scar, paler than the surrounding skin. This sequence of events is not, however, invariable. Fibrous tissue in the dermis may become grossly hypertrophic, red, and raised.

A more florid reaction is keloid scarring. In a keloid scar the tissue is grossly elevated, tends to spread, involving the surrounding normal skin, and may feel hot, tender, and itchy. Keloid scarring is more common in black- than white-skinned patients. Certain areas have a higher risk of producing keloid scars than do others, notably the presternal and deltoid areas, and vertical scars of the neck.

1.5   Skin grafts and flaps

Major tissue defects may be repaired surgically, using skin grafts or flaps.

A skin graft is a segment of epidermis and dermis separated from its blood supply and transferred to another part of the body.

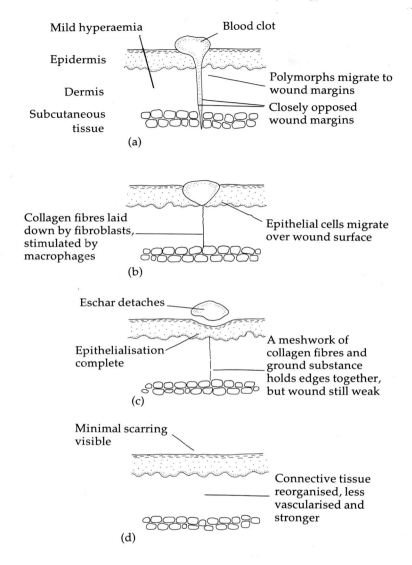

Figure 1.3. Wound healing by primary intention, such as a surgically closed wound or minor laceration closed with skin tapes. (a) Immediately, (b) 2–3 days later, (c) 10–14 days later, (d) 1 year later.

A whole-skin graft consists of the epidermis and the full thickness of dermis, while a split-skin graft consists of epidermis and a variable quantity of dermis. The translucency of the graft is the main indicator of its thickness, a very thin graft being translucent and not unlike tissue paper. Thicker grafts are increasingly opaque. The thickness of the graft

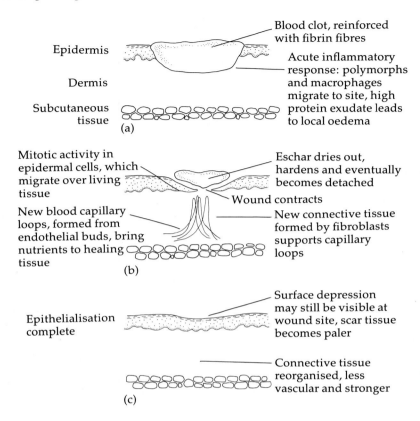

Epidermis

Dermis

Subcutaneous
tissue

(a)

Blood clot, reinforced
with fibrin fibres

Acute inflammatory
response: polymorphs
and macrophages
migrate to site, high
protein exudate leads
to local oedema

Mitotic activity in
epidermal cells, which
migrate over living
tissue

New blood capillary
loops, formed from
endothelial buds, bring
nutrients to healing
tissue

(b)

Eschar dries out,
hardens and eventually
becomes detached

Wound contracts

New connective tissue
formed by fibroblasts
supports capillary
loops

Epithelialisation
complete

Surface depression
may still be visible at
wound site, scar tissue
becomes paler

Connective tissue
reorganised, less
vascular and stronger

(c)

Figure 1.4. Wound healing by secondary intention. (a) 0–3 days, (b) 1 week later, (c) 6 months later.

has certain practical implications for healing, both for the donor and the recipient site, as indicated in *Table 10.2*. The actual healing process has some points of difference from the mechanisms described so far for healing by primary and secondary intention. The graft initially receives its nutritional requirements by diffusion from the plasma exuding from the recipient bed. The precise mechanisms of re-vascularisation are uncertain, but it is thought that capillary buds from the recipient bed rapidly unite with the cut capillaries on the deep surface of the graft. Fibroblasts infiltrate the area and produce fibrous tissue, which strengthens the attachment of the raw surfaces. In a healthy graft, capillary link-up is well under way by the third day and within 4 days the graft is usually sufficiently well anchored by fibrous tissue to be safely handled. Successful 'take' *depends* upon the rapid development of a new blood supply. Grafts fail because of:

- Inadequate blood supply in the recipient area.
- Haematoma, which prevents vascular link-up and increases the risk of infection.
- Shearing forces, which cause the graft to move, severing newly joined vessels.
- Infection, especially by *Streptococcus pyogenes* (beta haemolytic Streptococcus) and *Pseudomonas aeruginosa*.

Flaps differ from grafts in that both skin and subcutaneous tissue (with varying degrees of blood supply) are transferred from one site to another, usually without being completely detached from the donor site.

Flaps are named according to the tissue transferred, thus a skin flap consists of skin and superficial fascia, and a myocutaneous flap consists of muscle and the skin that overlays it. Although most flaps retain a vascular attachment to the body, a 'free' flap is occasionally used when the donor tissue is particularly well vascularised and the blood vessels can be anastomosed to suitable vessels in the recipient site.

A particularly readable review of the types of flap used to reconstruct a very wide range of primary defects is given by McGregor (1989). The secondary defect created by the transfer is usually closed by direct suture or covered with a free skin graft.

The use of flaps in the repair of excised pressure sores is illustrated in Chapter 6. The successful 'take' of a flap depends upon preventing vascular insufficiency, which can lead to necrosis, and upon the prevention of haematoma, which prevents vascular link-up between the flap and the bed, and increases the risk of infection.

1.6 Factors that can delay healing

Many factors can delay wound healing. These can be divided into patient-related (intrinsic) factors, such as adverse conditions at the wound site, and a number of medical conditions that can lead to a poor local environment for healing, and outside (extrinsic) factors, such as inappropriate wound management and the adverse effects of other therapies (*Figure 1.1*).

Overcoming the adverse effects of all these factors is required for optimum healing. This is a theme that will be returned to many times, in different circumstances, throughout this book.

1.6.1 Adverse local factors at the wound site
Adverse local factors at the wound site that can delay healing include hypoxia, dehydration, excess exudate, fall in temperature, necrotic tissue, excess slough, the presence of foreign materials, and recurrent trauma.

Poor blood supply and the effects of hypoxia   Wounds with a poor blood supply heal slowly. If factors essential to healing, such as oxygen, amino acids, vitamins and minerals, are slow to reach the wound because of impaired vasculature, healing is delayed, even in a well-nourished patient.

Some areas of the body, such as the face, have a good blood supply, which is hard to compromise, while other areas, such as the skin overlying the tibia, are poorly supplied with blood, so minimal trauma here can lead to intractable leg ulcers in some patients.

The growing edge of a wound is an area of high metabolic activity (Niinikoski, 1980). Hypoxia here inhibits mitosis in migrating epithelial cells and fibroblasts, collagen synthesis, and the ability of macrophages to destroy ingested bacteria (Silver, 1980). However, when the partial pressure of oxygen at the wound site is low, macrophages produce a factor that stimulates angiogenesis. By stimulating the growth of new blood capillaries, the local problem of hypoxia may be overcome (Cherry and Ryan, 1985). The paramount importance of the rapid re-establishment of an adequate blood supply to the 'take' of skin grafts and to the success of tissue flaps is described in Section 1.5.

Dehydration   If an open wound is exposed to the air the surface layers dry out. Epithelial cells at the wound margins move downwards, beneath these layers, until they reach moist conditions that favour mitosis and migration of the cells across the damaged surface (Silver, 1980). The long-term result of letting a wound dry out is more pronounced tissue loss and scarring, and delayed healing (Turner, 1985). If a wound is kept moist, under a semipermeable or occlusive dressing, healing occurs much more rapidly (Winter, 1978). There are, however, a few occasions when exposure of a wound may be the only practical solution, as in facial burns.

Excess exudate   There is a delicate balance between the need for a moist wound environment and the need to remove excess exudate that can result in sloughing of tissue. Exotoxins and cell debris present in the exudate retard healing by perpetuating the inflammatory response.

Fall in temperature   Phagocytic and mitotic activity are particularly susceptible to a fall in temperature at the wound site. Below about 28°C leucocyte activity can fall to zero (Myers, 1982). Long exposure of wet wounds during dressing changes, or while waiting for the doctor's round, can reduce the surface temperature to as low as 12°C. Recovery of the tissue to body temperature and full mitotic activity may take up to 3 hours (Turner, 1982).

Necrotic tissue, excess slough, and foreign bodies   The presence of necrotic tissue and excess slough at a wound site delays healing and increases the risk of a clinical infection developing. So, too, does the presence of any foreign body (Burke, 1980), including suture materials and wound drains. It is therefore important to remove organic and inorganic contaminants as quickly as possible but with the minimum of trauma to the intact tissues.

Haematoma   Where a wound has been surgically closed, whether by primary suture, skin grafting, or a transposed flap of tissue, a significant cause of delayed healing is the development of a haematoma. A haematoma can cause complications in several ways:

- It provides an excellent culture medium for micro-organisms, which might otherwise merely be commensal, increasing the risk of clinical infection and wound breakdown.
- It increases the tension on the wound.
- It acts as a foreign body, which can lead to excessive fibrosis and scar tissue.
- By preventing the rapid vascular link-up between the raw surfaces, it can cause skin graft and flap failure.

Recurrent trauma   In an open wound, mechanical trauma can easily damage highly vascular granulation tissue and delicate, newly formed epithelium and can cause the wound to revert to the acute inflammatory response phase of healing (*Table 1.1*).

Recurrent trauma can be caused in many ways. If a patient with a pressure sore is placed on the sore while in bed or in a chair, then the forces of pressure, shearing, and friction, which led to the breakdown of the overlying skin, will inevitably damage the even more delicate healing tissues, and the wound will enlarge. Trauma can also be caused by the careless removal of an adherent dressing. Even when the greatest care is taken, some trauma to the wound is probable if gauze is applied directly to its surface, as blood capillary loops grow through the mesh of cotton fibres and are torn off when the dressing is removed. Many supposedly low-adherent dressings can adhere to a wound if left in place too long, especially if strike-through of exudate occurs and the wound dries out. Bleeding of a wound on removal of a dressing is an obvious sign of trauma.

1.6.2   General pathophysiological factors

A number of medical conditions are associated with poor wound healing (*Table 1.2*). The mechanisms by which these conditions affect repair are often complex, but many delay healing by reducing the availability, at the wound site, of substances required for the healing processes, such as oxygen, amino acids, vitamins, and minerals.

Table 1.2 Some medical conditions associated with poor wound healing (Westaby, 1985, p.19)*

Poor nutritional state	Cardiovascular disorders
Malignancy	Arteriosclerosis
Inflammatory bowel diseases	Diabetes
Hepatic failure	Peripheral vascular disease
Vitamin deficiency (especially vitamins A and C)	Congestive cardiac failure
Mineral deficiency (especially iron and zinc)	
Anaemia	Respiratory disorders
Iron deficiency anaemia	
Pernicious anaemia	
Aplastic anaemia	
Haemolytic anaemia	
Haemorrhagic anaemia	
Decreased resistance to infection	Miscellaneous
Immune disorders	Cushing's disease
Diabetes	Addison's disease
Chronic infection	Rheumatoid arthritis
	Uraemia

* Many of these conditions affect repair through more than one mechanism.

Reduced oxygen supply   The adverse local effects of poor blood supply and hypoxia at the wound site are described in Section 1.6.1. Oxygen plays a critical role in the formation of collagen, new capillaries, and epithelial repair, as well as in the control of infection (La Van and Hunt, 1990). The amount of oxygen delivered to a wound depends on the partial pressure of oxygen in the blood, the degree of tissue perfusion, and the total blood volume.

The oxygen demands at a wound site are high. Reduced oxygen supply to the wound can be caused by:

- *Respiratory disorders*: reduced efficiency of gaseous exchange in the lungs, for whatever cause, can lead to a reduced partial pressure of oxygen (pO_2) in the blood and therefore reduced availability of oxygen to the tissues.
- *Cardiovascular disorders*: these can reduce the degree of tissue perfusion. This is especially significant where the peripheral circulation is compromised, as in diabetes mellitus where there is micro-angiopathy and in rheumatoid arthritis where there is arteritis, or

where there are damaged valves in the deep and perforating veins leading to chronic venous hypertension and local oedema.

- *Anaemia*: whatever the cause of the anaemia there is a reduction in the blood's oxygen-carrying capacity. This is particularly significant when associated with hypovolaemia following haemorrhage.
- *Haemorrhage*: to maintain adequate blood pressure and blood supply to the heart, brain, and other vital organs, peripheral vasoconstriction can accompany major haemorrhage. The degree of peripheral shutdown will depend upon the severity of the blood loss. Reduced peripheral blood supply leads to delayed healing until the blood volume is restored. This is normally a temporary phenomenon, but tissue necrosis can occur during this time.

Malnutrition   Whether a wound is traumatic, surgically made, or a chronic open wound, such as a pressure sore, one of the commonest causes of delayed healing is malnutrition.

Some studies of the incidence of malnutrition in patients in long-stay hospitals for the elderly, the mentally handicapped, and the mentally ill suggest that vitamin and mineral deficiencies are not uncommon in these vulnerable groups, but problems of poor nutritional status are not confined to long-stay patients. Hill *et al.* (1977) found that about 30% of surgical patients had evidence of malnutrition. The causes and extent of malnutrition in hospital patients are reviewed by Dickerson (1990).

A patient's protein and calorie requirements are likely to be higher than normal when a major wound is present (Kinney, 1980a, b). Amino acids are required for the synthesis of structural proteins such as collagen and for synthesising the proteins involved in the immune response. In the early stages following a major wound, various endocrine and nervous system responses to injury trigger catabolic processes that break down the body's own tissues to supply the materials required for urgent repair processes (Fleck, 1988). Patients with severe burns or trauma can suffer from dramatic muscle wasting and rapid weight loss within a few days. Protein, calorie, electrolyte, and fluid replacement are vital components of early treatment. Even in chronic open wounds such as pressure sores significant amounts of protein can be lost in the exudate (Bobel, 1987). Assessing a patient's nutritional status is an important part of overall patient assessment (Chapter 2).

Protein deficiency not only delays healing; it also results in healed wounds with diminished tensile strength (Steiger *et al.*, 1983). This can lead to dehiscence in an obese patient with a laparotomy wound or rapid breakdown of a newly healed pressure sore following even minor trauma.

Sufficient intake and absorption of certain vitamins and minerals is also required for optimum healing. Vitamin C is required for collagen synthesis. Scurvy is regarded as an uncommon phenomenon today, but sadly many elderly people show the early signs of vitamin C deficiency, whether through poverty, the difficulty of getting to the shops or the difficulty in eating fresh fruit and vegetables due to ill-fitting dentures.

Decreased resistance to infection   Decreased resistance to infection, as seen for example in patients with immune disorders, diabetes, or a chronic infection, delays healing, owing to reduced efficiency of the immune system. Chronic infection also results in catabolism and depletion of the protein pool, and is an ever-present source of endogenous wound infection (see Chapter 5).

1.6.3   *The physiological effects of the normal ageing processes*
There are significant differences in the structure and characteristics of skin across the life span which, coupled with normal age-associated physiological changes in other body systems, can affect predisposition to injury and the efficiency of the wound-healing mechanisms. Some of these differences and their clinical implications are discussed chronologically, beginning with the preterm infant.

Problems resulting from a defective skin barrier in the mature neonate are rare, but the preterm baby has a much less effective skin barrier system and the skin is very susceptible to trauma, due to a thin, poorly developed stratum corneum and to epidermal–dermal instability. This has important implications for many aspects of the nursing care of preterm babies (Gavin, 1990), including:

- The selection and use of soap, and bath frequency.
- The use of topical agents, such as antiseptics, steroid creams, and emollients, which may be excessively absorbed percutaneously.
- The prevention of pressure necrosis, especially on the occiput.
- The choice of methods for securing equipment and appliances. It is particularly important not to attach equipment to preterm babies with tapes that contain strong adhesives, as considerable epidermal damage can result on their removal.

Because of the relative incompetence of their immune system, preterm babies are particularly vulnerable to infection, including infection of the umbilical stump by gram-negative organisms and *Staph. aureus, Candida* infections, and infections that involve coagulase negative staphylococci, which would normally merely colonise the skin.

The skin of the full-term neonate is much more robust and less prone to infection, as the stratum corneum and dermis are much thicker than in the preterm baby and the immune system is more developed. Although the skin is virtually sterile at birth, colonisation occurs rapidly and within 6 weeks the infant's skin has a microbial flora comparable to that of an adult. The dermis increases in thickness during years 1–3 and doubles in thickness during years 4–7.

Intact skin in a healthy young adult is a good barrier to mechanical trauma and to infection, and the efficiency of the immune, cardiovascular, and respiratory systems means that wound healing is likely to be rapid. The different body systems 'age' at different rates, but over the age of 30 there begins to be a significant decline in some functions, such as reduced cardiac efficiency, vital capacity, and immune system efficiency, which in part contribute to longer healing times with increasing age. There are also significant, normal, age-associated changes in the skin that predispose to injuries such as pressure sores and to poor wound healing. Changes that worsen with increasing age include decreases in: epidermal cell replacement rate, inflammatory response to injury, sensory perception, mechanical protection, and barrier functions of the skin. Coupled to this is the increased frequency of age-associated pathological disorders, which can delay wound healing through many mechanisms (Section 1.6.2). Arterial disease and the development of chronic venous hypertension in the lower limb predispose to leg ulceration. Chronic sun damage increases the risk of skin cancer, and nutritional deficiencies, so common in the elderly, delay healing. Recognition of the increased vulnerability of the elderly to tissue damage is reflected in many risk-assessment scoring systems for pressure sores (Section 6.3), but whether sufficient recognition of the age-related phenomena just described is reflected in the planning and implementation of nursing care in general is a vexed question.

1.6.4 Psychosocial factors

Some of the psychosocial factors that may affect healing are shown in *Figure 1.5*. The closeness of the relationship between mind and body is being increasingly recognised. It has been demonstrated, for instance, that when patients are anxious the efficiency of their immune system is reduced and they are physiologically less able to deal with any pathological disturbances (Maier and Laudenslager, 1985).

Conversely, in a placebo study of a pressure sore treatment, Fernie and Dornan (1976) showed that positive attitudes of staff to the treatment had a highly significant part to play in healing.

1.6.5 Adverse effects of other therapies

Cytotoxic drugs, radiotherapy, and in some circumstances steroid therapy, can delay wound healing. Cytotoxic drugs such as vincristine have the most marked effect on wound healing as they interfere with cell proliferation. Prolonged steroid therapy can also delay healing, but only during the inflammatory and proliferative phases, by suppressing the multiplication of fibroblasts and collagen synthesis. Non-steroidal anti-inflammatory drugs appear to have a negligible effect on wound healing in normal therapeutic doses (Westaby, 1985).

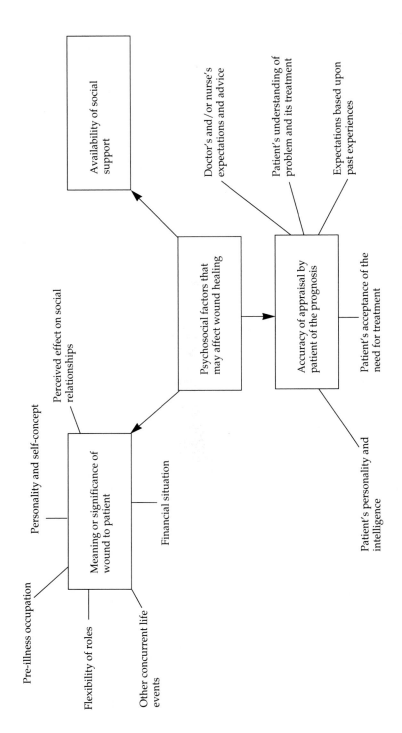

Figure 1.5. Psychosocial factors that may affect wound healing and recovery from illness (from Wilson-Barnett and Fordham, 1982).

Table 1.3   Inappropriate wound management

- Failure to *assess* a wound accurately and to *identify problems* that may be causing delayed healing
- Careless wound dressing *technique*
- Selection of *inappropriate or harmful* wound care *products*
- Changing the dressing regime before it has had time to be effective
- Failure to *chart healing* and to *evaluate* the effectiveness of a treatment regime
- Negative attitudes to healing

Radiotherapy, when used in the treatment of malignant disease, can produce local damage, can retard healing and can cause long-term weakness in tissues, especially in skin (Irvin, 1981). It may cause loss of vascularity and skin ulceration in extreme cases.

1.6.6   Inappropriate wound management

Failure to identify the underlying cause of a wound or to identify local problems at the wound site, the injudicious use of antiseptics, topical antibiotics, and other wound care preparations, and careless wound dressing technique are just some of the avoidable causes of delayed healing due to inappropriate wound management (*Table 1.3*). Patient assessment is discussed in Chapter 2. Guidance on the selection of the most appropriate primary dressings and wound cleansing agents is given in Chapters 3 and 4. Subsequent chapters are concerned with the assessment and treatment of particular types of wound.

Further reading

The physiology of wound healing

Fleck, A. (1988), Metabolic response to injury. In Ledingham, I. and MacKay, C. (eds), *Textbook of Surgical Physiology* (4th edn), pp. 55–65. Churchill Livingstone, Edinburgh.

Hirsch, J. and Kelton, J.G. (1984), Haemostasis and thrombosis. In Campbell, E.J.M. *et al.* (eds), *Clinical Physiology* (5th edn), pp. 290–309. Blackwell Scientific Publications, Oxford.

Hunt, T.K. and Van Winkle (1979), Normal repair. In Hunt, T.K. *et al.* (eds), *Fundamentals of Wound Management*, pp. 2–67. Appleton-Century Crofts, New York.

Irvin, T.T. (1981), *Wound Healing: Principles and Practice*, pp. 1–33. Chapman and Hall, London.

Physiology of wound healing in special tissues: tendon, bone, blood vessels, and nerves

Heppenstall, R.B. (1979), Fracture and cartilage repair. In Hunt, T.K. *et al.* (eds.), *Fundamentals of Wound Management*, pp. 524–551. Appleton-Century Crofts, New York.

Ketchum, L.D. (1979), Peripheral nerve repair. In Hunt, T.K. *et al.* (eds), *Fundamentals of Wound Management*, pp. 459–475. Appleton-Century Crofts, New York.

Ketchum, L.D. (1979), Tendon healing. In Hunt, T.K. *et al.* (eds), *Fundamentals of Wound Management*, pp. 500–523. Appleton-Century Crofts, New York.

Moore, W.S. and Malone, J.M. (1979), Vascular repair. In Hunt, T.K. *et al.* (eds), *Fundamentals of Wound Management*, pp. 476–499. Appleton-Century Crofts, New York.

References

Bobel, L.M. (1987), Nutritional implications in the patient with pressure sores. *Nurs. Clin. N. Am.*, **22**, 379–390.

Burke, J.F. (1980), The physiology of wound infection. In Hunt, T.K. (ed.), *Wound Healing and Wound Infection: Theory and Surgical Practice*, pp. 242–247. Appleton-Century Crofts, New York.

Cherry, G.W. and Ryan, T.J. (1985), Enhanced wound angiogenesis with a new hydrocolloid dressing. In Ryan, T.J. (ed.), *An Environment for Healing: the Role of Occlusion*, pp. 61–68. Royal Society of Medicine International Congress and Symposium Series (No. 88), London.

Dickerson, J.W.T. (1990), Hospital induced malnutrition: a cause for concern. In *The Staff Nurse's Survival Guide*, pp. 169–174. The Professional Developments Series, Austen Cornish, London.

Fernie, G.R. and Dornan, J. (1976), The problems of clinical trials with new systems for preventing or healing decubiti. In Kenedi, R.M. *et al.* (eds), *Bedsore Biomechanics*, pp. 315–320. Macmillan, London.

Fleck, A. (1988), Metabolic responses to injury. In Ledingham, I. and MacKay, C. (eds), *Textbook of Surgical Physiology* (4th edn), pp. 55–65. Churchill Livingstone, Edinburgh.

Gavin, G. (1990), Skin care considerations in the neonate for the ET nurse. *J. Enterostom. Ther.*, **17**, 225–230.

Hill, G.L., Blackett, R.L., Pickford, I. *et al.* (1977), Malnutrition in surgical patients: an unrecognised problem. *Lancet*, **i**, 689.

Irvin, T.T. (1981), *Wound Healing: Principles and Practice*. Chapman and Hall, London.

Kinney, J.M. (1980a), Catabolic influences in injury and sepsis. In Karran, S.J. and Alberti, K.G. (eds), *Practical Nutritional Support*, pp. 33–43. Pitman Medical, London.

Kinney, J.M. (1980b) Calorie and nitrogen requirements in catabolic states. In Karran, S.J. and Alberti, K.G. (eds), *Practical Nutritional Support*, pp. 81–93. Pitman Medical, London.

La Van, F. and Hunt, T.K. (1990), Oxygen and wound healing. *Clin. Plastic Surg.*, **3**, 463–472.

Maier, S.F. and Laudenslager, M. (1985), Stress and health: exploring the links. *Psychology Today*, **19**(8), 44–49.

McGregor, I.A. (1989), *Fundamental Techniques of Plastic Surgery and Their Surgical Applications*. Churchill Livingstone, Edinburgh.

Myers, J.A. (1982), Wound healing and the use of a modern surgical dressing. *The Pharmaceutical Journal*, **229**, 103–104.

Niinikoski, J. (1980), The effect of blood and oxygen supply on the biochemistry of repair. In Hunt, T.K. *et al.* (eds), *Fundamentals of Wound Management*, pp. 56–70. Appleton-Century Crofts, New York.

Silver, I.A. (1980), The physiology of wound healing. In Hunt, T.K. *et al.* (eds), *Fundamentals of Wound Management*, pp. 11–28. Appleton-Century Crofts, New York.

Steiger, *et al.* (1983), Post-operative intravenous nutrition: effects of body weight, protein regeneration, wound healing and liver morphology. *Surgery,* **73**(5), 686–691.

Turner, T.D. (1982), Synthaderm—an environmental dressing. *The Pharmaceutical Journal,* **228**, 206–208.

Turner, T.D. (1985), Which dressing and why? In Westaby, S. (ed.) *Wound Care,* pp. 58–69. Heinemann Medical Books, London.

Westaby, S. (ed.) (1985), *Wound Care*. Heinemann Medical Books, London.

Wilson-Barnett, J. and Fordham, M. (1982), *Recovery from Illness*. John Wiley, Chichester.

Winter, G.D. (1978), Wound healing. *Nursing Mirror,* **146**(10), (Supplement), pp. i–viii.

2 Patient Assessment

2.1 The four levels of patient assessment

The review of the physiology of wound healing in Chapter 1 high-lighted the wide variety of factors that can influence the rate at which wounds heal, including many medical conditions, adverse effects of other therapies, psychosocial factors, and adverse local conditions at the wound site. Before assessing the local conditions at the wound site it is therefore important to assess the patient as a whole to identify the wider problems that might have an adverse effect on the healing processes.

Assessment can be thought of on four levels, namely assessment of:

- *General patient factors* that could delay healing.
- *Immediate causes* of the wound and any *underlying pathophysiology*.
- *Local conditions* at the wound site.
- Potential *consequences* of the wound for the individual.

2.2 General patient assessment

2.2.1 General assessment

It is important to begin any assessment with a general assessment of the patient as a whole. Any such assessment of the patient should include assessment and documentation of, general physical condition, self-care abilities, skin appearance, mobility, nutritional status, continence, sensory functioning, cardiovascular status, respiratory function, presence or absence of pain, conscious state and mental alertness, emotional state, understanding of the current condition, current medication, allergies, and social circumstances.

Several different approaches to general patient assessment are reflected in the references given in the Further Reading section of Chapter 2. A more detailed account of the assessment of nutritional status, pain, and psychosocial factors is given below, because of their particular

Table 2.1 Nutritional assessment: common indices of protein/calorie malnutrition (Moghissi and Boore, 1983)

Method and parameters measured	*Indices of protein calorie malnutrition*
1. Anthropometry	
a. weight for height and sex[a]	< 60% of predicted ideal value
b. recent weight loss (percentage weight change)	> 10%[b]
c. triceps skinfold thickness (measure of body fat stores)	< 10 mm in males < 13 mm in females
d. mid upper arm muscle circumference (indirect measure of skeletal muscle mass and protein reserves)[c]	< 19 cm in males < 17 cm in females
2. Biochemical methods	
e.g., serum albumin[d]	< 35 g/100 ml
3. Blood cell count	
Lymphatic count	$< 1500 \times 10^6/l$
4. 24-hour urine tests	
a. Creatinine: height index	< 70% of normal value
b. Nitrogen excretion (combined with an accurate measure of dietary nitrogen intake)	nitrogen intake < nitrogen lost, i.e. negative nitrogen balance
5. Clinical examination	
6. Dietary history on admission	

Notes:
[a] Body weight values are meaningless in dehydrated patients or in those with fluid retention.
[b] Important evidence of protein/calorie malnutrition.
[c] Misleading in oedematous patients.
[d] The usefulness of this index in sick patients has been questioned (O'Keefe and Dicker, 1988; Dickerson, 1990).

significance to all wound healing. The importance of wider issues, such as mobility, continence, and cardiovascular status, will be addressed for particular types of wounds in later chapters.

2.2.2 Nutritional status

Malnutrition is a very important cause of delayed wound healing. A number of indicators of protein/calorie malnutrition are given in *Table 2.1*. The concurrent measurement of at least three variables is desirable (Goodinson, 1986). The importance of *closely* monitoring weight and other indicators of malnutrition in patients with severe injuries, following major surgery, and where septicaemia is present, is emphasised by Kinney (1980). Seek the dietician's advice if malnutrition is suspected.

2.2.3 Pain

Pain is a common and often underestimated problem for patients with wounds. Inadequately managed pain can lead to a vicious circle of muscle tension, fatigue, anxiety, and depression, which can delay healing by depressing the effectiveness of the immune system (Maier and Laudenslager, 1985).

Although undesirable and generally preventable, acute pain following major surgery does at least have a positive physiological function, acting as a warning that particular care must be taken to prevent further trauma to the area. Pain following surgery is normally of a predictable finite duration, lessening over time as natural repair to damaged tissue proceeds. By contrast, for a patient suffering with chronic pain, such as that associated with a fungating carcinoma, or for a patient with severe peripheral vascular disease and an ischaemic ulcer in the lower limb, pain serves no useful function and tissue healing may be an unrealistic goal.

Pain is a complex phenomenon that is influenced only in part by the degree of tissue injury or disease. There are many accounts of soldiers having sustained very severe traumatic injury and yet reporting little or no pain, while at the other extreme there are patients who experience intense pain in the absence of any identifiable organic cause. Patients' perceptions of pain are influenced by factors such as the meaning of the pain to them (Waugh, 1990), which is influenced in turn by social and cultural factors, personality, and current psychological state. Patients with cancer pain are faced with the possibility of imminent death. The uncertainty, fear, fatigue, and depression that can accompany terminal illness lowers the patient's pain threshold, increasing the perceived pain and the need for analgesia (Bond, 1984).

It is the complexity of the factors affecting pain perception and the inherent lack of absolute, objective measures of pain that make pain assessment so difficult. McCaffery's (1983) definition of pain is a useful starting point for pain assessment: 'Pain is what the patient says it is and exists when he says it does.' The assessment charts for open wounds (*Figure 2.1*) and closed wounds (see *Figure 9.9*) encourage the nurse to record the site of any pain, its frequency, and the patient's perception of its severity on a 0–10 scale. Possible causes of pain at the wound site and at dressing changes are summarised in *Table 2.2*, which suggests factors that may require further assessment and the evaluation of practice.

More sophisticated methods for assessing and documenting pain and the factors that relieve it, suitable for patients with chronic, intractable wound pain, include the King's College Hospital Pain Clinic Chart, the McGill Pain Questionnaire, and the London Hospital Pain Observation Chart. The use of these methods is reviewed by Latham (1990).

OPEN WOUND ASSESSMENT CHART

Type of wound (e.g. pressure sore, fungating carcinoma, etc.) ....

Location ....

How long has wound been open? ....

General patient factors which may delay healing (e.g. malnourished, diabetic, chronic infection) ....
....

Allergies to wound care products...

Previous treatments tried (comment on success/problems) ....

Special aids in current use (e.g. pressure-relieving bed, cushion)...
....
....

TRACE THE WOUND WEEKLY, ANNOTATING TRACING WITH NATURE OF WOUND BED, ORIENTATION OF WOUND, POSITION/EXTENT OF SINUSES, AND UNDERMINING OF SURROUNDING SKIN

All other parameters should be assessed at **every** dressing change.

Wound factors/Date									
1. **NATURE OF WOUND BED** a. healthy granulation b. epithelialization c. slough d. black/brown necrotic tissue e. other (specify)									
2. **EXUDATE** a. colour b. type c. approximate amount									
3. **ODOUR** Offensive/some/none									
4. **PAIN (SITE)** a. at wound site b. elsewhere (specify)									
5. **PAIN (FREQUENCY)** Continuous/intermittent/ only at dressing changes/none									
6. **PAIN (SEVERITY)** Patient's score (0–10)									
7. **WOUND MARGIN** a. colour b. oedematous									
8. **ERYTHEMA OF SURROUNDING SKIN** a. present b. max. distance from wound (mm)									
9. **GENERAL CONDITION OF SURROUNDING SKIN** (e.g. dry eczema)									
10. **INFECTION** a. suspected b. wound swab sent c. confimed (specify organism)									

WOUND ASSESSED BY:

Figure 2.1. Open wound assessment chart.

Table 2.2   Possible causes of pain at the wound site and at dressing changes

If the patient complains of pain at the wound site or experiences pain at dressing changes, the nurse should consider the following questions:

A. *Pain at the wound site*
1. *Is the wound infected?* Look for other local and systemic signs and symptoms of clinical infection (Chapter 5).
2. *Is any overlying conforming or compression bandage too tightly applied?* Has the bandage slipped? Are there tight bands of constriction overlying the wound or over any nearby bony prominence?
3. *Is there underlying ischaemia?* For example, in a patient with severe peripheral vascular disease even small open wounds can be very painful and there may be rest pain in the limb (see Chapter 7).

B. *Pain at dressing changes*
1. *Is the dressing adhering, causing tissue trauma on removal?* Even low-adherent dressings can adhere to the wound if they are left in place for too long, especially if exudate strikes through the dressing and then dries out. Fresh bleeding on dressing removal is an obvious sign of trauma.
2. *Has any prescribed analgesia been given in sufficient time to be effective* where it is anticipated that a dressing change may be painful?
3. *Is the most painless method of dressing removal being employed?* Removal of adhesive dressings or the tapes used to hold a dressing in place can be very painful if removal is against the lie of any hair present. Removing dressings and tapes in line with the hairs is virtually painless. If a dressing has adhered to the wound bed it should be gently soaked off, not ripped off 'quickly'.
4. *Is a cleansing solution being used that could be causing an irritant tissue response*, such as a hypochlorite? (See Chapter 4.)
5. *Is the nurse lacking in empathy?* Is the nurse underestimating the significance of the wound to the individual? (See Sections 1.6 and 2.2.3.)

2.2.4   Psychosocial factors

The significance of the mind–body relationship to healing was described in Section 1.6.4. *Table 2.3* is a useful checklist for identifying some of the positive and negative psychosocial factors that can facilitate or delay recovery from any illness and which may be significant to wound healing, and to the patient's ability and willingness to comply with and facilitate treatment.

2.3   Assessing the cause of the wound

Identifying the immediate cause of a wound and, where possible, any underlying pathophysiology, is a prerequisite to planning appropriate care and to preventing recurrence of the wound in the longer term. The following examples make this clear.

The primary cause of most pressure sores is usually unrelieved pressure, often accompanied by friction and shearing forces (Chapter

Table 2.3 Positive and negative psychosocial factors which can affect recovery from any illness

Positive factors	Negative factors
Good knowledge of illness/condition	Unwilling or unable to know about illness/condition
Active participation in treatment	Lack of belief in, and unwillingness to participate in, treatment
Good relationships with staff	Poor relationships with staff
Flexible coping methods	Passive dependence, persistent denial, or highly emotional disposition
Good supportive social relationships	Poor family relationships, living alone
Positive orientation to treatment and rehabilitation from members of the health care team (hospital and/or community)	Negative attitudes of staff to treatment and healing
	Additional recent life stress, e.g. bereavement, separation, loss of employment

6). Sensory loss associated with a cerebrovascular accident, paraplegia, multiple sclerosis, or diabetes may contribute to the development of a pressure sore and must be considered when planning immediate care and pressure sore prevention in the future. In the case of a leg ulcer, the immediate cause may be a minor traumatic injury, but the underlying problem is usually vascular (Chapter 7). If the underlying problem is not addressed, wound healing is unlikely. A foot ulcer in a diabetic patient may have been directly caused by ill-fitting footwear but slow healing may be due in part to micro-angiopathy (Chapter 8). Management of the diabetes and its side-effects is at least as important as choosing the best wound dressing to promote healing.

If the cause of any wounds and any underlying pathophysiology are ignored, treatment will merely be directed at alleviating the symptoms of the problem. Even if the wound does heal, there is a high probability that it will recur, whether the wound is a leg ulcer, a pressure sore, or a self-inflicted injury.

2.4 Local wound assessment and problem identification

After assessing the patient as a whole, the immediate cause of the wound, and any underlying pathophysiology, it is important to make an accurate assessment of the wound itself, in order to identify any local factors that might delay healing, such as necrotic tissue, excess slough, infection, or excess exudate (*Colour Plates* **1–4**). Accurate and ongoing wound assessment is essential to planning appropriate local wound management (Chapter 3) and to evaluating its effectiveness. It is also important to be able to recognise when healing is progressing well; that is, being able to recognise healthy granulation tissue and epithelialisation (*Colour Plates* **5–7**).

Charting observations makes them more accessible to other nurses and can help to develop the observational skills of students by highlighting the points that should be noticed. Two wound assessment charts are included in this book to aid accurate recording of the most important parameters. The first (*Figure 2.1*) is for open wounds that heal by secondary intention. This includes chronic wounds, such as pressure sores and leg ulcers, and surgically made open wounds, such as drained abscesses and excised pilonidal sinuses. The second chart (see *Figure 9.9*) is for closed wounds that heal by primary intention. The parameters recorded give a good indication of whether the wound is healthy or unhealthy, and whether healing is progressing well or with obvious delay.

2.4.1 Open wounds

Change in the wound surface area is a useful indicator of healing. Several methods for recording this accurately have been developed (see Eriksson *et al.*, 1979; Bohannon and Pfaller, 1983; Anthony, 1985; Bulstrode *et al.*, 1986). These methods use sophisticated equipment, but this level of accuracy is required only for clinical dressing trials. Some of these methods are costly and time consuming, and some can only cope with flat or saucer-shaped wounds. Many cannot be used to measure the undermining of tissue, which is a common phenomenon in chronic open wounds. A much simpler method is to trace the wound using a clear glove or acetate sheet and a fine permanent marker pen. The tracing can then be transferred to the nursing notes and annotated to include the nature of the wound bed; the extent of undermining of the surrounding skin; and the position of the wound relative to other structures. An example of a simple annotated tracing is given in *Figure 2.2*. Tracings can be shown to patients, which is particularly important where the wound is so sited that it cannot be seen by the patient, as in the case of a sacral pressure sore, or when the patient needs extra encouragement to participate fully in the treatment programme. It

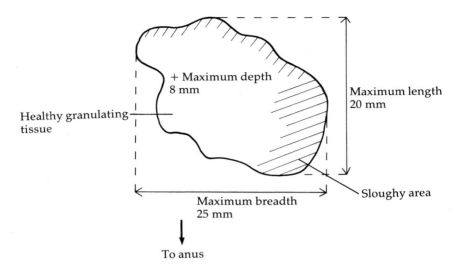

Figure 2.2. Example of a tracing of a sacral pressure sore. The maximum dimensions can be recorded separately on the wound assessment chart (Figure 2.1).

should be noted that in the initial stages of healing it is quite normal for a wound to enlarge as devitalised tissue is removed.

A method for determining the volume of a wound using an alginate dental impression material has been described by Resch *et al.* (1988). This can be used in clinical trials to evaluate the effectiveness of a treatment of a deep wound, as the surface area of the wound may not reduce significantly until the late stages of healthy healing. If Silastic Foam is used in the management of the wound the stents can be kept and compared and will be seen by the patient to be getting smaller as healing progresses (see *Colour Plate* **103**).

A crude estimate of the depth of a wound can be gained using two sterile probes. One probe is placed into the wound, perpendicular to the wound surface, and the distance to the other probe, placed across the wound surface, is measured.

Other parameters to record include the nature of any exudate, pain, odour, and erythema of the surrounding skin, as these parameters can indicate clinical infection (Chapter 5). They may also be distressing for the patient, and should be taken into account when selecting a wound dressing (Chapter 3). If pain is a problem, the cause of the pain should be sought (*Table 2.2*).

It is also worth recording the general condition of the skin surrounding the wound. This is so often neglected and yet may be a problem in itself, especially if the patient presents with extensive wet or dry eczema (*Colour Plate* 8), psoriasis, or a papery thin skin that is very susceptible to trauma.

2.4.2 Surgically closed wounds

It is important to identify infection as quickly as possible. Events in the operating theatre have an important bearing on whether a wound infection develops later (Chapter 9). In a closed wound, the only sign of infection, at first, may be spreading erythema, perhaps accompanied by pain, oedema, and an elevated body temperature (Section 9.4.2). Wound breakdown can be dramatic, but there are usually signs of problems developing long before dehiscence occurs. It can be useful to trace wounds where there is spreading erythema and to document observations of the wound systematically (see *Figure 9.9*).

2.5 Assessing the consequences of the wound

The cause of a wound has a direct bearing on the patient's feelings about it and its likely physical, social, and emotional consequences.

A young, otherwise fit, woman who requires a Caesarean section for the safe delivery of her child will suffer short-term discomfort, but the degree of discomfort is lessened by its association with a happy event, the birth of the baby. Often the wound is planned, and the long-term consequences are generally not serious.

By contrast, a young, otherwise fit, man who loses his leg following a motorcycle accident not only suffers considerable physical pain in the short term but also has to face the long-term effects of physical disability, with perhaps loss of job, loss of self-esteem, altered body image, altered social relationships, and restricted recreational opportunities.

The consequences of a wound can be broken down into:

- *Physical consequences*: Loss of function, scarring, chronic pain.
- *Emotional consequences*: Altered body image, problems with social relationships, sexual problems.
- *Social consequences*: Failure to perform certain social roles, such as carer or employee, or restriction of activities within these roles.

The nature of the problem is related not only to the type of wound and its site but also to the person's level of social support, economic independence, personality, and personal philosophy (see *Figure 1.5*).

The short- and long-term rehabilitation of patients, both physical and psychological, requires planning and sensitivity. Sympathetic counselling, involving the patient and his or her family, is an integral part of patient care from the outset (Chapter 12) and begins with assessing the patient's knowledge, cognitive abilities, and needs.

Further reading

General patient assessment

Brunner, L.S. and Suddarth, D.S. (1990), *The Lippincott Manual of Medical-Surgical Nursing* (2nd edn). Harper and Row, London.

Game, C., Anderson, R.E. and Kidd, J.R. (eds) (1989), *Medical-Surgical Nursing: a Core Text*. Churchill Livingstone, Melbourne.

Morton, P.C. (1990), *Health Assessment in Nursing*. Springhouse, Pennsylvania.

Roper, N., Logan, W. and Tierney, A. (1985), *The Elements of Nursing* (2nd edn). Churchill Livingstone, Edinburgh.

See also Chapters 6–11 for further reading on the assessment of patients with particular types of wound.

Nutrition and nutritional assessment

Burtis, G., Davis, J. and Martin, S. (1988), *Applied Nutrition and Diet Therapy*. W.B. Saunders, Philadelphia.

Huskisson (1985), *Applied Nutrition and Dietetics*. Current Nursing Practice Series, Baillière Tindall, London.

Karran, S.J. and Alberti, K.G. (1980). *Practical Nutritional Support*. Pitman Medical, London.

Taylor, S. and Goodinson-McLaren, S.M. (1992), *Nutritional Support: A team approach*. Wolfe Publishing, London.

Pain and pain assessment

McCaffery, M. (1983), *Nursing the Patient in Pain*. Harper and Row, London.

McCaffrey, M. and Beebe, A.(1989), *Pain: clinical manual for nursing practice*. C.V. Mosby, St Louis.

The consequences of the wound for the individual

David, J.A. (1986), The long-term effects of wounds. In *Wound Management: a Comprehensive Guide to Dressing and Healing*, pp. 170–177. Martin Dunitz, London.

Murray-Parks, C. (1975), Reaction to loss of a limb. *Nursing Mirror*, **140**(1), 36–40.

See also Chapter 12, Further Reading section, Patient Education and Counselling.

References

Anthony, D. (1985), Measuring pressure sores. *Nursing Times*, **81**(22), 57–61.

Bohannon, R.W. and Pfaller, B.A. (1983), Documentation of wound surface area from tracings of wound perimeters: clinical report on three techniques. *Physical Therapy*, **63**(10), 1622–1624.

Bond, M.R. (1984), *Pain: Its Nature, Analysis and Treatment*. Churchill Livingstone, Edinburgh.

Bulstrode, C.J.K., Good, A.W. and Scott, P.J. (1986), Stereophotogrammetry for measuring rates of cutaneous healing: a comparison with conventional techniques. *Clinical Science*, **71**, 437–443.

Dickerson, J.W.T. (1990), Hospital induced malnutrition: prevention and treatment. In *The Staff Nurse's Survival Guide*, pp. 175–178. The Professional Developments Series, Austen Cornish, London.

Eriksson, G., Eklund, A.E., Torlegard, K. *et al.* (1979), Evaluation of leg ulcer treatment with stereophotogrammetry. *Br. J. Dermatology*, **101**(2), 123–131.

Goodinson, S.M. (1986), Assessment of nutritional status. *Nursing*, **3**(7), 252–257.

Kinney, J.M. (1980), Catabolic influences in injury and sepsis. In Karran, S.J. and Alberti, K.G. (eds), *Practical Nutritional Support*, pp. 33–43. Pitman Medical, London.

Latham, J. (1990), Assessment, observation and measurement of pain. In *The Staff Nurse's Survival Guide*, pp. 179–185. The Professional Developments Series, Austen Cornish, London.

McCaffery, M. (1983), *Nursing the Patient in Pain*. Harper and Row, London.

Maier, S.F. and Laudenslager, M. (1985), Stress and health: exploring the links. *Psychology Today*, **19**(8), 44–49.

Moghissi, K. and Boore, J. (1983), *Parenteral and Enteral Nutrition for Nurses*. Heinemann Medical Books, London.

O'Keefe, S.J.D. and Dicker, J. (1988), Is plasma albumin concentration useful in the assessment of nutritional status in hospital patients? *European Journal of Clinical Nutrition*, **42**, 41–45.

Resch, C.S. *et al.* (1988), Pressure sore volume measurement, a technique to document and record wound healing. *J. Am. Geriat. Soc.*, **36**, 444–446.

Waugh, L. (1990), Psychological aspects of cancer pain. In *The Staff Nurse's Survival Guide*, pp. 194–201. The Professional Developments Series, Austen Cornish, London.

3 Priorities in Wound Management: Which Dressing?

3.1 The aim of local wound management

The cellular events involved in the four main phases of wound healing, as described in Chapter 1, are significantly affected by many factors, including the local conditions at the wound site, the patient's general physiological state, and the way the wound is managed (see *Figure 1.1*). The adverse local effects of poor blood supply, dehydration, excess exudate, fall in temperature, recurrent trauma, necrotic tissue, slough, and foreign bodies are discussed in Section 1.6.

> The aim of local wound management is to provide the optimum environment for the natural healing processes to take place.

What are the main priorities?

3.2 Priorities in local wound management

Priorities in the local management of wounds are essentially the same whatever the wound, namely: controlling bleeding (haemostasis); removing foreign bodies, which could act as foci for infection; removing devitalised tissue, thick slough, and pus; providing optimum temperature, humidity, and pH for the cells involved in the healing processes; promoting the formation of granulation tissue and epithelialisation; and protecting the wound from further trauma and from the entry of potentially pathogenic micro-organisms. The aims are to protect the individual from further physiological damage, to remove actual and potential causes of delayed healing, and to create an optimum local environment for vascular and connective tissue reconstruction and epithelialisation. This often necessitates covering a wound with a dressing.

3.3   The ideal dressing

Where skin is damaged a dressing is usually required to protect the underlying tissues from further damage and to take over temporarily many of the functions of intact skin. Characteristics of the ideal dressing are given in *Table 3.1*.

The problem of dressing selection   The problem today is that there is such a bewildering variety of dressings to choose from. No single dressing is suitable for all wounds; it is necessary to select the dressing that is most suited to the individual patient's needs. This requires assessment not only of the local conditions at the wound site (Section 2.4) but also of the patient's life style and where and by whom the wound will be re-dressed. Detailed knowledge is needed of the characteristics, uses, contraindications, and precautions for a wide range of dressings, if the most *appropriate* dressing is to be chosen.

The problem of choice is complicated by several factors:

- Products that *look* alike may have significantly different physical and chemical properties.
- Manufacturers may recommend *different types* of products for tackling the *same problem*; for example, hydrocolloid dressings, hydrogels, enzymatic preparations, acid creams, and chlorinated solutions have all been recommended at one time or another as means of removing thick slough.
- *Extensive, comparative clinical trials* on the uses of different wound management products in humans are relatively scarce.
- The effect of *therapeutic traditions*, strongly held by people in positions of influence, makes it difficult for others working in the same domain to use new products.
- There can be a *blurring of responsibility* for wound management between medical, nursing, and paramedical staff.
- The *economics* of wound management are complex—many newer dressings have relatively high unit costs but require changing less frequently than traditional dressings. They can therefore be more cost-effective and convenient for patients.
- New products are coming on the market all the time.

The value of a wound management policy   In an attempt to overcome the problems outlined above, many health authorities in the United Kingdom are developing *wound management policies*. Development of a policy is normally undertaken by the local drugs and therapeutics committee, who may set up a working party to advise them. On the working party there should be representatives from all members of the health care team who have responsibility for wound management.

Table 3.1 Characteristics of the ideal wound dressing

Non-adherent.
Impermeable to bacteria.
Capable of maintaining a high humidity at the wound site while removing
  excess exudate.
Thermally insulating.
Non-toxic and non-allergenic.
Comfortable and conformable.
Capable of protecting the wound from further trauma.
Requires infrequent dressing changes.
Cost-effective.
Long shelf life.
Available both in hospital and in the community.

The working party may be charged with drawing up a list of products to be routinely stocked by pharmacies, monitoring product use, and developing a continuing education programme to keep all those involved in prescribing up to date with new products and the latest research findings. The practicalities of setting up a policy are described by Morgan (1990a, b). Thomas (1990) has reviewed the main categories of wound dressings and their uses, providing a valuable reference when drawing up a policy.

The responsibility of individual prescribers   Whether or not a hospital or unit has a list of recommended wound care products the individual prescriber still has the final responsibility when it comes to dressing selection:

> **Before using any wound care product,**
> **ALWAYS consult the manufacturer's recommendations,**
> **contraindications, precautions, and warnings.**

This information can change, so it is worth re-reading the manufacturer's instructions at frequent intervals. If there is still any doubt about the suitability of a dressing, the doctor should be consulted or further advice obtained from the local pharmacist.

The section that follows gives a rationale for dressing selection based on the priorities outlined in Section 3.2.

An algorithm has been devised as an aid to teaching students the priorities in the management of open wounds (*Figure 3.1*). It summarises the main treatment options and gives some examples of each, based on the personal experience of the author. This algorithm is not intended to be fully comprehensive or exclusive and as new products appear on the market, it can be augmented.

In the United Kingdom, not all the wound dressings mentioned are available to patients whose wounds are being managed in the community. The GP is allowed to prescribe from a restricted list of products on the Drug Tariff. The number of products listed on the Drug Tariff is steadily increasing, but even when a dressing is available the number of sizes may be restricted (Bale, 1989). This can pose problems for the community nurse, and does not facilitate continuity of care when patients are transferred from hospital to the community.

3.4 Creating the optimum environment for healing

This section expands on the priorities for wound management listed in Section 3.2 and highlighted in the algorithm given in *Figure 3.1*. The following subsection headings are related directly to the relevant question in the algorithm where appropriate.

3.4.1 Haemostasis

Controlling bleeding is the first priority in wound management, but outside the Accident and Emergency Department or the GP's treatment room this is rarely a problem encountered by nurses. Methods of controlling bleeding in newly made skin graft donor sites are discussed in Chapter 10. Haemostasis, including the management of major haemorrhage in traumatic wounds, is discussed in detail in Chapter 11. In terminally ill patients with fragile open wounds—for example, patients with fragile, fungating breast carcinomas that bleed readily— haemostasis can generally be achieved by using alginate dressings, such as Kaltostat.

3.4.2 Removal of foreign bodies

Foreign bodies can act as a focus of infection in traumatic wounds, and methods of removing them are described in Chapter 11. Removing foreign bodies, such as non-absorbable sutures, that are inadvertently left in wounds is discussed in Section 8.4. The effects of leaving skin sutures and drains *in situ* for longer than is therapeutically required is discussed in Chapter 9.

3.4.3 Removing dead and devitalised tissue

The presence of necrotic tissue delays healing and promotes infection, and often hides the true extent of tissue damage. Surgical débridement under a general or local anaesthetic is the most rapid method of obtaining a clean wound bed (*Colour Plate 9*); it may not be appropriate for elderly or debilitated patients, however, where another method must be sought.

Figure 3.1. Algorithm summarising local treatment options for open wounds, such as pressure sores, leg and foot ulcers. The examples quoted are based on the personal experience of the author and are not to be regarded as an exhaustive or exclusive list of options. (See Section 3.4.)

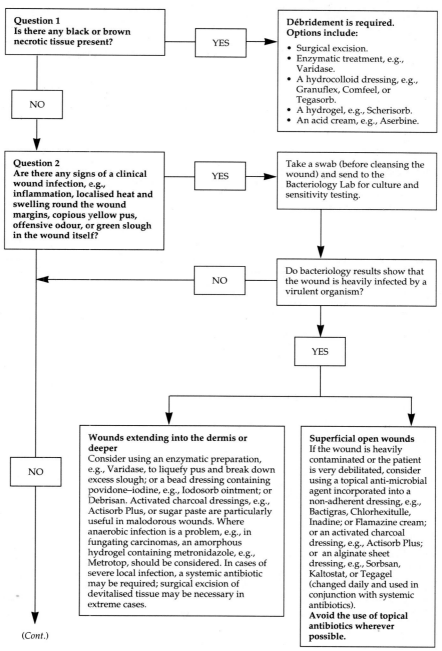

Question 1
Is there any black or brown necrotic tissue present?

YES

NO

Débridement is required.
Options include:

- Surgical excision.
- Enzymatic treatment, e.g., Varidase.
- A hydrocolloid dressing, e.g., Granuflex, Comfeel, or Tegasorb.
- A hydrogel, e.g., Scherisorb.
- An acid cream, e.g., Aserbine.

Question 2
Are there any signs of a clinical wound infection, e.g., inflammation, localised heat and swelling round the wound margins, copious yellow pus, offensive odour, or green slough in the wound itself?

YES

Take a swab (before cleansing the wound) and send to the Bacteriology Lab for culture and sensitivity testing.

NO

Do bacteriology results show that the wound is heavily infected by a virulent organism?

YES

NO

Wounds extending into the dermis or deeper
Consider using an enzymatic preparation, e.g., Varidase, to liquefy pus and break down excess slough; or a bead dressing containing povidone–iodine, e.g., Iodosorb ointment; or Debrisan. Activated charcoal dressings, e.g., Actisorb Plus, or sugar paste are particularly useful in malodorous wounds. Where anaerobic infection is a problem, e.g., in fungating carcinomas, an amorphous hydrogel containing metronidazole, e.g., Metrotop, should be considered. In cases of severe local infection, a systemic antibiotic may be required; surgical excision of devitalised tissue may be necessary in extreme cases.

Superficial open wounds
If the wound is heavily contaminated or the patient is very debilitated, consider using a topical anti-microbial agent incorporated into a non-adherent dressing, e.g., Bactigras, Chlorhexitulle, Inadine; or Flamazine cream; or an activated charcoal dressing, e.g., Actisorb Plus; or an alginate sheet dressing, e.g., Sorbsan, Kaltostat, or Tegagel (changed daily and used in conjunction with systemic antibiotics).
Avoid the use of topical antibiotics wherever possible.

(Cont.)

37

Figure 3.1 (cont.).

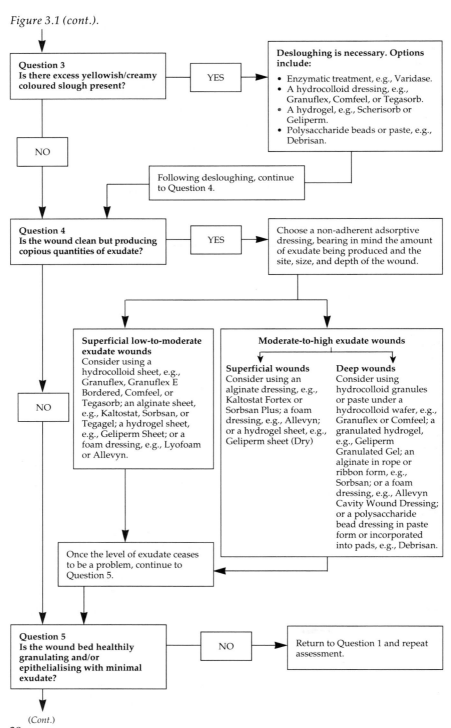

Figure 3.1 (cont.).

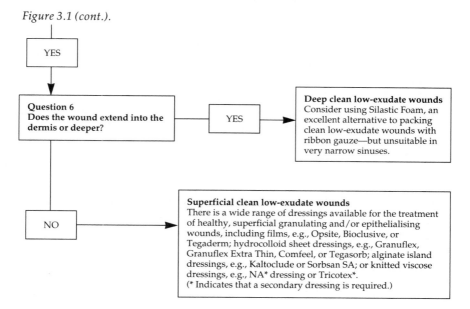

YES

Question 6
Does the wound extend into the dermis or deeper?

YES

Deep clean low-exudate wounds
Consider using Silastic Foam, an excellent alternative to packing clean low-exudate wounds with ribbon gauze—but unsuitable in very narrow sinuses.

NO

Superficial clean low-exudate wounds
There is a wide range of dressings available for the treatment of healthy, superficial granulating and/or epithelialising wounds, including films, e.g., Opsite, Bioclusive, or Tegaderm; hydrocolloid sheet dressings, e.g., Granuflex, Granuflex Extra Thin, Comfeel, or Tegasorb; alginate island dressings, e.g., Kaltoclude or Sorbsan SA; or knitted viscose dressings, e.g., NA* dressing or Tricotex*.
(* Indicates that a secondary dressing is required.)

In all cases
Your choice will be affected by:

- The site of the wound and the ease or otherwise of applying the dressing.
- The size of the wound.
- The frequency of dressing changes required.
- Comfort and cosmetic considerations.
- Where and by whom the dressing will be changed.
- The availability of the dressing in the size required—not all dressings are available to patients whose wounds are being managed in the community, and where a dressing is available on the community Drug Tariff it may not be available in all sizes.

Where all other considerations are equal, choose the **cheapest** dressing.

If in doubt about the suitability of a dressing for a particular situation, consult the manufacturer's instructions, the hospital or community pharmacist, and the patient's doctor.

Hard black or brown necrotic tissue (Question 1, *Figure 3.1*)   If the necrotic tissue is in the form of hard dry black or brown material, it should be rehydrated and conditions created that favour the body's natural debriding processes.

One effective treatment option is to use an enzymatic preparation, such as Varidase (*Colour Plates* **10–12**). This contains two enzyme systems that degrade fibrin fibres found in hard black necrotic material and in slough. The enzymes also liquefy pus and free white blood cells to phagocytose bacteria. Varidase can be made up in sterile saline and applied with gauze packing or made up with sterile water and mixed with sterile K-Y jelly. A film dressing can be used as a secondary dressing, provided the surrounding skin is not fragile. Alternatively, a low-adherent secondary dressing can be used to help to retain moisture at the wound site. If the manufacturer's instructions are carefully followed, Varidase can be injected under the necrotic tissue, causing it to separate rapidly (*Figure 3.2*).

Another approach is to use a hydrocolloid dressing, such as Granu-flex, or an amorphous hydrogel, such as Scherisorb Gel, covered with a semipermeable film or low-adherent secondary dressing. These dress-ings rehydrate the necrotic tissue and create conditions that encourage the body's natural debriding processes, without traumatising the tissue in the wound bed or damaging the surrounding skin. A hydrocolloid wafer, cut to shape, is particularly suitable for dressing awkwardly sited necrotic wounds, such as those on heels, and can often be left in place for several days. The Granuflex E bordered dressings come in a variety of shapes and sizes. A triangular dressing suitable for sacral pressure sores is illustrated in *Colour Plate* **13**. Hydrogels can easily be applied to large deep cavities containing necrotic material (*Colour Plate* **14**).

Acid creams, such as Aserbine, are effective debriding agents and do not harm viable tissue, but care is required to protect the surrounding skin from possible irritation and maceration.

Hypochlorite agents, such as Eusol, are not effective against hard necrotic material. Their disadvantages are considerable and are sum-marised in Chapter 4.

Thick slough (Question 3, *Figure 3.1*)   Any of the methods suggested for the removal of hard black necrotic tissue can be used to remove thick slough. Another approach, suitable in *moist* wounds, is to use polysac-charide beads or paste, such as Debrisan (*Colour Plate* **15**).

A saline soak, covered by a semipermeable film, is one of the simplest and least-expensive methods of removing slough if the other options are not available, but is unlikely to cause such rapid débridement as the use of a 'biologically active' treatment, e.g. Varidase.

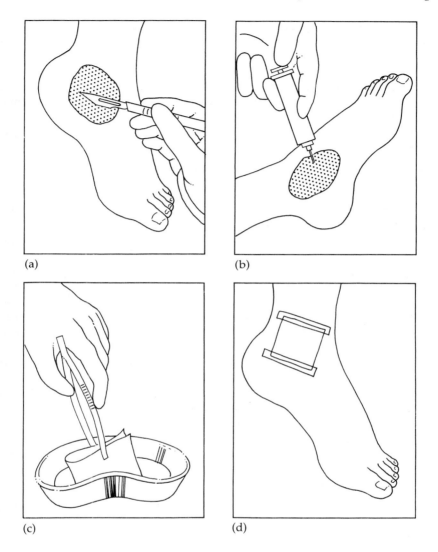

(a)

(b)

(c)

(d)

Figure 3.2. Methods of applying an enzymatic preparation, such as Varidase, to wounds with hard black necrotic material: (a) the hard black necrotic material can first be scored with a scalpel or (b) Varidase solution can be gently injected under the necrotic tissue. (c) Gauze can be soaked in Varidase, made up in sterile saline and (d) the gauze applied to the necrotic area and covered with a secondary dressing to aid rehydration.

3.4.4 Managing infected wounds (Question 2, Figure 3.1)

Most chronic open wounds are heavily colonised by micro-organisms that do not appear to delay the healing process. It is, therefore, only necessary to take a wound swab to identify micro-organisms and to determine their antibiotic sensitivity if a wound is showing the *clinical signs and symptoms of infection*, such as localised pain and erythema, local oedema, excess exudate, pus, and offensive odour (Chapter 5).

Many factors should be considered when deciding on the most appropriate management of a clinically infected wound:

- *How debilitated is the patient?* Is the patient's immune system likely to be able to deal with the infection with minimal outside assistance or is the effectiveness of the patient's immune system depressed by disease, by chemotherapy, or by another chronic infection?
- *How virulent is the organism?* Is it likely to spread systemically and cause widespread damage or are its effects localised?
- *How vulnerable are the other patients in the ward to infection?* Is source isolation necessary? (Chapter 5).

A systemic antibiotic may be prescribed by the physician if the patient is suffering from cellulitis (*Colour Plate* 16), a life-threatening infection, or is severely immunocompromised. The routine use of topical antibiotics is to be discouraged, as their injudicious use can encourage the emergence of multiple antibiotic-resistant strains of bacteria and their topical use can lead to local sensitivity reactions.

The body's natural immune system can normally cope with infection if it is not suppressed or disordered (Chapter 5), but it is, nevertheless, helpful to tip the balance in favour of the body's own mechanisms; for example, by removing the products of infected tissue, such as slough and pus, as described in the previous section. Improving the patient's nutritional status is also a high priority.

The local management of post-operative infection in surgical wounds is discussed in detail in Chapter 9. The rest of this section is concerned with the nursing management of open infected wounds, such as leg ulcers and pressure sores.

In severely debilitated patients or where the wound is dirty and obviously contaminated, an antiseptic-containing dressing may be indicated. The characteristics of the ideal antiseptic are given in Chapter 4. Povidone–iodine and chlorhexidine have a broad spectrum of activity. Iodosorb ointment, which contains povidone–iodine, is useful for treating deep infected wounds (*Colour Plates* 17, 18). Superficial infected traumatic wounds can be dressed with a simple non-adherent dressing, such as Inadine (*Colour Plate* 19), which contains povidone–iodine, or Bactigras, which contains chlorhexidine. With increasing evidence that many antiseptics delay parts of the healing process, the use of antiseptic preparations should be carefully considered.

Gross fungal infection of open wounds is unusual, except in very debilitated patients. The patient shown in *Colour Plates* **20, 21** developed an extensive secondary infection with a pin mould, following major trauma. The mould was successfully treated with Debrisan. There is a range of other antifungal treatments from which the doctor can choose, according to the organism involved and the patient's general physical condition.

Dressing malodorous wounds Malodorous wounds can be very distressing for patients, leading to self-imposed social isolation, loss of appetite, and depression. Treating the infection that leads to the malodorous exudate will eventually remove the odour, but in the interim an activated charcoal dressing, such as Actisorb Plus, can be an effective deodoriser (*Colour Plate* **22**); the silver in the dressing is bacteriostatic. If there is a moderate amount of exudate present, an absorbent foam dressing with a charcoal backing, such as Lyofoam C, may be appropriate. A gel containing metronidazole may be prescribed to help control odour in fungating wounds and in cases where there is severe anaerobic infection. Sugar pastes are regaining popularity in the management of infected and malodorous wounds; they are inexpensive and lack the toxicity of many antiseptics (Middleton, 1990).

While the infection, which is normally the cause of the odour, is being tackled, other simple remedies should not be forgotten, such as changing bed linen as soon as it becomes contaminated by leaking exudate, changing the dressing if strike-through of exudate occurs, offering the patient the option of a single room if this is possible, providing fresh air, using perfumes and, perhaps, aromatherapy, and encouraging relatives who understand the problem to bring in scented plants. There is more to providing the ideal environment for healing than choosing the most appropriate wound dressing.

3.4.5 *Managing high-exudate wounds* (Question 4, Figure 3.1)

Even when necrotic and obviously infected tissue has been removed from the wound bed, the wound may still produce copious volumes of exudate that can strike through non-occlusive dressings and increase the risk of wound infection. The exudate can also macerate the wound margins if the surrounding tissues become waterlogged.

The volume of exudate should lessen in time, but until this stage is reached an absorbent, non-adherent dressing is needed. As with all wounds, the choice of dressing will be affected by:

- The site of the wound and ease or otherwise of applying the dressing.
- The size of the wound.
- The frequency of dressing changes required.

- Comfort and cosmetic considerations.
- Where and by whom the dressing will be changed.
- The availability of the dressing in the size required—not all dress-ings are available to patients whose wounds are being managed in the community, and where a dressing is available on the community Drug Tariff it may not be available in all sizes.

Where all other considerations are equal, choose the *cheapest* dressing.

In *Figure 3.1*, wounds where levels of exudate are still a problem are somewhat arbitrarily divided into three categories, depending on their depth and the level of exudate being produced. Evaluation of the effectiveness of a dressing in coping with moderate-to-high levels of exudate will be required in each individual case and the following should be considered as a general guide.

For superficial low-to-moderate exudate wounds the dressing options include:

- A hydrocolloid sheet, e.g. Granuflex E (*Colour Plates* **23, 24**), Comfeel (*Colour Plates* **25, 26**), or Tegasorb (*Colour Plates* **27, 28**).
- An alginate sheet, e.g. Kaltostat, Sorbsan, or Tegagel.
- A hydrogel sheet, e.g. Geliperm Sheet.
- A foam dressing, e.g. Allevyn or Lyofoam.

The hydrocolloid sheet dressings require no secondary dressing and it is easy to see when the dressing needs changing. The Comfeel Pressure Relieving Dressing (*Colour Plate* **29**) has been specially designed to protect high-risk sites, such as heels, from further damage. As exudate levels lessen, the dressing can be left in place for increasing lengths of time. Angiogenesis is stimulated. The alginate hydrogel and foam dressings also provide a good local environment for healing.

For superficial moderate-to-high exudate wounds the dressing options include:

- An alginate dressing, e.g. Kaltostat Fortex or Sorbsan Plus (*Colour Plate* **30**).
- A foam dressing, e.g. Allevyn (*Colour Plate* **31**).
- A hydrogel sheet, e.g. Geliperm Sheet.

If high exudate levels show no signs of lessening in a superficial wound, it is well worth investigating whether there is an underlying problem that requires treatment. Many leg ulcers produce high levels of exudate. Attempting to control the exudate by the use of a dressing alone is futile. Any underlying vascular problems need to be identified to enable effective management to be planned (Chapter 7). For venous ulcers, elevating the legs above hip level at rest reduces exudate production by aiding venous return. Other causes of high levels of exudate in superficial wounds of the lower leg include congestive cardiac failure. Again, the underlying problem needs to be tackled if possible. There is a limit to what a dressing alone can achieve.

For deeper moderate-to-high exudate wounds the dressing options include:

- Hydrocolloid granules or paste, under a hydrocolloid wafer, e.g. Granuflex or Comfeel.
- A granulated hydrogel, e.g. Geliperm Granulated Gel.
- An alginate dressing, e.g. Tegagel (*Colour Plate* **32**); an alginate dressing in ribbon or rope form, e.g. Sorbsan (*Colour Plate* **33**), is useful for packing narrower wounds.
- A foam dressing, e.g. Allevyn Cavity Wound Dressing (*Colour Plate* **34**).
- A polysaccharide bead dressing in paste form or incorporated into a pad, e.g. Debrisan (*Colour Plate* **15**).

In deeper wounds it is important to assess at the outset the probable ease of removing the dressing. Beads and granules could be very difficult to retrieve from a deep, narrow sinus. The alginate dressings, such as Sorbsan, are biodegradable and the ribbon form comes with a probe to facilitate light packing. Ramifying deep sinuses are impossible to pack, and with the very real risk of deep abscess formation the surgeon may decide to excise the tissues (see Chapters 8 and 10). For saucer-shaped wounds the dressing should be easier to remove. Debrisan pads (*Colour Plate* **15**) and the Allevyn Cavity Wound Dressing (*Colour Plate* **34**) come in a variety of sizes and are easy and quick to remove from such wounds. Other dressings, such as the alginates, hydrocolloid granules, and hydrogels, can easily be removed by gentle irrigation.

The function of all these dressings is to maintain a *moist* environment at the wound site while removing excess exudate.

3.4.6 Managing clean deep low exudate wounds (Question 6, *Figure 3.1*)

Once the exudate levels are reduced, Silastic Foam is a useful way of dressing a clean deep saucer-shaped wound, such as an excised pilonidal sinus (see *Colour Plates* **101–103**), or a large sacral pressure sore. For more minor wounds many patients or their carers can manage the twice-daily surface disinfection of the foam stent or 'bung' themselves, at home, with new stents being made as required by the community nurse, who can monitor the wound's progress. This is certainly preferable to packing wounds with ribbon gauze. Not only is the gauze less easy to manage but it is also possible to do considerable damage to a wound inadvertently by heavy-handed over-packing. If the gauze dries out it will also adhere and the wound bed can easily be traumatised on the removal of the dressing. Blood capillary loops tend to grow through the gauze mesh and are damaged on dressing removal.

3.4.7 Managing clean superficial low exudate wounds (Question 6, Figure 3.1)

Many dressings are suitable for managing clean superficial wounds. Continuing to provide a moist environment encourages rapid epithelialisation and pain relief and protects the wound surface from further mechanical damage and from contamination. An ideal dressing is one that can be left undisturbed for several days, such as a semipermeable film, e.g. Tegaderm (Colour Plate 35), a hydrocolloid sheet, e.g. Granuflex Extra Thin or an alginate island dressing, e.g. Kaltoclude or Sorbsan SA (Colour Plate 36).

Many factors will influence the choice of dressing. The importance of comfort, convenience, and cosmetic acceptability to the patient should not be underestimated, especially in the terminally ill patient, where wound healing may not be a realistic goal. Figure 3.1 highlights the principal priorities and some of the treatment options. Most of the examples given have been on the market for several years and are well tried, but they are just a sample of those available. It is important to keep an open mind as new products appear, and to judge each new dressing on its merits.

3.5 Looking to the future

There are some very exciting developments on the horizon in wound management. Several new approaches to promoting healing are currently being assessed, including the use of growth factors to accelerate healing. Many growth factors have now been isolated, including: epidermal growth factor (EGF), platelet-derived growth factor (PDGF), fibroblast growth factors (FGFs), and transforming growth factor-beta (TGF-B). These growth factors have been reported to be highly potent agents in promoting healing in animal models, even in very low doses. They can now be manufactured in large quantities using recombinant DNA technology. Clinical trials in humans are well under way in many specialist centres in the USA, and are yielding some promising results. However, many questions remain to be answered, especially with regard to 'bioactive' products: At what stage in the healing process should they be used? What are the likely side-effects, and how does the body metabolise these substances?

Another exciting development, of particular relevance to the management of patients with extensive burns where insufficient skin donor sites are available for grafting, is the culture of skin grafts in the laboratory from the patient's own cells (Philips, 1988; Hancock and Leigh, 1989). The grafts are called keratinocyte autografts. Clinical trials have demonstrated that these grafts have major life-saving potential in the management of patients with very extensive skin loss. Also, they have been used successfully to treat both chronic wounds, such as leg ulcers, and skin disorders, such as epidermolysis bullosa.

Further reading

Thomas, S. (1990), *Wound Management and Dressings*. The Pharmaceutical Press, London.

References

Bale, S. (1989), Cost-effective wound management in the community. *Professional Nurse*, **4**(12), 598–601.

Hancock, K. and Leigh, I.M. (1989), Cultured keratinocytes and keratinocyte grafts. *Br. Med. J.*, **299**, 1179–1180.

Middleton, K. (1990), Sugar pastes in wound management. *The Dressings Times*, **3**(2), 1–3. (Obtainable from the Surgical Materials Testing Laboratory, Bridgend General Hospital, Mid-Glamorgan, Wales.)

Morgan, D. A. (1990a), Development of a wound management policy: Part 1. *Pharm. J.*, **244**, 295–297.

Morgan, D.A. (1990b), Development of a wound management policy: Part 2. *Pharm. J.*, **244**, 358–359.

Phillips, T. (1988), Cultured skin grafts. *Arch. Dermatol.*, **124**, 1035–1038.

Thomas, S. (1990), *Wound Management and Dressings*. The Pharmaceutical Press, London.

4   Wound Cleansing: Which Solution?

4.1   Introduction

A review of written records dating back 4000 years suggests that man has used many methods of wound cleansing (Forrest, 1982).

About 4000 BC, Hippocrates was recommending that wounds should be washed in tepid water. If a wound was grossly contaminated he suggested that it should be washed in much diluted wine or vinegar. Wine and vinegar were amongst the first antiseptics in everyday use. Galen, a surgeon to the gladiators in the second century AD, washed wounds in sea water as this was relatively uncontaminated compared with the urban water supplies. Both doctors used simple solutions to remove gross contaminants physically, and in so doing probably did their patients little harm.

Fortunately, some less innocuous ancient cleansing agents such as lizards' dung, pigeons' blood, and boiling oil have gone out of fashion. Unfortunately, other harmful agents such as Eusol, which dates back to World War I, are still to be found in use in some hospitals today.

4.2   The purpose of wound cleansing

The purpose of wound cleansing is to remove organic and inorganic debris prior to the application of a wound dressing, thus maintaining an optimum environment at the wound site for healing (Chapter 3).

The continued presence of debris, which includes foreign bodies, devitalised soft tissue, slough, and necrotic tissue, might delay healing and act as foci for infection.

4.3   Approaches to cleansing in different wounds

4.3.1   Contaminated traumatic wounds and devitalised soft tissue

Where tissue is heavily contaminated by dirt and bacteria or is devitalised, surgical removal is often the treatment of choice (Haury *et al.*, 1980; see *Colour Plate* **9**). Devitalised soft tissue acts as a culture medium, promoting bacterial growth and inhibiting the ability of white blood cells to ingest bacteria and kill them.

Decontamination of traumatic wounds is usually done in the Accident and Emergency Department, where treatment methods will generally be decided by the casualty officer. In some cases, débridement may need to be carried out in the operating theatre under general anaesthetic. Removal of more trivial foreign bodies, such as splinters, fish hooks, and superficial grit and grease, may be left to the nurse (see Chapter 11). In brief, the aim is to remove gross contaminants with the minimum of pain to the patient and trauma to the tissues. For trivial injuries, the best practical approach is to immerse the injured part in water or saline at body temperature, which eases the pain and helps to loosen debris. For minor traumatic wounds, asepsis is unnecessary until all gross contamination is removed.

4.3.2 Closed surgical wounds

A different approach is needed when cleansing closed surgical wounds, which are initially 'clean'. Here, strict asepsis is needed at the outset to prevent endogenous or exogenous wound infection. If a wound infection does develop, however, the cause can almost always be traced back to the time of the surgery itself. After 2–3 days, when the wound has sealed, it should generally be possible for the patient to take a shower (see Chapter 9).

4.3.3 Chronic open wounds

When cleansing chronic open wounds, such as pressure sores and leg ulcers, there is some controversy surrounding the need for strict asepsis, especially in the community. The patient's home is likely to harbour far fewer pathogens than lurk in the physical environment in many hospital wards! For a patient with a leg ulcer that is being managed at home, cleansing the whole leg in a bowl can be therapeutic, especially if the patient's leg has been encased in a compression bandage all week, when cleansing is essential for hygiene (see Chapter 7).

When a clean, rather than an aseptic, technique is employed, there is always the risk that the nurse could unwittingly act as a vector for cross-infection, which could have serious consequences if organisms such as β-haemolytic streptococci or pseudomonads are involved. It is therefore wise to adopt a strictly aseptic technique when cleansing chronic wounds in hospital wards and to take special care with the disposal of waste materials, both in hospital and in the community. Scrupulous attention to washing hands is essential in both settings (see Chapter 5).

4.4 Methods of wound cleansing

4.4.1 Removing necrotic tissue and slough

Methods for removing necrotic tissue, such as hard dry black eschar and thick slough, in chronic wounds, were discussed in detail in Chapter 3. In brief, the main treatment options are:

- Surgical excision.
- An enzymatic treatment, e.g. Varidase.
- A hydrocolloid dressing, e.g. Granuflex or Comfeel.
- A hydrogel, e.g. Scherisorb Gel.
- An acid cream or solution, e.g. Aserbine.
- A hypochlorite solution.

The dangers of using hypochlorite solutions are explained in more detail in Section 4.5.

4.4.2 Removing stale exudate and loose debris

Assuming that the wound is not covered with necrotic tissue or thick slough, which solution should be used to remove loose debris and stale exudate?

For wounds that are not grossly contaminated, sterile water or a 0.9% saline solution are the cleansing agents of choice. These simple solutions, or an approximation of them, have been in use for the last 2000 years. They are non-toxic and inexpensive.

Where there is a reasonable-to-high risk of wound infection, for instance in contaminated traumatic wounds and burns, in severely debilitated patients, or where wounds are so sited that they are likely to have become contaminated by urine or faecal material, then an antiseptic solution may be indicated. Which are the safer solutions?

4.5 A review of the uses and hazards of antiseptic solutions

The characteristics of the ideal antiseptic are given in *Table 4.1*. When choosing an antiseptic, its effectiveness as a bactericidal or bacteriostatic agent must be balanced against the likely degree of damage to healthy human tissues.

Lister's introduction of the antiseptic carbolic acid into the operating room greatly reduced the incidence of wound infection, septicaemia, and death following surgery, but his use of dressings over open wounds kept permanently wet with carbolic acid, by various ingenious means, yielded disappointing results because the acid killed healthy cells as well as micro-organisms.

Eusol was introduced as a cleansing solution for treating heavily contaminated wounds during World War I. Dakin used hypochlorite

Table 4.1   Characteristics of the ideal antiseptic

Kills a wide range of micro-organisms.
Effective over a wide range of dilutions.
Non-toxic to human tissues.
Does not easily give rise to sensitivity reactions, either locally or systemically.
Acts rapidly.
Works efficiently, even in the presence of organic material (e.g. pus, blood, or soap).
Inexpensive.
Long shelf life.

solutions with great effect at this time to prevent wound sepsis and to remove necrotic tissue, but he used quite different methods of applying these solutions compared with the methods generally used today. In recognition of the fact that the hypochlorites are rapidly inactivated by pus and slough he recommended that 5–10 ml of hypochlorite solution should be introduced into small wounds every 2 hours and that up to 2 litres of hypochlorite solution should be applied to more extensive necrotic wounds by continuous or frequent irrigation (Thomas, 1991). Since it often took 2–3 days for soldiers with heavily contaminated wounds to travel from the front line to a field hospital, the risk of death from septicaemia in those days was very great. Before the advent of antibiotics and antiseptics of low toxicity to human tissues, Eusol and other hypochlorite solutions undoubtedly saved lives, but should we still be using them today?

Three reviews of the debate on the use of hypochlorite solutions in open wounds are given in the Further reading section of Chapter 4. Feelings on the matter can run high. After an extensive literature search undertaken to try to establish the place of Eusol in wound management, which was commissioned by the South-Western Regional Health Authority following 'a series of disputes about Eusol', Farrow and Toth (1991) concluded: 'There is clear evidence that Eusol should not be applied to healing tissue. That it remains in use is a minor scandal.'

There is a paucity of first-rate experimental evidence in humans but there are many indications of the possible harmful effects of hypochlorites on healthy tissue. A moderate-to-severe irritant response to hypochlorites has been reported in humans within 4–5 days of commencement of use. In animal models, toxicity to fibroblasts, delayed production of collagen, impaired epithelial migration, and inhibition of microcirculation have been reported (Brennan and Leaper, 1985; Brennan *et al.*, 1986).

In the absence of experimental proof of its efficacy and cost-effectiveness, neither would Farrow and Toth (1991) recommend Eusol as a debriding or a desloughing agent. This view is shared by Thomas (1991), who stated, 'When applied to necrotic wounds in the form of packs or soaks which are changed daily, it is unlikely that hypochlorite is present in sufficient concentration to exert any significant chemical debriding effect.'

It is unlikely that with current methods enough available chlorine is introduced into the wound either to dissolve slough or necrotic tissue or to exert an appreciable antibacterial effect.

There are certainly much safer antiseptics to use than the hypochlorites. Indeed, there is a strong argument for saying that except for the initial cleansing of some dirty, traumatic wounds in the Accident and Emergency Department, antiseptic cleansing solutions are rarely required.

Even if it were possible to surface-sterilise a wound, there is considerable evidence that the wound surface does not need to be sterile for healing to take place (e.g. Eriksson, 1985; Van Rijswijk, 1985). Paradoxically, the presence of certain micro-organisms may promote healing, perhaps by out-competing potential pathogens. However, if an antiseptic solution is indicated, what are the safer options?

Aqueous chlorhexidine solutions have many of the characteristics of the ideal antiseptic. They have a low toxicity to living tissues in animal models and are effective against a wide range of gram-positive and gram-negative organisms, but they are not effective against acid-fast bacilli, bacterial spores, fungi, or viruses and their activity, like the activity of the hypochlorites, is reduced by organic matter such as blood, pus, and soap (Reynolds, 1982).

Povidone–iodine is a potent antimicrobial agent used widely and effectively in pre- and post-operative skin disinfection and cleansing, in the outpatient management of dirty traumatic wounds (Helm, 1978), and to reduce wound sepsis in burns (Zellner and Bugyi, 1985).

In a burn injury there may be irreversible damage to the microcirculation so that neither the body's own immune system components nor parenterally administered antibiotics are able to penetrate rapidly to the site where they are most needed, and micro-organisms can proliferate in the nutrient medium provided by the dead tissue. Wound sepsis remains the commonest cause of death in such patients and local treatment of infected burns with antiseptics is sometimes needed.

The value of antiseptics in the management of other open wounds is more difficult to assess, and further studies of the interactions between antiseptics, bacteria, and the immune system are needed in humans to determine the situations where their use is most beneficial (Leaper and Simpson, 1986).

A number of solutions that are still to be found in some ward cupboards are of limited usefulness, and are positively harmful in certain situations. These include the following:

- *Hydrogen peroxide* (3%) Still used for cleansing and deodorising infected wounds, but its effect lasts only for the short period during which oxygen is being released. It is dangerous to instil large volumes of hydrogen peroxide into closed cavities in which the escape of released oxygen is impaired—gas embolism has been reported. More commonly, an irritant skin response is seen in some patients.

- *Silver nitrate*   Owes its use to the antibacterial properties of silver. A 0.5% silver nitrate solution was used routinely in the 1960s for the prophylactic treatment of severe burns, being particularly effective against *Pseudomonas* spp., but it can cause methaemoglobinaemia, argyria, and metabolic disturbances. It has largely been replaced by silver sulphadiazine. Although still occasionally used in the stick form to treat hypergranulation, silver nitrate is caustic and prolonged use is not recommended.

- *Potassium permanganate solution* (1 in 8000 dilution)   Still prescribed by some dermatologists for cleansing and deodorising suppurating eczematous wounds and acute dermatoses, and may be useful prophylactically where there is a risk of secondary infection. However, concentrated solutions are caustic and even fairly dilute solutions can be an irritant to tissues. Potassium permanganate stains the skin brown and although bactericidal *in vitro*, its clinical value as a bactericide is minimised by its rapid deactivation in the presence of body fluids.

- *Crystal violet*   Formerly used because of its activity against *Staphylococcus* spp. and some pathogenic yeasts, such as *Candida*. But its use on broken skin is now banned in the United Kingdom, because it can interact with DNA in living cells and has been proved to be carcinogenic in animal studies.

Do antiseptics, used as cleansing agents, have time to be effective?   This brief review of the antiseptics that have been used for wound cleansing for many years and are readily available to nurses has indicated how hazardous they can be if inappropriately used. It is also very questionable whether antiseptics have time to bring about the desired effect!

Antiseptics require time in contact with bacteria if they are to kill them or inhibit their division. Where an antiseptic is used only in passing, as a cleansing solution, and does not remain in contact with the wound after the wound toilet is completed, then it may not have time to be effective. If bacteria are merely being removed by the physical action of cleaning, at a dressing change, then normal saline should be as effective a cleansing agent as any, and has no unwanted side-effects.

For further information on the uses of antiseptics incorporated into primary dressings, see Chapter 3.

4.6 Applying the cleansing solution

There are two basic methods for mechanically cleansing a wound: irrigation and direct 'scrubbing' with a cotton wool ball or gauze. The difficulty with irrigation is how to apply the cleansing solution under sufficient pressure to dislodge the debris without damaging the underlying tissue (Westaby, 1985). It is also possible to damage wound tissue by rough handling with cotton wool balls or gauze swabs.

Many different swabbing techniques are practised in Britain and the United States but a study by Thomlinson (1987) found that of the three methods she tested in discharging surgical wounds no technique was significantly better at cleaning than any other, and all techniques merely resulted in the redistribution of micro-organisms. This raises the question of whether we need to cleanse wounds at every dressing change.

4.7 Do we need to cleanse wounds at every dressing change?

If a wound is grossly contaminated by foreign material, slough, or necrotic tissue, wound cleansing is necessary at every dressing change to prevent delayed healing. If, however, a wound is clean, there is little exudate, and it is healthily granulating, repeated cleaning may do more harm than good; it may traumatise newly produced and delicate tissues, reduce the surface temperature of the wound, and remove exudate that has bactericidal properties (Hohn *et al.*, 1977).

Further reading

General review

Thomas, S. (1990), Wound cleansing agents. In *Wound Management and Dressings*, pp. 74–80. The Pharmaceutical Press, London.

Reviews of the debate on the use of hypochlorite solutions on open wounds

Farrow, S. and Toth, B. (1991), The place of eusol in wound management. *Nurs. Stand.*, **5**(22), 25–27.

Morgan, D.A. (1989), Wound care. Chlorinated solutions—useful or useless? *Pharm. J.*, **243**, 219–220.

Thomas, S. (1991), Evidence fails to justify use of hypochlorite. *Journal of Tissue Viability*, **1**(1), 9–10.

References

Brennan, S.S. and Leaper, D.J. (1985), The effect of antiseptics on the healing wound: a study using rabbit earchamber. *Br. J. Surg.*, **72**(10), 780–782.

Brennan, S.S., Foster, M.E. and Leaper, D.J. (1986), Antiseptics toxicity in wounds healing by secondary intention. *J. Hosp. Infect.*, **8**(3), 263–267.

Eriksson, G. (1985), Bacterial growth in venous leg ulcers—its clinical significance in the healing process. *An Environment for Healing: The Role of Occlusion*. Congress and Symposium Series No. 88, Royal Society of Medicine.

Farrow, S. and Toth, B. (1991), The place of eusol in wound management. *Nurs. Stand.*, **5**(22), 25–27.

Forrest, R.D. (1982), Early history of wound treatment. *Journal of the Royal Society of Medicine*, **75**, 198–205.

Haury, B. *et al.* (1980), Débridement: an essential component of traumatic wound care. In Hunt, T.K. (ed.), *Wound Healing and Wound Infection: Theory and Surgical Practice*. pp. 229–240. Appleton-Century Crofts, New York.

Helm, P.A. (1978), Outpatient wound management with Betadine products (povidone-iodine). *The Proceedings of the World Congress on Antisepsis*, pp. 105–108. New York H.P.

Hohn, D.C. *et al.* (1977), Antimicrobial systems of the surgical wound. *Am. J. Surg.*, **133**(5), 597–600.

Leaper, D.J. and Simpson, R.A. (1986), The effect of antiseptics and topical antimicrobials on wound healing. *Journal of Antimicrobial Chemotherapy*, **17**(2), 135–137.

Reynolds, J.E.F. (ed.) (1982), *Martindale: The Extra Pharmacopoeia*. The Pharmaceutical Press, London.

Thomas, S. (1991), Evidence fails to justify use of hypochlorite. *Journal of Tissue Viability*, **1**(1), 9–10.

Thomlinson, D. (1987), To clean or not to clean? *Nursing Times*, March 4, 71–75.

Van Rijswijk *et al.* (1985), Multicentre clinical evaluation of a hydrocolloid dressing for leg ulcers. *Cutis*, **35**, 173–176.

Westaby, S. (ed.) (1985), *Wound Care*. Heinemann Medical Books, London.

Zellner, P.R. and Bugyi, S. (1985), Povidone-iodine in the treatment of burn patients. *J. Hosp. Infect.*, **6** (supplement), 139–146.

5 Wound Infection

5.1 The cost and prevalence of hospital-acquired infection

Wound infections delay healing and can greatly add to the cost of hospital care, especially if the infection involves an orthopaedic prosthesis or follows major cardiac or abdominal surgery. At the least, the patient is inconvenienced by a prolonged period of hospitalisation, which may involve economic and social hardship to the whole family; at the worst, the patient may die from septicaemia.

Infections in chronic wounds can be costly too. Hibbs (1988) estimated that a patient with a complicated hip fracture, who had developed a severely infected Grade IV pressure sore, cost the health authority £25,905 during her 180-day stay. Another way of measuring the cost is in terms of the opportunities lost to operate on or treat other patients. Assuming no undue complications, 17 people could have received hip or knee replacements in the time that one patient was in hospital with an infected wound.

The hospital environment is not a particularly safe one in which to recover from illness! The physical environment may harbour pathogenic micro-organisms that have developed resistance to a wide range of antibiotics. Infected patients in nearby beds are another potential source of infection, as are the staff, who are much more likely to be carriers of some diseases than the general population. The resistance of patients to infection is likely to be reduced because of the disease or disorder that brought them to hospital, and during their stay patients' natural defence mechanisms are commonly bypassed by therapeutic procedures, such as catheterisation and surgery.

A study to determine the prevalence of hospital-acquired infection found that the most common infections were those involving the urinary tract, followed in frequency by infections in wounds and in the lower respiratory tract (Meers *et al.*, 1981). It was not possible to estimate what proportion of these infections was preventable.

5.2   The changing pattern of hospital-acquired infection

Before the advent of antibiotics the incidence of death from septicaemia following surgery or traumatic injury was high and was mainly due to the systemic effects of β-haemolytic streptococci. These organisms are still occasionally isolated from patients with cellulitis and chronic wounds, but, except in severely debilitated patients, they are now generally not life threatening if treatment is initiated promptly, because they are still sensitive to penicillin.

The development of multiple antibiotic resistance by strains of *Staphylococcus aureus*, which began to be noticed in the 1950s, has since caused a major problem for some patients. Critically ill patients with implants, cannulae, drains, or catheters are particularly at risk (Whipp, 1990a). Between 1976 and 1984 epidemics of methicillin-resistant *S. aureus* (MRSA) were reported world-wide. Guidelines for the control of epidemic MRSA were drawn up by a joint working party of the Hospital Infection Society and the British Society for Antimicrobial Chemotherapy (1986). Methods for preventing and controlling the spread of MRSA are summarised by Taylor (1990) and Whipp (1990b).

A study by Meers (1981) of hospital-acquired infection showed that *S. aureus* was by far the pathogen most frequently isolated from wounds, followed by *Escherichia coli, Proteus* spp., the faecal streptococci, and *Pseudomonas aeruginosa*. A summary of the micro-organisms most commonly involved in wound infections and their sources is given in *Table 5.1*. Most are commensal organisms living in the gut or in the upper respiratory tract.

5.3   Clinical signs and symptoms of wound infection

A potentially pathogenic organism may be present in a wound without causing any clinical signs of infection. It is therefore important to distinguish between organisms that colonise a wound but cause no tissue damage and organisms that cause a tissue response.

In the early stages of infection there may be no clinically visible signs, but the organism may already have triggered an immunological memory. In this case, the infection is said to be subclinical.

Where there are visible signs and symptoms of infection, such as pyrexia, localised pain, and erythema, local oedema, excess exudate, pus, and offensive odour, the wound is clinically infected (*Colour Plates* **4, 37, 38**). In these cases it is advisable to take a wound swab for identification of the organism and antibiotic-sensitivity testing, especially in an elderly, debilitated, or in any way immunocompromised patient. The sample should be collected before the wound is cleaned, avoiding the surrounding skin and mucous membranes, which may well be colonised by different organisms from the one(s) in the wound causing infection. Bacteriologists should be given as much information as possible to enable them to provide the best service. The site of the wound, its probable cause, any systemic antibiotics currently being taken for whatever reason, and whether or not the wound has deteriorated rapidly should all be stated on the Bacteriology form.

In the very young and the very elderly, the classic signs of wound infection, described so far, may not be seen due to an immature or impaired immune system. Lethargy and refusal of feeds may be the only indications of a life-threatening post-operative infection in a young baby. In the very elderly, the first evidence of infection may be generalised septicaemia accompanied, perhaps, by a subnormal temperature.

The manner in which a clinical infection presents will also depend on the nature of the pathogen. The infection may remain localised and give rise to a discrete abscess or it may spread via the lymphatic system causing lymphangitis and lymphadenitis, with perhaps abscesses in distant sites. Wound observation and assessment of patients for infection following surgery are discussed in more detail in Section 9.4.2.

5.4   How infection spreads

Some of the means by which infection spreads are shown in *Figure 5.1*.

5.4.1   Sources of infection
The source of infection can be endogenous, that is from the patient himself, or exogenous, that is from an infected case or carrier.

As *Table 5.1* illustrates, many potential pathogens are commensal, living in the gut or upper respiratory tract. Gut flora can readily contaminate nearby wounds, such as sacral pressure sores or leg ulcers, especially in a faecally incontinent, confused patient. Skin commensals can enter via a break in the skin. Thus, patients can infect themselves.

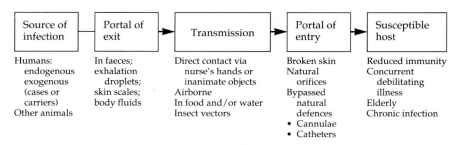

Source of infection	Portal of exit	Transmission	Portal of entry	Susceptible host
Humans: endogenous exogenous (cases or carriers) Other animals	In faeces; exhalation droplets; skin scales; body fluids	Direct contact via nurse's hands or inanimate objects Airborne In food and/or water Insect vectors	Broken skin Natural orifices Bypassed natural defences • Cannulae • Catheters	Reduced immunity Concurrent debilitating illness Elderly Chronic infection

Figure 5.1. How infection spreads.

Table 5.1 Micro-organisms most commonly involved in wound infection

Micro-organism	Potential sources	Remarks
Staphylococcus aureus	Present in nose of 20–30% of normal population.	The commonest cause of hospital-acquired wound infections.
β-Haemolytic streptococci (Lancefield group A)	Present in 5% of the population and in the throats of individuals with tonsillitis.	Can cause skin-graft failures and puerperal sepsis in maternity units.
Escherichia coli *Proteus* spp. }	Normal gut flora of healthy individuals.	Can cause infection after spillage of bowel contents during surgery.
Klebsiella spp. *Pseudomonas* spp. }	In the bowel and also free-living in moist environments.	Can cause infections in genito-urinary and respiratory tracts.
Clostridium welchii	Bowel and in soil.	May cause gas gangrene in deep, dirty traumatic wounds or where prostheses are implanted, especially in sites where blood supply is poor.
Clostridium tetani	Soil.	Can cause tetanus in traumatic wounds.
Bacteroides spp.	Bowel.	Can cause peritonitis and pelvic abscesses if bowel contents leak into peritoneal cavity.

Alternatively, the source of an infection may be other patients. Patients who have recovered from an infection may still be convalescent carriers. The most dangerous carriers are, however, those who have never exhibited any outward signs or symptoms of disease and have therefore never been identified as being carriers.

Animals can also be sources of infection. For example, anthrax and brucellosis can be contracted by humans from infected cattle, the initial symptoms depending on the way the organisms gained entry to the host.

5.4.2 Transmission

The most common vehicles of transmission from a source to a susceptible host are nurses' hands, followed by contaminated inanimate objects, such as instruments and clothes. Dust particles containing organisms from shed skin, and exhalation droplets from patients with upper respiratory tract infections, are suspended in the air and can be breathed in by another patient, or can land on an open wound surface. Pathogens can be transmitted in contaminated food or, less commonly in this country, in contaminated water, or by insect vectors. Some ways of preventing the transmission of infection are summarised in Section 5.5.

5.4.3 Entry into the susceptible host and the immune response
For an infectious agent to become established, it must gain entry to a susceptible host, evade or neutralise the body's immune defences, and multiply.

Pathogens can gain entry via natural orifices, especially when breached by 'therapeutic' procedures, such as catheterisation, or through breaches in the body's non-specific defence mechanisms, such as intact skin and mucous membranes (*Table 5.2*).

A surgical wound is, in a sense, a special case, since here a gross breach in the innate defences is deliberately created. The factors that influence whether or not a clinical infection develops in a surgically made wound are summarised later (see *Figure 9.4*). By far the most important factors are the degree of contamination of the wound at the time of surgery and the use or not of prophylactic antibiotics. In a dirty wound the infection rate is likely to be 25-times higher than in a clean wound (Cruse and Foord, 1980) (see *Table 9.3*). Some surgical wound infections are hard to avoid, especially if the surgeon encounters pus or a perforated viscus. Further discussion of the epidemiology of surgical wound infection and its implications for pre- and post-operative patient care is given in Chapter 9.

If the pathogen penetrates the body's primary defences by whatever means, a specific or acquired response may be triggered (*Figure 5.2*). Components of the specific immune response system, the B- and T-lymphocytes, work closely with polymorphs and macrophages of the non-specific immune system (*Table 5.2*) to neutralise the invading organism and eliminate it. The specific immune response differs from non-specific immunity in two fundamental characteristics: specificity and memory. Specificity refers to the fact that the specific immune system is only immediately effective against a pathogen or material that it has encountered before. Build-up of an effective response can take several days from the first encounter with the pathogen. Memory of a previous encounter allows the specific defence mechanisms to act more rapidly on second and subsequent occasions. The efficiency of this system, and therefore the resistance of the host to infection, is decreased with increasing age, and in people with immune disorders or existing chronic infections, especially if they are also malnourished.

Table 5.2 Defence mechanisms: non-specific (innate) immunity

Mechanism	Mode of action	Breached or weakened by
1. Intact skin	Mechanical barrier, adverse physical environment and bacteriostatic skin secretions; a healthy outer commensal microbial flora inhibits pathogen multiplication by direct competition.	Surgery, trauma, injections, intravenous cannulae, severe inflammatory skin disorders, poor peripheral circulation.
2. Intact mucous membranes, e.g. lining of lungs, digestive system, and reproductive organs.	Secrete inhibitory chemicals, e.g. lysozyme; mucous traps organisms, but less of a physical barrier than 1; again, commensals inhibit multiplication of pathogens by direct competition.	Inhaling or ingesting noxious chemicals, artificial ventilation, commensal microbial flora upset by antibiotics.
3. Cilia, in upper respiratory tract.	Rhythmic movement wafts mucous containing trapped micro-organisms to throat, where it is swallowed.	Smoking, anaesthetic agents.
4. Acidity, in stomach.	Very low pH (1.5–3.5) kills most ingested micro-organisms.	Gastrectomy, some acid secretion inhibiting drugs.
5. Acidity, in vagina.	Caused by lactobacilli, inhibits infection.	Natural commensal flora upset by antibiotics, and in pregnancy.
6. Flushing by natural body secretions and/or excreted fluids.	Regular flushing of eyes by tears and urinary tract by passage of urine.	Reduced secretion of tears with increasing age, bypassing of urethra by urinary catheter.

Table 5.2 (*cont.*)

Mechanism	Mode of action	Breached or weakened by
7. Phagocytosis.	Polymorphs and macrophages, which are attracted to a site of tissue damage, ingest micro-organisms and destroy them and remove other debris; they also facilitate specific immunity-defence mechanisms.	Various immune-system disorders.
8. Complement.	A series of plasma proteins which, when activated by antigen–antibody complexes, facilitate bacterial lysis and phagocytosis.	Natural variation in amounts of complement produced by individuals.
9. Interferons.	Released from cells when they become infected by viruses, making nearby cells resistant to viral infection.	

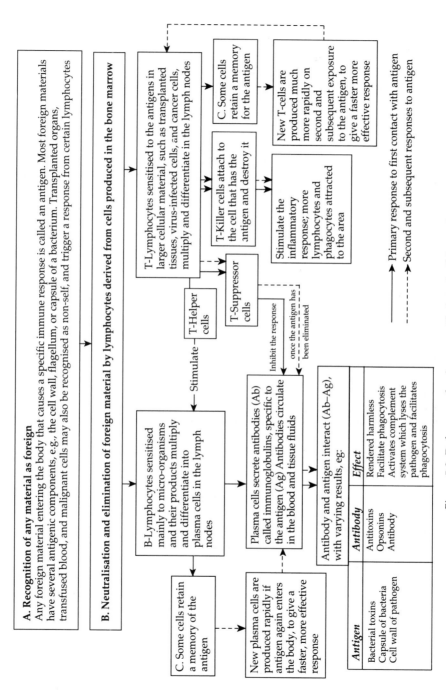

A. Recognition of any material as foreign
Any foreign material entering the body that causes a specific immune response is called an antigen. Most foreign materials have several antigenic components, e.g., the cell wall, flagellum, or capsule of a bacterium. Transplanted organs, transfused blood, and malignant cells may also be recognised as non-self, and trigger a response from certain lymphocytes

B. Neutralisation and elimination of foreign material by lymphocytes derived from cells produced in the bone marrow

T-Lymphocytes sensitised to the antigens in larger cellular material, such as transplanted tissues, virus-infected cells, and cancer cells, multiply and differentiate in the lymph nodes

C. Some cells retain a memory for the antigen

New T-cells are produced much more rapidly on second and subsequent exposure to the antigen, to give a faster more effective response

T-Killer cells attach to the cell that has the antigen and destroy it

Stimulate the inflammatory response; more lymphocytes and phagocytes attracted to the area

Stimulate — T-Helper cells

T-Suppressor cells

Inhibit the response once the antigen has been eliminated

B-Lymphocytes sensitised mainly to micro-organisms and their products multiply and differentiate into plasma cells in the lymph nodes

Plasma cells secrete antibodies (Ab) called immunoglobulins, specific to the antigen (Ag) Antibodies circulate in the blood and tissue fluids

C. Some cells retain a memory of the antigen

New plasma cells are produced rapidly if antigen again enters the body, to give a faster, more effective response

Antibody and antigen interact (Ab–Ag), with varying results, eg:

Antigen	Antibody	Effect
Bacterial toxins	Antitoxins	Rendered harmless
Capsule of bacteria	Opsonins	Facilitate phagocytosis
Cell wall of pathogen	Antibody	Activates complement system which lyses the pathogen and facilitates phagocytosis

⟶ Primary response to first contact with antigen
⟶ Second and subsequent responses to antigen

Figure 5.2. Defence mechanisms: specific (acquired) immunity.

63

The other major factor that determines whether or not a susceptible host develops a clinical infection is the virulence of the organism; that is, its ability to evade the host's defence mechanisms and spread. Some micro-organisms have capsules, and others have components in their cell walls which protect them from phagocytosis. Some secrete enzymes which dissolve the 'cement' between cells, facilitating their spread. Others produce enzymes which de-activate white blood cells or lyse red cells.

The damaging effects of micro-organisms are caused by direct tissue destruction by the organism, the body's response to the organism, or the effect of toxins released by them. Exotoxins secreted by the organism into the host cause such conditions as gas gangrene, tetanus, and botulism. Endotoxins, released on the death of the pathogens, can have equally dramatic effects, in the extreme leading to septicaemic shock, which can prove fatal if not recognised quickly and treated. Septicaemic shock is characterised by peripheral vasodilation and a profound drop in blood pressure.

5.5   Preventing wound infection

The principles of preventing wound infection are based on breaking the chain of events which lead to an organism passing from a source into a susceptible host and multiplying there (*Figure 5.1*). The chain can be broken in several places, for instance by:

- Isolating potential sources of infection, by barrier nursing.
- Effectively cleansing and disinfecting the physical environment.
- Effective hand washing by nurses and other carers.
- Aseptic wound dressing technique.
- Protecting the susceptible patient, who may need to be reverse barrier nursed.

5.5.1   Barrier nursing (source isolation)
Some form of isolation may be needed to prevent the spread of infection from patients with communicable diseases, or from patients harbouring organisms, such as MRSA, which could pose a hazard to others (Taylor, 1990). The type of isolation required depends on the virulence of the organism and its mode of transmission, the severity of the resulting illness if acquired, and the level of immunity of the surrounding patients (Brettle and Thomson, 1984). Each hospital has its own policy for infection control. Advice should be sought from the infection control nurse or the hospital's principal bacteriologist as to the best method of source isolation in a particular case. The main elements of effective isolation are summarised in *Table 5.3*. Nurses are normally aware of the need to take precautions when caring for patients with hepatitis B,

Table 5.3   The principles of effective barrier nursing

1. *Isolate the patient.*   This is most easily achieved by nursing the patient in a single room, with hand washing and toilet facilities and, ideally, an anteroom for protective clothing. Remove all inessential furniture, and furniture that cannot easily be cleaned, in advance. Keep a thermometer, sphygmomanometer, water jug, and eating utensils in the room for the patient's exclusive use. Set up a trolley outside the room to hold disposable gloves, gowns, and caps as required and the patient's TPR and fluid balance charts.

2. *Notification of infection.*   The infection control nurse, the patient, all members of the ward team, including domestic staff, visitors, and the Occupational Health Department must be informed. Careful explanation of the precautions to the patient encourages the patient's informed co-operation and can reduce anxiety. A simple card on the patient's door, asking all visitors to report first to the ward staff, alerts visitors to the need for and nature of precautions. The minimum number of staff should be involved in nursing the patient.

3. *Waste.*   The precautions required will depend on the organism involved. Follow the hospital policy for disposal of soiled bed linen, 'sharps', dressings, contaminated utensils, urinals, and bed pans. Suitable bags and containers should be kept in the room.

4. *Clothing.*   For staff, disposable plastic gowns that cover the parts of the body that come into closest contact with the patient substantially reduce contact transfer of micro-organisms. Caps, masks and coverings for footwear may be required in some circumstances. Seek advice on the degree of protection required for all those entering the room from the infection control nurse or hospital bacteriologist. Keep the patients' personal property to a minimum, advise them to wear hospital clothing.

5. *Hand washing.*   Close-fitting disposable gloves will be required for all intimate procedures. Before leaving the room, thorough hand washing with a preparation containing a disinfectant, such as Hibiscrub, reduces the number of transiently acquired micro-organisms dramatically.

6. *Disinfection of the physical environment on patient discharge.*   The nature of the precautions required will depend upon the organism involved. Seek advice from the infection control nurse or hospital bacteriologist on the methods required for cleaning curtains, furniture, walls, and floor.

salmonellosis, or with wounds known to harbour multiple antibiotic-resistant strains of *S. aureus*. The risks posed by a patient admitted to a general surgical or orthopaedic ward with a discharging abscess or heavily infected pressure sore are often underestimated.

5.5.2   Cleansing and disinfecting the physical environment
The physical environment of the hospital is a potential source of many pathogens. The moist environment found in toilets, showers, and even

in vases of flowers beside a patient's bed, is a particularly inviting habitat for many organisms, such as *Pseudomonas* spp. Skin scales harbouring commensals, which can be opportunistic pathogens, are found in bedding and are shed onto the floor and kicked up in dust. Exhaled droplets of moisture containing upper respiratory tract pathogens, such as *Streptococci* spp., are suspended in the air and can be breathed in by others.

Furthermore, the organisms which survive in the hospital environment have often developed multiple antibiotic resistance. Hospitals normally now have a policy that clearly states the methods to be used for cleansing and, where necessary, disinfecting the physical environment to keep the level of micro-organisms to within safe limits. Special precautions are required in treatment rooms, bathrooms, and sluice areas. The policy should describe methods for dealing with spillages of body fluids and excreta, especially from patients who are HIV positive, or who have hepatitis B.

Ideally, wounds should be re-dressed in a well-ventilated treatment room, with the most heavily infected wound being treated last. If a dressing change must be carried out in the ward it is important to avoid times when there are large numbers of airborne organisms. Dressings should therefore be carried out at least one hour after bed making and vacuum cleaning have been completed. Bed-screening curtains, harbouring airborne dust particles and skin scales, should be disturbed as little as possible. The patient's bed can be moved to one side before the dressing trolley is brought in, to allow plenty of working space and to prevent curtains from contaminating the contents of the trolley.

5.5.3 Hand washing

Effective hand washing greatly reduces the risk of transferring pathogenic organisms from one patient to another by direct contact or by contamination of inanimate objects that are shared (Lowbury *et al.*, 1974). However, hand washing is often performed inadequately: right-handed people tend to wash their right hand less thoroughly than the left (Fox, 1974), and such areas as wrists, under fingernails, and the skin under rings are often missed. Although improvements in hand-washing frequency and technique can be measured after staff have undergone an intensive training programme, there is a tendency for staff to lapse into their old ways in time unless the teaching is periodically reinforced.

A detergent solution such as Hibiscrub, which also contains the antiseptic chlorhexidine, is useful for removing dirt and contaminants before and after any procedure involving intimate patient contact or contact with body fluids or excreta. When carrying out a dressing alone, it is useful to have an alcoholic solution such as Hibisol on the bottom of the dressing trolley, to allow a degree of surface disinfection of the hands after opening dressing packs. Not all the micro-organisms will be killed, but their numbers will be significantly reduced.

5.5.4 Aseptic dressing technique

The aim of any aseptic technique is to prevent pathogenic organisms from being transferred to a susceptible host, by direct or indirect contact. In open wounds, which have lost their very effective epidermal barrier to the entry of micro-organisms, very low doses of contaminants can lead to the development of a clinical infection, especially if the organism is virulent and the host has a poor resistance to infection, because of a deficiency in the immune system.

Although health authorities recommend slightly different wound dressing procedures, the principles are basically the same, aimed at preventing organisms from coming into contact with the wound from the nurse's hands, from inanimate objects, such as forceps, from cleansing solutions, or from the immediate physical environment (Section 5.5.2). Strict adherence to wound dressing rituals, which become part of the tradition handed down to new student nurses, can lead to a false assessment of the patient's safety from infection.

A number of different swabbing techniques are practised in different parts of Britain and the United States. Nurses may argue vehemently that their method is the best, but Thomlinson (1987) found that, of the three methods she tested for cleansing discharging surgical wounds, no technique was significantly better than any other and all techniques merely resulted in the redistribution of micro-organisms. Furthermore, strict adherence to ritualistic practices discourages nurses from using their common sense to find the best way of applying a dressing to a difficult site while still applying the principles of asepsis. It is very difficult to handle some modern dressings with forceps, and alternative methods must be sought which are practical and yet preserve the principle that only uncontaminated materials should come in contact with an open wound surface. A practical approach to wound cleansing in different types of wounds was discussed in Chapter 4.

A disposable plastic apron can protect the patient from organisms that inevitably contaminate a nurse's uniform, but paper masks, which are sometimes worn in an attempt to prevent organisms from the nurse's upper respiratory tract from alighting on the wound surface, are ineffective (Lowbury et al., 1975).

One of the best ways of reducing the risk of infection is to expose the wound for the shortest possible time. Clean wounds should be dressed before contaminated ones. Great care should be taken with the disposal of dirty dressings, and hands should be washed *effectively* at the beginning and the end of the procedure (Section 5.5.3).

Table 5.4   The principles of effective reverse barrier nursing for patients in general hospital wards

1. *Isolate the patient.*   Use a single room, with toilet and washing facilities.

2. *Notification of precautions when entering the room.*   The patient's principal visitors should be encouraged and should be taught the precautions required when visiting. Casual visitors should be discouraged. No one with a known infection of any kind should be allowed entry.

3. *The physical environment.*   The room, including walls, floor, and furniture, should be kept clean, using appropriate disinfectant and detergent agents as recommended by the infection control nurse or hospital bacteriologist. Damp dusting reduces airborne organisms, but wet surfaces should then be dried, as many organisms thrive in damp conditions. Bed linen should be changed frequently.

4. *Clothing.*   A disposable apron or gown should be worn for all nursing procedures and may be recommended for all visitors; caps and coverings for footwear may be recommended. Gloves should be worn for all intimate procedures.

5. *Hand washing.*   Before entering the room, everyone should thoroughly wash their hands with an antiseptic solution to remove transient contaminating micro-organisms.

6. *Food.*   Raw fruit and vegetables should be avoided, but cooked food from the hospital menu is acceptable.

7. *Vital signs.*   Four-hourly recording of temperature, pulse, and blood pressure helps to detect the development of an infection at an early stage. In an immune-suppressed patient the inflammatory response to injury is damped down, and the first sign of septicaemia may be hypotension.

5.5.5   Reverse barrier nursing (protective isolation)

Barrier nursing is designed to isolate a patient with a serious infection, or who harbours a multiple antibiotic-resistant pathogen, to protect other patients in the vicinity. The aim of *reverse* barrier nursing is to protect a particularly susceptible *patient* from the infectious agents carried by others. Patients with disorders of the immune system, such as acute leukaemia, or in the late stages of Hodgkin's disease, are particularly at risk, as are patients with neutropenia, whose immune system has been artificially suppressed by cancer chemotherapy or by drugs following transplant surgery to prevent organ rejection. Patients with severe and extensive burns are also at high risk of acquiring an infection: the integrity of their skin has been severely breached and the endocrine response to such severe trauma tends to damp down the inflammatory response phase of healing.

The degree of protection required by the susceptible patient will depend upon the degree to which their immune system has been compromised and will be determined by the physician and by the resources available. Successful reverse barrier nursing depends on the complete and informed co-operation of hospital staff, patients, and their relatives. In extreme cases, a laminar flow system will be needed, or an isolation tent, with sterile materials being passed through the portholes. The precautions appropriate in less severe cases are outlined in *Table 5.4*. Many of the precautions are the same as for barrier nursing, but here the emphasis is on preventing pathogenic organisms from entering the patient's environment rather than from leaving it.

5.6 The management of infected wounds

The local management of infected wounds is discussed in Chapter 3. The management of infection in closed surgical wounds is discussed in Chapter 9.

Further reading

Brettle, R.P. and Thomson, M. (1984), *Infection and Communicable Diseases*. Heinemann Medical Books, London.

Duerden, B.I., Reid, T.M.S., Jewsbury, J.M. and Turk, D.C. (1987), *A New Short Textbook of Microbial and Parasitic Infection*. Hodder and Stoughton, London.

Westaby, S. and White, S. (1985), Wound infection. In Westaby, S. (ed.), *Wound Care*, pp. 70–83. Heinemann Medical Books, London.

References

Brettle, R.P. and Thomson, M. (1984), *Infection and Communicable Diseases*. Heinemann Medical Books, London.

Combined working party of the Hospital Infection Society and the British Society for Antimicrobial Chemotherapy (1986), Guidelines for the control of methicillin resistant *Staphylococcus aureus*. *Journal of Hospital Infection* 7, 193–201.

Cruse, P.J.E. and Foord R. (1980), The epidemiology of wound infection – a 10 year prospective study of 62,939 wounds. *Surgical Clinics of North America*, **60** (1), 27–40.

Fox, M.K. (1974), How good are hand washing practices? *American Journal of Nursing*, **74**, 1676–1678.

Hibbs, P.J. (1988), *Pressure Area Care for the City and Hackney Health Authority*. St Bartholomew's Hospital, London.

Lowbury, E.J. *et al.* (1974), Disinfection of hands: removal of transient organisms. *Br. Med. J.* **2**, 230–233.

Lowbury, E.J. *et al.* (1975), *Control of Hospital Infection – a practical handbook*. Chapman and Hall, London.

Meers, *et al.* (1981), Wound infections. *Journal of Hospital Infection*, **2**, Supplement, 29–34.

Taylor, L.J. (1990), Infection control at your finger tips: procedures for preventing and controlling MRSA. *The Professional Nurse*, **5**(10), 547–551.

Thomlinson, D. (1987), To clean or not to clean? *Nursing Times*, **83**(9), 71–75.

Whipp, P. (1990a), *Staph. aureus*: resistance to antibiotics. In *The Staff Nurse's Survival Guide*, pp. 143–146. The Professional Developments Series, Austen Cornish, London.

Whipp, P. (1990b), MRSA: methods of prevention and control. In *The Staff Nurse's Survival Guide*, pp. 147–151. The Professional Developments Series, Austen Cornish, London.

6 Pressure Sores

6.1 Epidemiology

6.1.1 The size of the problem

Pressure sores have been a problem encountered by the chronically ill, the debilitated, and the disabled for millennia, and even today are a common secondary affliction of hospital patients.

Research has shown that of the general adult hospitalised population, 6.5 – 9.4% of patients have at least one pressure sore at any one time (Barbenel *et al.*, 1977; Jordan and Nicol, 1977; David *et al.*, 1983). The incidence of pressure sores in the elderly hospitalised population can be much higher (Exton-Smith, 1987).

Successful surgical treatment of pressure sores began during World War II when doctors were faced with increasing numbers of young patients with spinal cord injuries. At the same time the need for high protein diets to overcome negative nitrogen balance in patients with chronic open wounds was recognised (Mulholland *et al.*, 1943).

Since then, although pressure sore prevention and treatment have been widely researched, over the last 30 years there is little evidence to show a decline in the incidence of pressure sores or an improvement in their treatment. In a major study published in 1983, nurses were found to be using 98 different substances to treat pressure sores (David *et al.*, 1983). Many were merely a waste of time and effort, while others were positively harmful to healing. Other recent studies demonstrate a lack of understanding of wound healing among nurses, and those teaching them (Gould, 1985, 1986). Our existing knowledge of pressure sore aetiology, prevention, and treatment would appear to be under-utilised.

The incidence of pressure sores can be greatly reduced where a health authority or hospital has developed a pressure sore prevention and treatment policy that is known and carried out by all staff (Livesley, 1987; Hibbs, 1988) (Section 6.8). The need to introduce a properly organised and audited pressure sore prevention and treatment service has been recognised by the Royal College of Physicians (1986) but pressure sore prevention and management is not seen by most doctors as their responsibility (*Lancet* editorial, 1990).

6.1.2 *The cost of pressure sores*

The cost of delayed wound healing can be high, both for the individual and for the hospital. At the least, the patient is inconvenienced by a prolonged period of hospitalisation, which may have social and economic consequences for the whole family. At the worst, the patient may die from septicaemia.

It has been estimated that the total cost of treating pressure sores in the United Kingdom each year is £150–200 million, or £750,000 for each health district at 1982 prices (Livesley, 1987). Allowing for inflation and the increasing numbers of people living to be over 80 years of age, the cost in 1990 may easily be double this figure. The total cost of hospital care for one patient with a Grade IV pressure sore who was in hospital for 180 days was calculated to be £25,905 (Hibbs, 1988). Furthermore, patients who develop pressure sores may sue health authorities for negligence. Damages of £100,000 were awarded to one successful claimant (Silver, 1987) and the number of cases of litigation brought to the courts is increasing.

Since most pressure sores are preventable, the cost of pressure sores can also be thought of as a significant 'loss of opportunity' for treating patients with non-life-threatening conditions who must wait longer for their treatment because of a blocked bed. As a result of the development of an avoidable pressure sore, many people suffer, as well as the patient.

6.2   Aetiology

6.2.1   *What is a pressure sore?*

A pressure sore has been defined as (Chapman and Chapman, 1986, p. 106):

> a localised area of cellular damage resulting either from direct pressure on the skin, causing pressure ischaemia, or from shearing forces . . . causing mechanical stress to the tissues.

Pressure and shearing forces interrupt the local tissue microcirculation, and the resulting hypoxia and build-up of metabolic wastes can cause necrosis.

A number of classification systems have been developed (Forrest, 1980; Barton and Barton, 1981; Torrance, 1983) based on the cause, macroscopic appearance, and clinical manifestations of the sore. *Table 6.1* summarises Torrance's developmental classification, describing the clinical presentation of the sore at each stage. *Colour Plates* **39–43** illustrate these stages.

Table 6.1 Developmental classification of pressure sores (Torrance, 1983)

Stage 1 Blanching hyperaemia. Momentary light finger pressure onto the site of erythema, following a prolonged period of pressure on the skin, causes the skin to blanch, indicating that the skin is intact.

Stage 2 Non-blanching hyperaemia. The erythema remains when light finger pressure is applied, indicating some microcirculatory disruption. Superficial damage, including epidermal ulceration, may be present.

Stage 3 Ulceration progresses through the dermis. It progresses to the interface with the subcutaneous tissue.

Stage 4 The ulcer extends into the subcutaneous fat. Underlying muscle is swollen and inflamed. The ulcer tends to spread laterally, temporarily impeded from downward progress by deep fascia.

Stage 5 Infective necrosis penetrates down to the deep fascia. Destruction of muscle now occurs rapidly.

6.2.2   Factors affecting pressure sore development

The major factors in the development of pressure sores are summarised in *Figure 6.1*.

Nearly all pressure sores are primarily due to unrelieved pressure, usually in relatively or totally immobile patients (Barbenel, 1990), where skin and the underlying tissues are directly compressed between bone and another hard surface such as a bed, chair, operating table, or trolley (Versluysen, 1986). The most common site for pressure sores is the sacrum, followed by the trochanter of the femur, ischial tuberosities, and heels (*Figure 6.2*) (Petersen, 1976; Jordan and Nicol, 1977).

There is no scientific agreement about the time a given amount of pressure can be exerted before injury begins. Prolonged low pressure can be at least as hazardous as short-term high pressure (Kosiak, 1959). It has generally been assumed in the past that any period of pressure exceeding 2 hours is likely to cause trauma. For cachectic, debilitated, or terminally ill patients, tissue damage may occur in much less time than this.

Normally the patient experiences shearing forces and friction as well as pressure (Bennet and Lee, 1985), which can be especially important in paraplegic, debilitated, or any elderly patients when in a semirecumbent position (*Figure 6.3*). Paraplegic patients are particularly at risk because they cannot feel damage occurring (Thiyagarajan and Silver, 1984; Capen 1985). In general, chair-bound patients are more likely to develop pressure sores than those who are bed-bound (Barbenel *et al.*, 1977).

The effect of shearing forces is to disrupt the local microcirculation by displacing, distorting, or severing blood vessels as the skin strata move

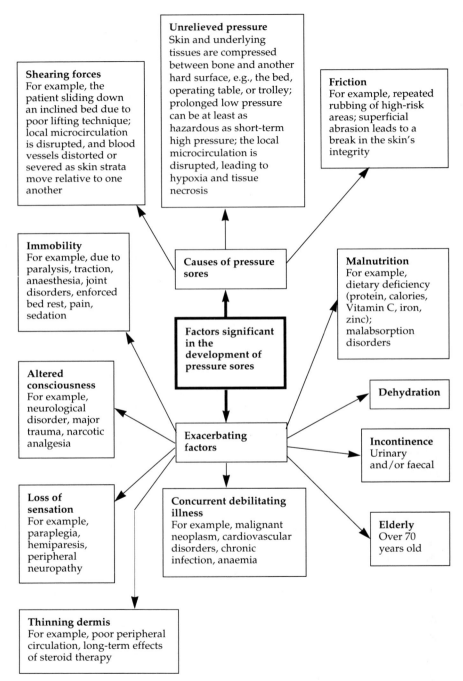

Unrelieved pressure
Skin and underlying tissues are compressed between bone and another hard surface, e.g., the bed, operating table, or trolley; prolonged low pressure can be at least as hazardous as short-term high pressure; the local microcirculation is disrupted, leading to hypoxia and tissue necrosis

Shearing forces
For example, the patient sliding down an inclined bed due to poor lifting technique; local microcirculation is disrupted, and blood vessels distorted or severed as skin strata move relative to one another

Friction
For example, repeated rubbing of high-risk areas; superficial abrasion leads to a break in the skin's integrity

Immobility
For example, due to paralysis, traction, anaesthesia, joint disorders, enforced bed rest, pain, sedation

Causes of pressure sores

Malnutrition
For example, dietary deficiency (protein, calories, Vitamin C, iron, zinc); malabsorption disorders

Factors significant in the development of pressure sores

Altered consciousness
For example, neurological disorder, major trauma, narcotic analgesia

Dehydration

Exacerbating factors

Incontinence
Urinary and/or faecal

Loss of sensation
For example, paraplegia, hemiparesis, peripheral neuropathy

Concurrent debilitating illness
For example, malignant neoplasm, cardiovascular disorders, chronic infection, anaemia

Elderly
Over 70 years old

Thinning dermis
For example, poor peripheral circulation, long-term effects of steroid therapy

Figure 6.1. Intrinsic and extrinsic factors significant in the development of pressure sores.

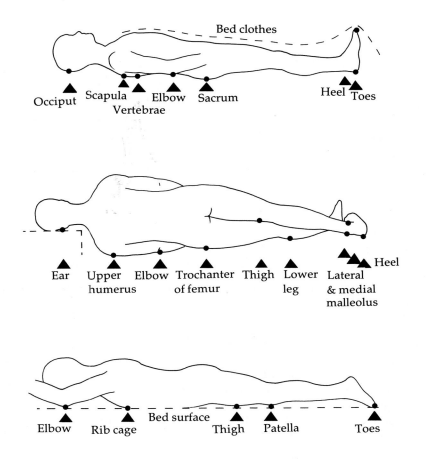

Figure 6.2. Areas of the body at highest risk of developing pressure sores (● pressure points). Any area subject to sufficient unrelieved pressure may develop pressure sores, but certain areas are at particular risk (Torrance, 1983).

relative to one another (Chow *et al.*, 1976). The mechanisms involved in the pathogenesis of pressure sores are reviewed by Scales (1990).

The importance of immobility in the development of pressure sores, whether through paralysis, anaesthesia, pain, or sedation, cannot be overemphasised. Other exacerbating factors include incontinence, malnutrition, and loss of sensory functioning due to paraplegia or hemiparesis.

There is a high correlation between incontinence and pressure sores (Exton-Smith, 1987). Urine can cause maceration and excoriation of skin, and superficial abrasion by friction becomes much more likely.

Malnutrition does not directly cause pressure sores, but is a very

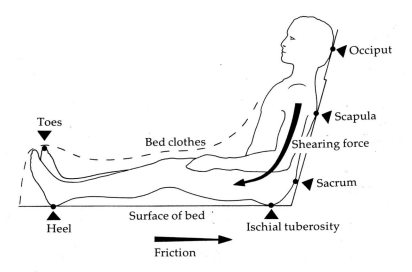

Figure 6.3. Shearing forces, friction, and pressure in a semirecumbent patient (• pressure points).

important exacerbating factor (Agarwal *et al.*, 1985) in pressure sore development.

The incidence of pressure sores is highest in elderly patients who may have multiple age-related pathologies. The skin of elderly patients is predisposed to injury and to poor wound healing because of these conditions and because of the normal age-associated physiological changes in the tissues described in Section 1.6.3.

6.3   Patient risk assessment

It has been suggested that one of the major reasons why pressure sores form and are often so slow to heal is that insufficient care is taken with assessing a patient's risk of developing them (Abruzzese, 1985).

According to Agate (1976, p. 33), 'There is hardly one pressure sore which could not be prevented.' Prevention, however, can be costly, both in nursing time and in equipment. It is therefore vital that nurses' efforts at pressure sore prevention are targeted at those patients most at risk. A valid and reliable method of assessing pressure sore risk is needed that can discriminate between patients who have no risk, low risk, medium risk, and high risk.

Some studies have attempted to group variables related to factors known to predispose patients to pressure sores (*Figure 6.1*) into assessment scales for use in determining a patient's risk. The best known and simplest scale (*Table 6.2*) was devised by Norton *et al.*, (1962), who

Table 6.2   The Norton scale for pressure sore risk assessment

Physical condition		Mental state		Activity		Mobility		Incontinence	
Good	4	Alert	4	Ambulant	4	Full	4	None	4
Fair	3	Apathetic	3	Walks with help	3	Slightly limited	3	Occasional	3
Poor	2	Confused	2	Chairbound	2	Very limited	2	Usually urinary	2
Very bad	1	Stuporous	1	Bedfast	1	Immobile	1	Double	1

Patient total score:
Implications:

found an almost linear relationship between the patient's score and the incidence of pressure sores, a fact confirmed by Exton-Smith (1987) in a much more recent study in a geriatric unit. Patients scoring 14 or under were found to be at risk, with those scoring less than 12 particularly at risk.

There have been a number of criticisms of the Norton scale. Goldstone and Goldstone (1982) found that it tended to overpredict pressure sore risk in some patients. They showed that the sum of just the 'physical condition' and 'incontinence' scores was as successful in predicting patients' risk as the full Norton score. As Chapman and Chapman (1986) point out, Norton's scale was devised from a study of patients aged 65 years and over and so is only valid for this age group. It has been found to be ineffective in at least two groups of patients: children under 6 years old and people of all ages who are only at risk for part of the day (Horsley *et al.*, 1981). Pritchard (1986) found the scale underestimated risk in patients recovering from a myocardial infarction, who had been given high-dose analgesia. It may be a less appropriate tool in acute areas (Jones, 1986).

The Norton scale has also been criticised for not including any reference to nutrition or pain (Barratt, 1988). In Norton's defence, patients' nutritional status will be partly reflected by their 'physical condition'. A cachectic or otherwise anorexic patient is likely to score poorly in this category. A separate, detailed nutritional assessment by the dietician is, however, a useful adjunct to the Norton assessment in any patient where malnutrition is suspected (Section 2.2.2). The presence or absence of pain is likely to be reflected in the 'mobility' score, and the effects of powerful analgesia in 'mental state'. So long as its limitations are borne in mind, especially when assessing patients in an acute setting who may be at risk for only part of the time, the Norton scale, which has stood the test of time through its simplicity, remains a valuable adjunct to the nurse's direct observation and clinical judgement.

Table 6.3 Waterlow's (1988) pressure sore risk assessment scoring system. Ring scores in the table and add total; several scores per category can be used where appropriate. Cards are obtainable from, Newtons, Curland, Taunton TA3 5SG, UK

Build/weight for height	*	Skin type and visual risk areas	*	Sex and age	*	Special risks	*
Average	0	Healthy	0	Male	1		
Above average	1	Tissue paper	1	Female	2	*Tissue malnutrition*	*
Obese	2	Dry	1	14–49	1	e.g. Terminal cachexia	8
Below average	3	Oedematous	1	50–64	2	Cardiac failure	5
		Clammy (Temp↑)	1	65–74	3	Peripheral vascular disease	5
Continence	*	Discoloured	2	75–80	4	Anaemia	2
Complete/catheterised	0	Broken/spot	3	81+	5	Smoking	1
Occasional incont.	1						
Cath./incont. of faeces	2	*Mobility*	*	*Appetite*	*	*Neurological deficit*	*
Doubly incontinent	3	Fully	0	Average	0	e.g. Diabetes, M.S., CVA,	
		Restless/fidgety	1	Poor	1	Motor/sensory, paraplegia	4–6
		Apathetic	2	N.G. tube/fluids only	2		
		Restricted	3	NBM/		*Major surgery/trauma*	*
		Inert/traction	4	anorexic	3	Orthopaedic	
		Chairbound	5			Below waist, spinal	5
						On table > 2 hours	5
						Medication	*
						Steroids, cytotoxics	
						High dose	
						Anti-inflammatory	4

Score	10+ At risk	15+ High risk	20+ Very high risk

There have been several attempts to refine Norton's scale by including more parameters. Gosnell (1973) included skin appearance, tone, and sensation but did not give these parameters a numerical rating. More recent assessment tools devised by Abruzzese (1985) and Waterlow (1985) have included nutritional factors, assessment of skin type, and a 'weighting' for predisposing diseases, especially those involving sensory deprivation, and cardiovascular disorders, which could contribute to tissue ischaemia. Waterlow's risk assessment card (*Table 6.3*) was updated and refined in the light of the findings of two local major pressure sore surveys (Waterlow, 1988). It has a wide applicability and is a useful aid for developing student nurses' awareness of pressure sore risk, observational skills, and clinical judgement.

As Waterlow points out, no risk assessment scale is any substitute for sound clinical judgement, and it is of little use if the risk is not recalculated regularly as the patient's condition changes. Which risk assessment tool to use is largely a matter for personal preference, so long as the user is aware of its limitations. The problem seems to be to get nurses to use any assessment system at all! (Torrance 1983; Spenceley, 1988).

Risk assessment involves **an ongoing assessment of the patient as a whole** and includes assessing the patient's:

- general physical condition
- skin appearance
- mobility
- nutritional status
- continence
- debilitating concurrent illness (where this exists)

- sensory functioning
- cardiovascular status
- conscious state and mental alertness
- physical and social environment

6.4 Assessing the wound

Where tissue damage has occurred, the next step is to identify any local problems that may delay healing, such as necrotic tissue, excess slough, infection, or excess exudate. The importance of accurate and ongoing wound assessment as a prerequisite to planning appropriate care and to evaluating its effectiveness was emphasised in Chapter 2, where it was demonstrated that charting wound healing facilitates accurate recording of observations (see *Figure 2.1*).

6.5 Assessing current local practice for pressure sore prevention

If a patient develops a pressure sore after admission to the ward and its cause cannot readily be traced to events immediately prior to admission (such as lying unconscious at home in a diabetic coma or lying for a prolonged period in one place due to a fractured neck of femur), it is worth reviewing current local practices for pressure sore prevention (*Table 6.4*). It takes only one lapse in turning a high-risk patient for a pressure sore to develop, which is why it is so important that all nurses in a ward achieve the same high standards in patient care achieved by the best. A 10-point action plan for the prevention and management of pressure sores is given in *Figure 6.4*.

6.6 Treatment options

6.6.1 *General treatment options*

No definitive treatment for pressure sores has yet emerged but the general principles of management are:

- **To remove the extrinsic factors significant in the develop-ment and delayed healing of pressure sores, such as unre-lieved pressure, shearing, and frictional forces.**
- **To alleviate the effects of the intrinsic exacerbating factors that can contribute to tissue breakdown, such as malnutri-tion, incontinence, and concurrent illness.**
- **To provide the optimum local environment for healing at the wound site.**

The 10-point action plan given in *Figure 6.4* reflects these principles.

6.6.2 *Ongoing patient assessment*

The action plan in *Figure 6.4* emphasises the importance of early and ongoing risk assessment. Which risk assessment tool to use is largely a matter of personal preference, so long as the user is aware of the tool's limitations (Section 6.3), but it is of paramount importance that the patient is assessed as soon as possible after admission, and that the risk is reassessed whenever there is a material change in the patient's condition.

The underlying tissue damage that can lead to a pressure sore can occur very rapidly; for example, when a patient is waiting to be seen in the Accident and Emergency Department or waiting to be transferred from there to a ward (Hibbs, 1989), or is in the X-ray Department during a special procedure that requires the patient to be placed on a hard

Table 6.4   Assess current local practice for pressure sore prevention

1. *Within one hour* of admission to the ward, is *every* patient assessed for the risk of developing a pressure sore, using a reliable and valid assessment tool?
2. Is the patient's risk *re-assessed* whenever there is a material change in his/her condition (especially if it involves reduced mobility or altered consciousness)?

For patients assessed as being at risk

3. Is the patient put on a support system appropriate to his/her risk, *within 1 hour* of admission to the ward?
4. Is an *individualised pressure sore prevention plan* drawn up, and documented in the nursing notes, within 6 hours of admission?
    Have the factors which put the patient at particular risk been identified?
    Has the patient been involved in drawing up the plan?
5. Where the patient requires to be re-positioned by staff on a regular basis, is the *re-positioning schedule charted*? Does the schedule take full account of the patient's need for sleep, visiting times and meals?
6. Are patient lifting/re-positioning techniques that *minimise* the friction and shearing forces applied to the skin used at all times?
7. If a patient is able to mobilise, but reluctant to do so, or requires some assistance, is a *mobility chart* kept? Has the *physiotherapist's* advice been sought where mobility is a problem?
8. Are the high-risk sites *inspected* regularly, e.g. when re-positioning the patient?
9. If the patient has a problem with urinary or faecal incontinence, have the *causes* of this been fully assessed? Are measures being undertaken to overcome the problems identified?
10. If a patient is found to have been incontinent of urine or faeces, is the skin cleansed *at once*, using minimum friction?
11. Is the patient observed for signs of *dehydration* within 2 hours of commencement of each shift?
12. Has the patient's *nutritional status* been assessed within 24–48 hours of admission? Has the dietician been contacted for advice if malnutrition is suspected?
13. If the patient is having problems *sleeping* in hospital, have the causes been identified and are they being addressed?
14. If the patient is *anxious, fearful or bewildered,* have any measures been taken to alleviate these feelings?

If you can answer *YES* to ALL these questions, your patients are unlikely to develop avoidable pressure sores while in your care.

surface or is on the operating theatre table and trolley. Some patients are at risk for only part of the day, during the acute phase of an illness, or for a few hours immediately post-surgery. Whether through pain or sedation, these patients move less than they normally would.

Nursing interventions need to keep pace with the changing nature of the patient's problems.

Nursing management of wounds

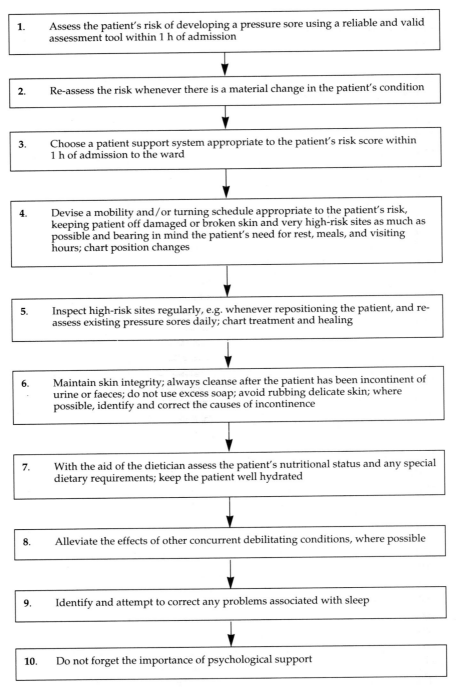

1. Assess the patient's risk of developing a pressure sore using a reliable and valid assessment tool within 1 h of admission

2. Re-assess the risk whenever there is a material change in the patient's condition

3. Choose a patient support system appropriate to the patient's risk score within 1 h of admission to the ward

4. Devise a mobility and/or turning schedule appropriate to the patient's risk, keeping patient off damaged or broken skin and very high-risk sites as much as possible and bearing in mind the patient's need for rest, meals, and visiting hours; chart position changes

5. Inspect high-risk sites regularly, e.g. whenever repositioning the patient, and re-assess existing pressure sores daily; chart treatment and healing

6. Maintain skin integrity; always cleanse after the patient has been incontinent of urine or faeces; do not use excess soap; avoid rubbing delicate skin; where possible, identify and correct the causes of incontinence

7. With the aid of the dietician assess the patient's nutritional status and any special dietary requirements; keep the patient well hydrated

8. Alleviate the effects of other concurrent debilitating conditions, where possible

9. Identify and attempt to correct any problems associated with sleep

10. Do not forget the importance of psychological support

Figure 6.4. Prevention and management of pressure sores: a 10-point action plan.

6.6.3   Relief of pressure, shearing and friction

Positioning the patient   It is a commonly quoted adage that the nurse can put anything on a pressure sore – except the patient. To encourage healing, all pressure should ideally be removed from the site. In practice, however, this is usually not possible, especially in severely deformed patients where repositioning can put undue pressure on other very vulnerable sites. The ideal way to reduce pressure on high-risk areas is to encourage early mobility, but for patients who are sedated or unconscious, who are on a form of treatment that restricts mobility (such as traction) or who are on enforced bed rest for medical reasons, regular repositioning by nurses may be required.

Pressure over high-risk sites must be reduced, so that irreversible tissue breakdown is prevented. A number of turning schedules have been devised (Lowthian 1979). The '30° tilt technique' (*Colour Plate* **44**) is particularly effective, since the pressure is transferred to low-risk 'soft' sites, such as the gluteal muscles, which can tolerate pressures up to three and a half times higher than those tolerated over bony prominences (Preston, 1988). This makes 4-hourly turning feasible for many patients. Extended periods of 8 hours or more are possible for some, allowing a complete night's sleep. As sleep favours the anabolic healing processes, wound healing should be facilitated.

Although pressure on high-risk sites can be relieved by turning patients and careful positioning, as just described, this can be a time-consuming procedure, especially in a busy ward with a high proportion of high-dependency patients. A number of pressure-relieving beds and mattresses are now available which reduce or remove the need for regular manual turning of high-dependency patients (Livesley, 1986), and some of these will now be described.

The ideal support system   The standard 4-inch NHS mattress may be suitable for the agile, low-risk patient, but the pressure-relieving characteristics of such a mattress are poor. The foam within the mattress has a finite life and 'grounding' or 'bottoming out' is not uncommon. Tiny tears in the plastic mattress cover may allow body fluids to accumulate inside the mattress, creating a potential health hazard. A planned and budgeted mattress replacement programme is advisable, with new mattresses date-stamped to check their length of life.

When embarking on a general purpose mattress replacement programme for low-risk patients it is well worth considering replacing NHS mattresses with Omnifoam (Huntleigh Health Care) or Vaperm (Slumberland Medicare) mattresses, which have superior pressure-relieving characteristics (Scales *et al.*, 1982) and are likely to last longer. The Omnifoam mattress has a 'turntable' guide to assist staff to keep a specified mattress-turning routine to prolong mattress life.

In most wards a variety of pressure-relieving beds and mattresses will be required, depending on the range of pressure sore risk of the patient population, including some more sophisticated systems.

Selecting a support system appropriate to the patient's risk of developing a pressure sore, within 1 hour of admission to the hospital or ward, is a very important means of reducing the incidence of avoidable pressure sores. For high-risk patients, the ideal support system should:

- **Distribute pressure evenly, or provide frequent relief of pressure by varying the areas under pressure.**
- **Minimise friction and shearing forces.**
- **Provide a comfortable, well-ventilated patient–support interface which does not restrict movement unduly.**
- **Be acceptable to the patient.**
- **Not impede nursing procedures.**
- **Be easily maintained.**

The advantages and disadvantages of a number of commonly available pressure-relieving beds, mattresses, and overlays, and the principles behind their use are given in *Table 6.5*, and a number of them are illustrated in *Colour Plates* **45–54**.

Once a patient is able to mobilise it is often assumed that he is at far lower risk of developing a pressure sore than when bed bound, but this is certainly not so. The risks may actually be greater.

Elderly and debilitated patients are often left to sit for prolonged periods in chairs that have not been specially designed with their needs in mind and which fail to promote good posture (Lowry, 1989; Dealey *et al.*, 1991). The patient may be reluctant or unable to get out of the chair without assistance and this situation is made worse if the chair itself is too low or too high. If the patient's feet cannot touch the ground, he is likely to adopt a slumped position, sliding down the chair. This leads to considerable shearing forces being applied to the tissues. When these forces are combined with the very high pressures exerted over the ischial tuberosities in the sitting position the risk of deep-seated tissue breakdown is high.

The physiotherapist's advice should be sought to identify the most appropriate type of chair to meet the individual patient's needs and to develop a programme to maximise the patient's mobility. It can be helpful to keep a mobility chart for debilitated patients, delegating a specific nurse on each shift to take responsibility for this, and for other aspects of the patient's care.

The patient–cushion interface is also a very important factor, especially for patients confined to wheelchairs (Ferguson-Pell *et al.*, 1986; Rithalia, 1989), as it affects the local climate at the skin surface

Table 6.5 Some pressure-relieving beds, mattresses, and overlays

Type	Examples (Manufacturers)	Description and principles behind use	Uses and advantages
I *Devices to alternate the area of the body under pressure*			
Alternating pressure mattresses and overlays.	Nimbus Dynamic flotation system (Huntleigh Health Care).	A low-pressure system with figure-of-eight shaped cells to achieve a pressure rating below 20 mm Hg for over 60% of the 10 min cycle. Can be used in dynamic or static mode for certain procedures. Sensor pad ensures that patient is automatically supported at optimum pressures, regardless of weight distribution or position.	1. Very high risk, critically ill patients; patients with severe burns; following major surgery; and patients with existing grade 4–5 pressure sores. 2. A high-performance, low-pressure system at relatively low cost. 3. Fits on top of all standard hospital beds and most domestic beds. 4. Useful for transporting patients to and from X-ray and theatre; mattress can be isolated from pump and will stay inflated for over 24 h.
	Pegasus Airwave System (Pegasus Airwave).	Two layers of air cells; produces a deep rhythmic wave effect from feet to head by deflating every third cell in a 7.5 min cycle. A continuous air flow ventilates the mattress and reduces problems caused by sweat and urine.	1. For very high risk patients; the critically ill; patients for whom normal lifting is contra-indicated; and patients with existing pressure sores. 2. Regular zero skin pressure, for about 2 min in every 7.5 min cycle, which allows blood re-circulation and prevents local ischaemia over high-risk sites. 3. Low interface pressures minimise forward slide and hammocking. 4. Feet-to-head airwave effect aids venous return. 5. Reliable, durable, and easy to clean.

Table 6.5 (cont.)

Type	Examples (Manufacturers)	Description and principles behind use	Uses and advantages
	Alpha Xcell (Huntleigh Health Care) Double Bubble and Alphacare Plus Pump (Huntleigh Health Care).	Alternates the area of the body under pressure. The mattress consists of air cells, which are alternately inflated and deflated by means of an electric pump, controlled on a time switch.	1. Can be very effective in preventing pressure sores in moderate-risk patients; also useful for patients with existing sores, even where positional change is restricted, e.g., traction; large-cell mattresses more effective than medium- or small-cell types. 2. Inexpensive, durable, reliable, and easy to use. 3. Degree of support can be altered according to patient weight and size.
II Devices to reduce and distribute pressure more evenly			
1. Water beds	Beaufort–Winchester (Paraglide).	Patient's weight is evenly distributed in a controlled volume of water (based on Pascal's law) so that there are no pressure gradients and tissue distortion does not occur. Only in deep-tank models is there a sufficient volume to displace the patient's mass without developing tension on the enveloping membrane.	1. Good systems are capable of providing the total hydrostatic support needed for very high-risk patients; for patients with existing pressure sores; and for patients with severe burns. 2. Patients find them comfortable. 3. Pain relief often reported.

2. *Air-fluidised beds*	Clinitron (Support Systems International).	Uses dry flotation to provide hydrostatic support. A flow of warm air is pumped through fine particles, e.g., sand or glass microspheres, to provide fluid-like support characteristics.	1. Provides true hydrostatic support, suitable for intensive care, e.g., a patient with severe burns, multiple trauma, or a critically ill patient who cannot tolerate manual lifting. 2. Air temperature can be controlled. 3. System can absorb exudate, so providing a healthy skin environment. 4. Air fluidisation can be continuous or intermittent; patient handling is easier when fluidisation is switched off. 5. Fluidisation can be stopped instantly in case of cardiac arrest.
3. *Low air-loss bed systems* (LALBS)	Mediscus (Mediscus).	The LALBS consists of waterproof, but vapour permeable, sacks arranged in groups, with pressure valves controlling each group to suit body contours. The bed is hinged, and bellows at the head and foot control posture. There is automatic deformation of the bed to accommodate body form.	1. Uniform pressure on maximum body surface area; therefore suitable for very high-risk patients and patients with existing sores. 2. Low shear stresses. 3. Water can evaporate from the support surface. 4. Temperature and humidity are controllable. 5. Air sacks are easily removable for washing/disinfection. 6. Minimum lifting of patient; variable positions possible. 7. Mobile.

Table 6.5 (cont.)

Type	Examples (Manufacturers)	Description and principles behind use	Uses and advantages
4. *Low pressure air bed*	Simpson–Edinburgh (Kellie).	Consists of two standard air beds placed one on top of the other on a wooden base and with padded sides. An air pump inflates the mattresses to a pre-set pressure and, when the patient is placed on the bed, air is discharged to keep the pressure constant.	1. Low- to moderate-risk patients. 2. Prevents the patient from grounding. 3. Adjustable pressure control ensures the bed is not over-inflated. 4. Relatively inexpensive.
5. *Cut foam mattress*	Polyfloat (Talley).	Consists of two layers of foam bonded together with the upper layer cut into almost independent blocks to reduce the hammock effect from the tension in the otherwise solid foam mattresses.	1. Low-risk patients. 2. Inexpensive, light, and easy to use. 3. Considerable improvement on solid foam mattresses, reducing shearing, but effectiveness is greatly reduced if sheets are tucked in.

6. *Bead Pillow overlays*	Beaufort Bead Pillow Support System (Paraglide).	Patient sinks into the transverse pillows and the beads conform to the patient's shape, instantly adjusting to movement and repositioning.	1. For low-risk patients, and patients with arthritic, rheumatic, and muscular pain. 2. Suitable for both home and hospital use. 3. Very easy to use and adaptable for patients with deformities. 4. Comfortable. 5. Machine washable.
7. *Silicone fibre overlays*	Spenco (Spenco Medical). Superdown (Huntleigh Health Care).	Made up of horizontal fibre-filled compartments.	1. Low-risk patients. 2. Easy to use and maintain, machine washable (with care). 3. Comfortable.
III *Devices to aid turning* Net Suspension beds	Mecabed (Arjo-Mecanaids).	Patient is supported on a slightly elastic open-mesh net suspended from a frame, which fits over the bed. Operated by two winding handles.	1. Moderate- to high-risk patients, especially those unable to tolerate physical handling for turning. 2. Bed conforms to body contours. 3. Provides a ventilated skin environment. 4. One nurse can easily turn even heavy patients.

(temperature and humidity) as well as the forces acting on tissues at high risk of developing tissue necrosis. The aim is to provide uniform pressure distribution over a maximum support area, to reduce shearing, and to provide the optimum local climate for the skin. For some patients a cushion may need to be individually designed to reduce or remove pressure over particularly sensitive areas (Bader and Hawken, 1990). Some examples of pressure-relieving cushions that are suitable for use on wheelchairs are given in *Colour Plates* **55–57**.

For the initial pressure relief of high-risk patients arriving at the Accident and Emergency Department, and for the continuity of pressure relief when it is not possible to keep a patient in his own bed during transfer between departments, a pressure-relieving trolley mattress is very valuable (*Colour Plate* **58**).

For further information on the biomechanics of pressure-relieving aids, nurses are referred to Bader (1990), Young (1990), and Webster (1991).

The beneficial effects of even the most sophisticated support systems can be counteracted if nurses handle patients carelessly. Good lifting technique is very important. It is also a nursing responsibility to understand when a support system is not functioning properly so that it can be reported for repair.

The value of inexpensive and well-tried alternatives should not be underestimated. Sheepskin fleeces under the buttocks and heels can reduce frictional forces. Paraplegic patients can be taught to relieve pressure from the sacral area while in bed by using monkey poles and rope ladders. Bed cradles should be used to remove the pressure of bed clothes from the lower limbs of vulnerable patients, especially those with peripheral vascular problems, who are particularly susceptible to trauma (and where the consequences of a pressure-induced wound could be severe enough to precipitate amputation).

It seems unlikely that there will ever be enough high-technology beds for all our high-risk patients. It is therefore important to make the best use of existing resources, matching those at greatest need to the best pressure-relieving aids. It is also important to prolong the useful life of even the humblest equipment, such as the basic hospital mattress.

6.6.4 *Nutrition*

Malnutrition is second only in importance to excessive pressure in the aetiology, pathogenesis, and non-healing of pressure sores (Agarwal *et al.*, 1985).

Protein deficiency produces a wound with diminished tensile strength, and collagen synthesis is impaired when there is a deficiency of vitamin C (Section 1.6.2). It is therefore essential that the patient's nutritional status should be assessed as soon as possible after admission (Section 2.2.2), with the help of the dietician where necessary, and any deficiencies corrected. The patient should also be kept well hy-drated.

6.6.5 Incontinence

Urinary and faecal incontinence can predispose patients to pressure sores, and delay their healing, by macerating the skin and causing excoriation. Identifying the causes of the incontinence and alleviating them where possible is very important for the patient's overall well-being as well as for pressure sore prevention and treatment. When the patient is incontinent the skin should be cleansed without delay and without applying undue friction (through rubbing the skin).

6.6.6 Debilitating concurrent illness

A number of medical conditions are known to exacerbate the extrinsic factors that cause pressure sores, and to be associated with poor wound healing (see *Table 1.2*) (Westaby, 1985). The prevention and manage-ment of pressure sores involve helping patients to achieve their potentially highest level of 'wellness'—physically, psychologically, and socially—by tackling their wider physical and psychosocial problems.

6.6.7 Local wound management

Removing the primary causes of pressure sores, such as excessive pressure, shearing, and frictional forces (*Colour Plates* **59, 60**), and correcting or alleviating the effects of the factors that exacerbate skin breakdown, such as incontinence and malnutrition (*Figure 6.1*), are the first priorities in pressure sore management, but it is important at the same time to create the optimum local conditions at the wound site to promote healing.

Adverse local conditions at the wound site are summarised in *Figure 1.1*. Priorities in local wound management and the principles behind the selection of the most appropriate primary wound dressing to overcome the problems identified are described in Chapter 3. Methods of wound cleansing are discussed in Chapter 4 and the principles behind the management of clinical wound infection are described in Chapter 5.

Allowing a wound to heal by secondary intention can be a very slow process for a patient with a large full-thickness pressure sore. The alternative to conservative treatment is to surgically close the wound, if the patient's condition permits. The wound should be clean prior to surgery (Buntine and Johnstone, 1988). The ulcer is excised and the wound closed by a graft or by a cutaneous or myocutaneous flap (*Figure 6.5*) (Black and Black, 1987; McGregor, 1989). The decision to repair a pressure sore surgically can be a difficult one to make and will be influenced by many factors, including the patient's general physical condition, the site and extent of the ulcer, and the presence of deep

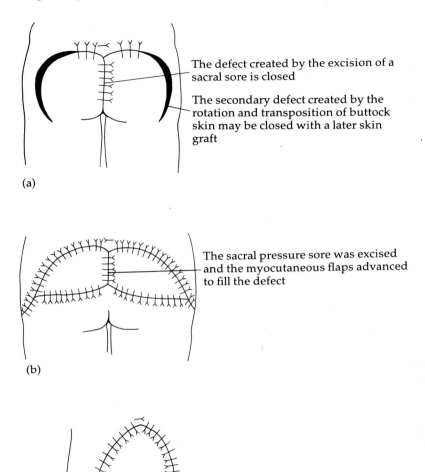

The defect created by the excision of a sacral sore is closed

The secondary defect created by the rotation and transposition of buttock skin may be closed with a later skin graft

(a)

The sacral pressure sore was excised and the myocutaneous flaps advanced to fill the defect

(b)

Secondary defect created by transposition of the skin flap

(c)

Figure 6.5. The use of skin flaps and myocutaneous flaps in the surgical repair of pressure sores: (a) a sacral pressure sore is excised and repaired with bilateral rotation—transposed flaps of buttock skin; (b) repair of an excised sacral pressure sore with a bilateral advancement gluteus maximus myocutaneous flap; (c) a transposed skin flap of posterior thigh skin was used to repair a defect resulting from the excision of an ischial ulcer (based on McGregor, 1989).

infection (including osteitis). Most importantly, the patient must be capable of keeping pressure off the ulcer following surgery. If this cannot be achieved, then flap or graft breakdown is likely in the short term and, even should the graft take, there is a high probability of recurrence of ulceration in the longer term. If it is estimated that the patient can keep pressure off the site, it is also necessary, when planning surgery, to consider whether the positions that the patient must maintain for a successful result could result in further pressure sores elsewhere. This risk in itself could preclude surgical intervention.

Assuming that the patient is suitable for surgical intervention, there are a number of methods of repair from which to choose. Occasionally, excision of a small ulcer and direct suture may be employed. If there is little or no undermining of the skin and the ulcer is relatively large and shallow, the defect may be skin grafted following excision of the ulcer. Deeper defects, especially when accompanied by significant undermining, are usually repaired by means of a skin or myocutaneous flap.

The flap selected will depend on the site, size, and shape of the ulcer. In the non-paraplegic patient, repair of a sacral sore can be achieved by a bilateral rotation flap of buttock skin (*Figure 6.5a*). Flaps incorporating the gluteus maximus muscle may be used to increase the thickness of tissue over the sacral area (*Figure 6.5b*). Ischial ulcers can be repaired using a transposed flap of posterior thigh skin (*Figure 6.5c*). Ulcers over the trochanter of femur are often extensively undermined and are usually repaired with a skin flap or a myocutaneous flap from the lateral aspect of the thigh.

It cannot be emphasised too strongly that keeping the patient off the newly repaired area is of paramount importance for the successful take of the graft or flap. A very high priority should be given to pressure-sore prevention for all sites of the body at risk (Section 6.6.3). In the case of a paraplegic patient, the prevention of pressure sores will be a life-long concern.

6.7   Patient education

The patient's role in pressure sore prevention should not be underestimated (Morison, 1989b).

The benefits of patient education and some basic principles are described in Chapter 12. The Appendix to Chapter 6 is in the form of an information leaflet which nurses may find appropriate for the more alert patient or the carers of a high-dependency patient being nursed at home.

6.8 Developing a pressure sore prevention and treatment policy

If relevant research into the prevention and management of pressure sores is to be put into practice, then its results must be made available to nurses at ward level by nurse educators (Morison, 1989a). The role of management in ensuring that theory is put into practice should not, however, be underestimated. It is, after all, the budget holders who ultimately determine how much is spent on pressure sore prevention and care and senior nurse managers who have considerable infuence on how the money is spent. If a hospital is given, say, £10,000 from a local charity appeal, is it better to spend the money on one low air-loss bed, four Airwave alternating pressure air mattresses, 60 large-cell ripple mattresses, 500 full-length sheepskin fleeces, or some combination of these? There is no easy answer to this question; it depends on what equipment the hospital already has and any special needs that are identified. However, the situation is eased where a health authority has a pressure sore prevention and treatment policy, based on the latest research, which is known and carried out by all staff and which includes monitoring equipment in use, planning equipment acqui- sition, and deciding on priorities for the future (Hibbs, 1988).

The steps involved in developing a pressure sore prevention and management policy are clearly described in a booklet produced by the working party of the Pressure Sore Study Group at the King's Fund Centre for Health Services Development (Livesley, 1989).

Developing an effective pressure sore prevention and management strategy requires the following five measures.

The formation of a multi-disciplinary pressure sore group at unit or health district level This group comprises representatives from the departments of medicine and surgery, nursing, physiotherapy, diet- etics, occupational therapy, pharmacy, education, and management. The group determines its aims, develops a plan of action, and a timetable to reflect its short-, medium- and long-term goals.

Collection of baseline data This includes:

- *Pressure sore point prevalence studies:* Assess the extent of the problem, support the need for a strategy, and give baseline data against which future prevalence data can be compared after a pressure sore prevention policy has been in place for some time.
- *Pressure sore risk survey:* Identify where the highest risk patients are to be found and allocate resources, such as pressure-relieving aids, accordingly.
- *Inventory of pressure-relieving aids:* Determine what is available,

where the equipment is to be found, whether the equipment is in working order, and whether it is in use!

- *Assessment of nurses' knowledge:* Examine the principles behind pressure sore prevention and treatment.

It is also helpful to keep an ongoing pressure sore register in each ward. If a patient with a pressure sore is transferred to a ward, the site and grade of the sore are noted, together with the source of admission. Pressure sores developing after admission are also noted, together with any pre-admission factors that may have led to the tissue damage.

Interpretation of data Data interpretation and the identification of actual or potential problems—for example, the availability and use of resources, the quality of patient care and nurses' knowledge of pressure sore prevention and management methods.

Developing and implementing a plan This may include developing a policy on pressure sore risk assessment, how to select the most appropriate support surfaces, equipment maintenance, procedures for lifting and turning, etc., and monitoring whether the policy is being carried out in practice, as well as devising an in-service training programme to meet local needs.

Evaluating the effectiveness of the plan The plan's success in reducing the incidence of pressure sores and improving the appropriateness of care when pressure sores do arise.

An example of a nursing standard on pressure sore prevention, developed by nursing and paramedical staff at Stirling Royal Infirmary, is given in *Table 6.6*. Further information on quality assurance, quality control, standard setting, and nursing audit can be found in Morison (1991a) and Morison (1991b).

National guidelines

At present, in the UK the emphasis is on the local development of standards, nursing audit, and quality assurance programmes. In the USA a somewhat different approach is being taken for some areas of clinical interest. In 1989 the United States Department of Health and Human Services created a new independent arm: The Agency for Health Care Policy and Research (AHCPR). This agency was charged with creating a process for the development of national treatment guidelines for certain health-related conditions. In 1990, seven conditions were selected as priorities for study: pressure sores, incontinence, cataracts, benign prostatic hypertrophy, pain, depression, and Sickle Cell disease. Interestingly, the first national health guidelines to be developed in the history of the United States were for the prediction,

TABLE 6.6 Core nursing standard on pressure sore prevention (Stirling Royal Infirmary)

TOPIC: Individualised care.
SUB TOPIC: Prevention of pressure sores
CARE GROUP: All hospital patients (other than Theatre, Recovery, Accident & Emergency,
X-Ray Departments, where a satellite standard applies)
STANDARD STATEMENT: Patients receive care appropriate to their risk of developing a pressure sore in order to prevent tissue damage.

ACHIEVE STANDARD BY: ....
REVIEW STANDARD BY: ....
SIGNATURE OF DNS: ....
SIGNATURE OF SENIOR NURSE: ....
DATE ....

STRUCTURE	PROCESS	OUTCOME
1. All nursing staff will have a knowledge of: a. primary causes of pressure sores and exacerbating patient factors. b. sites of the body at particular risk. c. principal methods of pressure-sore prevention. d. correct lifting and patient positioning techniques. e. correct use of pressure-relieving aids. f. the Waterlow and Norton risk-assessment scales.	1. All patients will be assessed for their risk of developing a pressure sore using the Waterlow scoring system, within 1 h of admission, by a registered nurse. 2. The risk will be reassessed whenever there is a significant change in the patient's condition (especially mobility or altered consciousness). 3. Pressure sore risk score. General condition of skin. Site, depth and condition of existing sores on admission or transfer. } will be documented in the nursing notes and on any transfer document, including the theatre check-list.	The risk of a patient developing a pressure sore is minimised. Patients are positioned comfortably. Whenever possible the patient understands and participates in developing the pressure sore prevention programme. Records show that patients with a Waterlow score of 10 or more have been identified within 1 h of admission and appropriate care initiated.
2. A registered nurse will be available to assess or supervise the assessment of the patient's skin condition and pressure sore risk within 1 h of admission to ward.	**FOR PATIENTS IDENTIFIED AS BEING AT RISK (WATERLOW ≥ 10):** 4. Patient will be placed on a pressure-relieving aid appropriate to their risk within 1 h of admission to or transfer within the hospital.	There is continuity of care. The best use is made of available pressure relieving equipment.
3. Pressure relieving equipment will be accessible throughout the 24 h period.	5. An individualised pressure-sore prevention plan will be decided upon with the patient whenever possible, and documented within 8 h of admission to include: • patient support system • mobilisation/positioning regime • nutrition and hydration • skin care • continence and will be updated whenever there is a material change in the patients condition.	
4. Waterlow risk assessment sheets will be available in the ward.	6. Referral will be made to other members of the multi-disciplinary team, e.g., physiotherapist, dietician or continence adviser, when the need is identified.	

prevention, and early treatment of pressure sores, following a review of all the scientific information on pressure sores by a panel of research experts. The priority given to pressure sores is perhaps a reflection of the estimated annual health-care costs in the USA that are attributable to this largely preventable problem, of 3.5–7.0 billion dollars! The National Pressure Ulcer Advisory Panel (NPUAP) presented an educational programme to release the AHCPR guidelines in March 1991, and professional bodies are being consulted for comments on methods of implementation.

APPENDIX

A typical patient information leaflet is shown.

Help us to heal your pressure sore

What is a pressure sore?

A pressure sore is an area where the skin and tissues have been damaged because of:

- Direct pressure on the skin. This can be through sitting or lying in one position for too long, putting pressure on one area.
- Shearing and friction. This can happen when you slide down the bed and rub the skin against the sheets.

You are more likely to develop a pressure sore if:

- You are not eating enough of the right kinds of food to meet your body's present needs.
- You are drowsy or in pain and feel reluctant to move.
- You are unable to move around freely; for instance, if you have a broken bone and you are on traction or if you are on bed rest because of a medical problem.
- You are elderly.
- Your skin is damp, due to perspiration or incontinence.

How common is the problem?

Pressure sores are more common than you might think. Of every 100 patients in hospital, between six and 10 are likely to have a pressure sore at any one time. The risk of developing a pressure sore increases as you get older.

Helping the pressure sore to heal

Whether you develop a pressure sore while in hospital, or already have one before entering hospital, there is a great deal that we can do to help you. We can keep the sore clean and re-dress it as required to reduce the discomfort, but unless we can eliminate the cause of the sore, healing will be very slow indeed.

We need your help!

As most pressure sores are the result of staying in one position for too long, the answer is to:

Relieve the pressure by changing position

Ideally, you should get up out of bed or your chair at least once every 2 hours during the day, and take a short walk. This activity also helps your blood circulation and stops your muscles getting lazy.

If you are confined to a chair you should lift your bottom off the seat for a few moments every half hour by pushing up on the arms of the chair.

If you have to stay in bed, then your bed may be fitted with a 'monkey pole' or rope ladder—the nurse will show you how to use this to lift yourself off the bed.

If your pressure sore is extensive or deep, or your movement is very restricted, a special movement chart will be devised for you by the nursing staff to keep you off the sore as much as possible, and you may be given a special bed or mattress.

Eating the right foods

When you are not feeling well your appetite can be poor, but if you have a pressure sore it is important to get enough of the right nutrients to help the healing process. The dietician may come and talk to you about your diet and can give you special advice to suit your particular needs. As a general rule, unless you are advised otherwise:

- Try to choose food you find appetising.
- Clear your plate at mealtimes, even if you feel 'off your food'.
- Eat plenty of protein (e.g. meat, eggs, fish, cheese), which is needed to make new healthy tissue.
- Take some fresh fruit and vegetables every day—these provide the vitamins and minerals that are needed for healing and the fibre that helps prevent constipation.

Sleep

Most healing occurs when you are asleep at night. If you are having difficulty with sleeping, talk to one of the nurses about it, or mention it to the doctor.

Don't be afraid to ask questions

Don't be afraid to ask the nurses or doctor how things are progressing, especially if the wound is in a place where you cannot see it! It is not usually possible to say when healing will be complete, but we are very happy to tell you what we are doing to help the healing process.

Further reading

General review

Torrance, C. (1983), *Pressure Sores: Aetiology, Treatment and Prevention.* Croom Helm, Beckenham, Kent.

General reviews and biomechanics

Bader, D.L. (ed.) (1990), *Pressure Sores: Clinical Practice and Scientific Approach.* Macmillan, London.

Developing a pressure sore prevention and management policy

Hibbs, P. (1988), Pressure area care for the City and Hackney Health Authority. (Available from Chief Nursing Officer, St. Bartholomew's Hospital, West Smithfield, London, EC1A 7BE.)

Livesley, B. (ed.) (1989), The Prevention and Management of Pressure Sores within Health Districts. Working party of the Pressure Sore Study Group at The King's Fund Centre for Health Services Development. (Available from The Academic Unit for the Care of the Elderly, Charing Cross Hospital, Fulham Palace Road, London W6 8RF.)

References

Abruzzese, R.S. (1985), Early assessment and prevention of pressure sores. In Lee, B.K. (ed.), *Chronic Ulcers of the Skin*. McGraw-Hill, New York.

Agarwal, N. *et al.* (1985), The role of nutrition in the management of pressure sores. In Lee, B.K. (ed.), *Chronic Ulcers of the Skin*. McGraw-Hill, New York.

Agate, J. (1976), Skin care: medical factors in the causes of pressure sores. *Modern Geriatrics*, May, 33–37.

Bader, D.L. (ed.) (1990), *Pressure Sores—Clinical Practice and Scientific Approach*. Macmillan, London.

Bader, D.L. and Hawken, M.B. (1990), Ischial pressure distribution under the seated person. In Bader, D.L. (ed.), *Pressure Sores—Clinical Practice and Scientific Approach*. Macmillan, London.

Barbenel, J.C. (1990), Movement studies during sleep. In Bader, D.L. (ed.), *Pressure Sores—Clinical Practice and Scientific Approach*, pp. 249–260. Macmillan, London.

Barbenel, J.C., Jordan, M.M., Nicol, S.M. *et al.* (1977), Incidence of pressure sores in the Greater Glasgow Health Board Area. *The Lancet*, 2, 548–550.

Barratt, E. (1988), A review of risk assessment methods. *Care—Science and Practice*, 6(2), 49–52.

Barton, A. and Barton, M. (1981), *The Management and Prevention of Pressure Sores*. Faber and Faber, London.

Bennet, L. and Lee, B.K. (1985), Pressure versus shear in pressure sore causation. In Lee, B.K. (ed.), *Chronic Ulcers of the Skin*, McGraw-Hill, New York.

Black, J.M. and Black, S.B. (1987), Surgical management of pressure ulcers. *Nurs. Clin. N. Am.*, 22, 429–438.

Buntine, J.A. and Johnstone, B.R. (1988), The contributions of plastic surgery to care of the spinal cord injured patient. *Paraplegia*, 26, 87–93.

Capen, D.A. (1985), Evaluation and treatment of skin pressure sores in the spinal cord injured patient. In Lee, B.K. (ed.), *Chronic Ulcers of the Skin*, pp. 69–76. McGraw-Hill, New York.

Chapman, E.J. and Chapman, R. (1986), Treatment of pressure sores: the state of the art. In Tierney, A.J. (ed.), *Clinical Nursing Practice*, pp. 105–124. Recent Advances in Nursing Series, Churchill Livingstone, Edinburgh.

Chow, W.W. *et al.* (1976), Effects and characteristics of cushion covering membranes. In Kenedi, R.M. *et al.* (eds), *Bedsore Biomechanics*. Macmillan, London.

David, J.A. *et al.* (1983), *An Investigation of the Current Methods used in Nursing for the Care of Patients with Established Pressure Sores*. Nursing Practice Research Unit, Harrow.

Dealey, C., Earwacker, T. and Eden, L. (1991), Are your patients sitting comfortably? *J. Tissue Viability*, **1**(2), 36–39.

Exton-Smith, N. (1987), The patient's not for turning. *Nursing Times*, **83**(42), 42–44.

Ferguson-Pell, M.W. *et al.* (1986), Development of a modular wheel chair cushion for spinal cord injury persons. *J. Rehab. Res. Dev.*, **23**, 63–76.

Forrest, R.D. (1980), The treatment of pressure sores. *Journal of International Medical Research*, **8**(6), 430–435.

Goldstone, L.A. and Goldstone, J. (1982), The Norton Score: an early warning of pressure sores? *Journal of Advanced Nursing*, **7**(5), 419–426.

Gosnell, D.J. (1973), An assessment tool to identify pressure sores. *Nursing Research*, **22**, 55–59.

Gould, D. (1985), Pressure for change. *Nursing Mirror*, **161**(16), 28–30.

Gould, D. (1986), Pressure sore prevention and treatment: an example of nurses' failure to implement research findings. *Journal of Advanced Nursing*, **11**(4), 389–394.

Hibbs, P.J. (1988), *Pressure Area Care for the City and Hackney Health Authority*. St Bartholomew's Hospital, London.

Hibbs, P.J. (1989), *Strategy for Fractured Neck of Femur Patients*. City & Hackney Health Authority.

Horsley, J.A. *et al.* (1981), *Preventing Decubitus Ulcers*. Grune and Stratton, New York.

Jones, J. (1986), An investigation of the diagnostic skills of nurses on an acute medical unit relating to the identification of risk of pressure sore development in patients. *Nursing Practice*, **1**(4), 257–267.

Jordan, M.M. and Nicol, S.M. (1977), *Incidence of Pressure Sores in the Patient Community of the Borders Health Board Area on 13 October 1976*. University of Strathclyde Bioengineering Unit and Borders Health Board, Glasgow.

Kosiak, M. (1959), Etiology and pathology of ischaemic ulcers. *Archives of Physical Medicine and Rehabilitation*, **40**, 62–69.

Lancet Editorial (1990), Preventing pressure sores. *Lancet*, **335**, 1311–1312.

Livesley, B. (1986), Airwaves take the pressure. *Nursing Times*, **82**(32), 67–71.

Livesley, B. (1987), Pressure sores: an expensive epidemic. *Nursing Times*, **83**(6), 79.

Livesley, B. (ed.) (1989), *The Prevention and Management of Pressure Sores within Health Districts*. Working party for the Pressure Sore Study Group at The King's Fund Centre for Health Services Development. (Available from the Academic Unit for the Care of the Elderly, Charing Cross Hospital, Fulham Palace Road, London W6 8RF.)

Lowry, M. (1989), Are you sitting comfortably? *Professional Nurse*, **5**(3), 162–164.

Lowthian, P. (1979), Turning clocks system to prevent pressure sores. *Nursing Mirror*, **148**(21), 30–31.

McGregor, I.A. (1989), *Fundamental Techniques of Plastic Surgery and Their Surgical Applications*. Churchill Livingstone, Edinburgh.

Morison, M.J. (1989a), Delayed pressure sore healing can be prevented. *Professional Nurse*, **4**(7), 332–336.

Morison, M.J. (1989b), Pressure sore management: The patient's role. *Professional Nurse*, **5**(3), 134–141.

Morison, M.J. (1991a), The Stirling model of nursing audit: its relationship to standard setting and quality assurance. *Professional Nurse*, **6**(7), 366–370.

Morison, M.J. (1991b), The Stirling model of nursing audit. *Professional Nurse*, **6**(7), Wallchart.

Mulholland, M. *et al.* (1943), Protein metabolism and bedsores. *Annals of Surgery*, **118**, 1015–1023.

Norton, D. *et al.* (1962), *An Investigation of Geriatric Nursing Problems in Hospital.* National Corporation for the Care of Old People, London.

Petersen, N.C. (1976), The development of pressure sores during hospitalisation. In Kenedi, R.M. *et al.* (eds), *Bedsore Biomechanics*, pp. 219–224. Macmillan, London.

Preston, K.W. (1988), Positioning for comfort and pressure relief: the 30 degree alternative. *Care: Science and Practice*, **6**(4), 116–119.

Pritchard, V. (1986), Calculating the risk. *Nursing Times*, **82**(7), 59–61.

Report of the Royal College of Physicians (1986), Physical disability in 1986 and beyond. *Journal of the Royal College of Physicians*, **20**(3), 28–29.

Rithalia, S.V.S. (1989), Comparison of pressure distribution in wheel chair cushions. *Care: Science and Practice*, **7**(4), 87–92.

Scales, J.T. (1990), Pathogenesis of pressure sores. In Bader, D.L. (ed.), *Pressure Sores—Clinical Practice and Scientific Approach*, pp. 15–26. Macmillan, London.

Scales, J.T., Lowthian, P.T., Poole, A.G. *et al.* (1982), 'Vaperm' Patient support system: a new general purpose hospital mattress. *Lancet*, **2**, 1150–1152.

Silver, J. (1987), Letter. *Care: Science and Practice*, **5**(3), 30.

Spenceley, P. (1988), Norton v. Waterlow, *Nursing Times*, **84**(32), 52–53.

Thiyagarajan, C. and Silver, J.R. (1984), Aetiology of pressure sores in patients with spinal cord injuries. *Br. Med. J.*, **289**, 1487–1490.

Torrance, C. (1983), *Pressure Sores: Aetiology, Treatment and Prevention.* Croom Helm, Beckenham, Kent.

Versluysen, M. (1986), How elderly patients with femoral fractures develop pressure sores in hospital. *Br. Med. J.*, **2**, 1311–1313.

Waterlow, J. (1985), A risk assessment card. *Nursing Times*, **81**(48), 49–55.

Waterlow, J. (1988), The Waterlow card for the prevention and management of pressure sores: towards a pocket policy. *Care: Science and Practice*, **6**(1), 8–12.

Webster, J.G. (ed.) (1991), *Prevention of Pressure Sores: Engineering and Clinical Aspects.* Adam Hilger, Bristol.

Westaby, S. (ed.) (1985), *Wound Care.* Heinemann Medical Books, London.

Young, J.B. (1990), Aids to prevent pressure sores. *Br. Med. J.* (14 April), 1002–1004.

7 Leg Ulcers

7.1 Epidemiology

7.1.1 The size of the problem

Large-scale studies, both in the United Kingdom and in Europe, suggest that about 1% of the population develop a leg ulcer at some point in their lives (*Table 7.1*), with one-fifth of those people having an open ulcer at any one time.

The incidence of leg ulceration rises with age. Over the age of 65, women are at far higher risk of developing a leg ulcer than men. The reasons for this are uncertain, but hormonal changes after the menopause have been implicated.

Table 7.1 Epidemiology of leg ulcers

Prevalence (open or healed)	
Ten per thousand of the adult population, rising to 36 per thousand of the population over 65 years of age	
Sex ratio	**Male: Female**
under 65	1:1
65–74	1:2.6
75–84	1:4.8
85+	1:10.3
Recurrence rates (%)	
1 episode	33
2–5 episodes	46
over 6 episodes	21
Healing rates (%)	
Time to heal	
up to 3 months	21
3 months to 1 year	29
1–5 years	40
over 5 years	10

Lothian and Forth Valley Leg Ulcer Study (after Dale and Gibson, 1986)

Leg ulcers are notoriously slow to heal: 50% of ulcers are open for more than 1 year (Cornwall *et al.*, 1986; Dale and Gibson, 1986) and 10% are open for more than 5 years (*Table 7.1*). Chronic leg ulceration may plague some people for virtually the whole of their adult life. The recurrence rate for ulceration is also depressing, with about two-thirds of patients experiencing two or more episodes and 21% of patients over six episodes of ulceration. There is an old adage:

Once an ulcer patient always a potential ulcer patient.

This is borne out by surveys that show that half the patients with an ulcer have a history of ulceration dating back at least 10 years (Callam *et al.*, 1987b).

7.1.2   Who carries out the care?

There are very few specialist leg ulcer centres, with outpatient clinics, in the United Kingdom. The majority of patients are cared for in the community by district nurses, at GPs' surgeries or by relatives who may or may not be adequately instructed or supervised.

7.1.3   The cost of caring

Caring for leg ulcers can be very costly. One survey found that 50% of patients with ulcers were having their dressings changed every 1–2 days, 16% twice a week, and 26% once a week (Dale and Gibson, 1986).

Determining the cost of treatment is difficult. Any costing must include costs of:

- District Nurses' time and travelling.
- Wound dressing materials, such as dressing packs, cleansing solutions, primary and secondary dressings, and bandages.
- Hospitalisation for ulcers that will not heal, where patients require complete bed rest, for vascular surgery, or skin grafting.

Staff at the Charing Cross Hospital's leg ulcer service have estimated the current annual cost per patient of treating a leg ulcer at between £2,700 and £5,200. It has been estimated that leg ulcers cost the National Health Service £400–800 million annually, for the United Kingdom as a whole.

7.2   The causes of leg ulcers

7.2.1   Introduction

A number of factors, some acting together, can lead to the development of leg ulcers (*Table 7.2*). While a minor traumatic incident is generally the immediate cause of the ulcer, the *underlying* problem is usually vascular.

Table 7.2 Causes of leg ulcers

A. Principal causes
1. *Chronic venous hypertension.* Usually due to incompetent valves in the deep and perforating veins.
2. *Arterial disease.* Atherosclerotic occlusion of large vessels or arteritis of small vessels, leading to tissue ischaemia.
3. *Combined venous hypertension and arterial disease.*

B. Unusual causes (less than 1% in total)
1. *Malignancy.* Squamous cell carcinoma, melanoma or basal cell carcinoma.
2. *Infection.* Tuberculosis, leprosy, syphilis, deep fungal infections (all rare causes in the UK but still seen in the tropics).
3. *Blood disorders.* Polycythaemia, haemoglobinopathies.
4. *Metabolic disorders.* Pyoderma gangrenosum, pretibial myxoedema.
5. *Lymphoedema.* Normally only associated with ulceration when venous hypertension is also present or following cellulitis.
6. *Trauma.* Usually the immediate cause of ulceration in most cases, and the primary cause in a few cases where there is no clinically significant underlying vascular problem.
7. *Iatrogenic.* Over-tight bandaging, or ill-fitting plaster cast.
8. *Self-inflicted.*

Over 70% of leg ulcers encountered in the United Kingdom are primarily the result of *chronic venous hypertension. Poor arterial blood supply* accounts for about 10% of leg ulcers, and a further 10–15% of ulcers are of *mixed arterial and venous origin.*

More unusual causes of ulceration, amounting to no more than 1% of causes, include malignancy, infection, lymphoedema, blood disorders, and certain metabolic disorders.

A few leg ulcers are primarily due to trauma, some are a secondary complication of treatment, and an unknown proportion are self-inflicted.

Identifying the underlying cause of the ulcer has important implications for treatment. To understand the major causes of ulceration requires an understanding of the anatomy of the vascular system of the lower limb and the mechanics of blood flow there.

7.2.2 Venous ulcers

The anatomy of the venous system in the lower limb and the mechanics of blood flow   Both superficial and deep systems of veins are found in the leg (*Figure 7.1*).

The superficial long and short saphenous veins are designed to carry blood under low pressure and have many valves to prevent back flow.

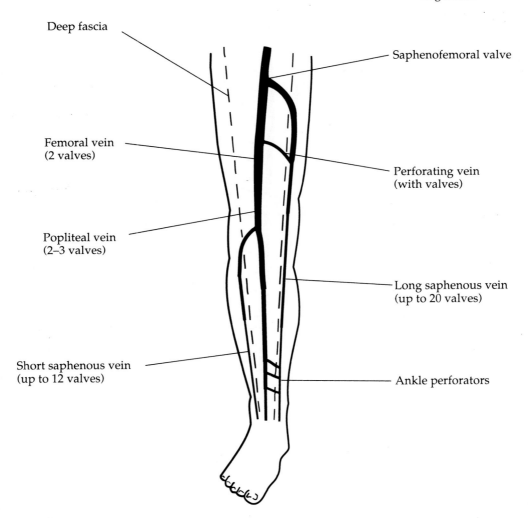

Deep fascia

Saphenofemoral valve

Femoral vein
(2 valves)

Perforating vein
(with valves)

Popliteal vein
(2–3 valves)

Long saphenous vein
(up to 20 valves)

Short saphenous vein
(up to 12 valves)

Ankle perforators

Figure 7.1. A diagrammatic representation of the normal anatomy of the venous system of the leg (based on Orr and McAvoy, 1987).

They lie outside the deep fascia and drain into the deep venous system, which comprises the popliteal and femoral veins. The deep veins are designed to carry blood back to the heart under much higher pressure and they have fewer valves. The superficial and deep systems are connected by perforating veins which pass through the fascia. Blood is returned to the heart from the periphery, via the venous system, by a combination of mechanisms acting together, including muscle contraction, capillary pressure, and variations in intra-abdominal and intra-thoracic pressure.

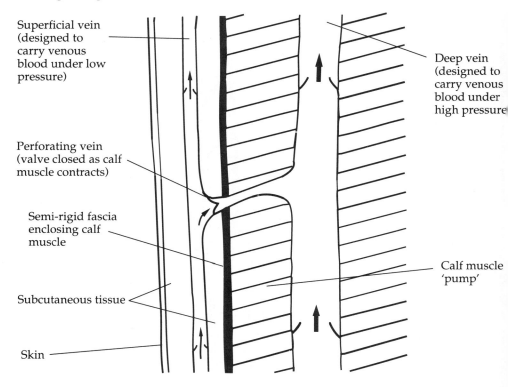

Superficial vein (designed to carry venous blood under low pressure)

Deep vein (designed to carry venous blood under high pressure)

Perforating vein (valve closed as calf muscle contracts)

Semi-rigid fascia enclosing calf muscle

Calf muscle 'pump'

Subcutaneous tissue

Skin

Figure 7.2. Healthy, intact valves prevent backflow of blood from the deep to the superficial veins.

Active calf muscles, in their semi-rigid fascial envelope, act as a *pump*, forcing deep venous blood upwards towards the heart. When healthy and intact, the valves in the perforating veins prevent back-flow of blood to the superficial system (*Figure 7.2*). During periods of muscle relaxation, blood flows from the superficial veins to an area of temporarily lower pressure in the deep veins (beneath the closed valves), filling them, before the calf muscle pump acts again to force this blood centrally away from the extremities.

If the valves in the perforating veins become incompetent (*Figure 7.3*), the back-pressure is transmitted directly to the superficial venous system, damaging more distal valves and eventually leading to varicose veins. Damaged valves in the deep and perforating veins result in *chronic venous hypertension* in the lower limb, the high back-pressure causing *venous stasis* and *oedema*.

The role of the calf muscle pump in aiding venous return has been described. The ankle movement involved in walking is also important,

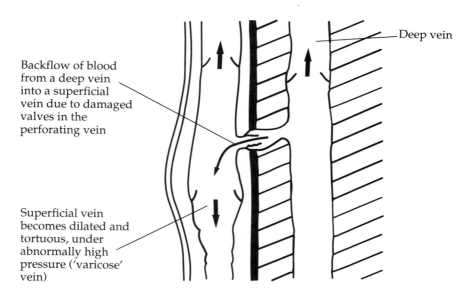

Backflow of blood from a deep vein into a superficial vein due to damaged valves in the perforating vein

Deep vein

Superficial vein becomes dilated and tortuous, under abnormally high pressure ('varicose' vein)

Figure 7.3. An incompetent valve in a perforating vein allows backflow of blood from the deep to the superficial venous system.

as tensioning the Achilles tendon alternately stretches and relaxes the calf muscle, independently of calf muscle contraction, further aiding venous return.

Another mechanism is involved in aiding venous return from the foot. Emptying of the foot veins is facilitated by external pressure as the heel strikes the ground during walking (Gardner and Fox, 1986).

In patients who are 'off their feet' neither the foot pump nor the calf muscle pump can operate, and the efficiency of venous return is markedly impaired.

Some patients' mobility is limited by restricted ankle movement, as seen in people with, for example, extensive ulceration in the gaiter area, lipodermatosclerosis (hardening of the dermis and underlying subcutaneous fat), or with extensive fibrosis. Restricted ankle movement makes venous return of blood to the heart much less efficient.

The clinical signs of chronic venous hypertension Some of the complications arising from chronic venous hypertension, which are summarised in *Figure 7.4*, are described below.

Varicose veins Varicose veins are a common problem, found in 10–20% of the adult population. People in occupations which involve prolonged

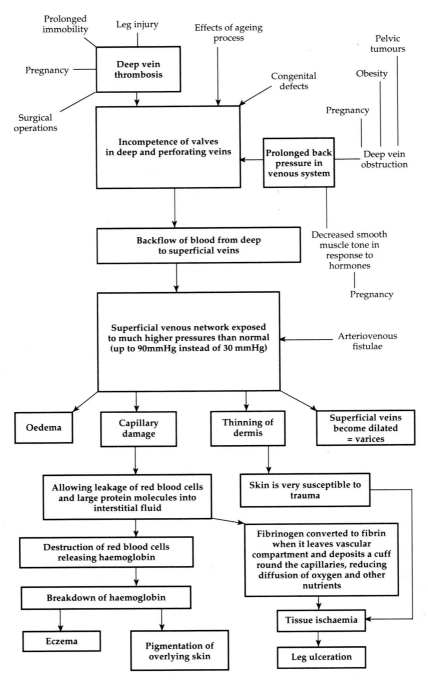

Figure 7.4. Venous ulcers: pathophysiology—a tentative model.

Table 7.3   Factors thought to predispose the development of varicose veins

1. *Family history.*
2. *Occupation:* those involving standing in warm conditions.
3. *Gender:* more common in women than men with increasing age.
4. *Pregnancy.*
5. *Low fibre diet.*
6. *Obesity.*

standing in warm conditions, such as nurses, airline stewardesses, teachers, and storemen are particularly at risk (*Table 7.3*).

Varicose veins are a sign of chronic venous hypertension in the lower limb, which is usually due to damage to the valves in the leg veins. The damage may be congenital or acquired (*Table 7.4*). The result is that the superficial venous network is exposed to much higher pressures than normal (up to 90 mmHg instead of 30 mmHg). The superficial veins, especially the relatively thin-walled tributaries of the long and short saphenous veins, become dilated, lengthened, and tortuous. About 3% of patients with varicose veins go on to develop leg ulcers.

Table 7.4   Causes of varicose veins and raised venous pressure in the lower leg

1. *Primary*	• Due to congenital defect in the vein wall (collagen defect). • Due to valve cusps absent or abnormal.
2. *Secondary*	• *Obstructed venous return* due to pregnancy, pelvic tumours or ascites; leads to prolonged back pressure in the venous system and incompetent deep and perforating vein valves. • *Distortion of the valve cusps* caused by deep vein thrombosis (resulting, for example, from leg injury, prolonged immobility, pregnancy and surgery).

Staining of skin in the gaiter area   Chronic venous hypertension leads to distension of the blood capillaries, with resulting damage to the endothelial walls and leakage of red blood cells and large protein molecules into the interstitial fluid (*Figure 7.4*). Destruction of the red blood cells releases breakdown products of haemoglobin, which leads to pigmentation of the overlying skin (*Colour Plate* **61**).

Ankle flare   Chronic venous hypertension can cause distension of the tiny veins on the medial aspect of the foot. This is particularly noticeable where the valves in the perforating veins in the ankle and lower calf are incompetent and is sometimes referred to as 'ankle flare' (*Colour Plate* **61**).

Atrophy of the skin Browse and Burnand (1982) have put forward the hypothesis that when blood capillaries are exposed to high pressures fibrinogen leaks out of damaged capillaries and is deposited around them as a fibrin cuff. This is thought to inhibit diffusion of oxygen and nutrients to surrounding tissues and the removal of metabolic waste products. Diffusion is further impaired by the presence of excess interstitial fluid in oedematous limbs.

Thinning of the dermis, associated with a poor blood supply, makes the skin very susceptible to trauma. Other trophic changes include stasis eczema and lipodermatosclerosis.

Eczema Wet or dry eczema is often associated with a poor peripheral blood supply and can be aggravated by a number of wound care products (see Section 7.4.5).

Lipodermatosclerosis 'Woody' induration of the tissues and fat necrosis is seen as an end-stage phenomenon. The leg often assumes the shape of an 'inverted champagne bottle', wide at the knee and very narrow at the ankle.

Ulceration is the end point of the trophic changes described above, affecting about 1% of the adult population and about 3% of the people with varicose veins. It is often precipitated by a *minor traumatic event*, such as a knock while alighting from a car, which would not cause significant skin breakdown in a person with healthy circulation in the leg.

7.2.3 Arterial ulcers

There are many causes of ischaemia in the lower leg, the most common being atherosclerosis. The co-existing atheroma and arteriosclerosis are degenerative changes often associated with advancing age. The severity of atherosclerosis is higher in *males*, and other risk factors include *hypertension* and *smoking*.

Other causes of ischaemia include rheumatoid arthritis (*Colour Plate* **62**) and diabetes mellitus, which tends to affect smaller distal arteries, *Buerger's disease*, and *Raynaud's disease*. Arterial embolism and trauma can cause acute ischaemia, which is potentially the most damaging (as well as life-threatening) because the body has not had time to develop a collateral circulation to compensate.

The relationship between arterial disease and arterial ulcers is summarised in *Figure 7.5*. Tissue ischaemia that results from a narrowing or distortion of arterioles predisposes to necrosis and ulceration following minor trauma. The skin surrounding the ulcer is often shiny, hair loss is common, but there is no brown staining in the gaiter area unless there are also venous problems (*Colour Plates* **63, 64**).

The significance of an arterial component in leg ulcer aetiology is being increasingly recognised. Both Cornwall *et al.* (1986) and Callam *et al.* (1987a) estimated that about 21% of patients presenting with leg ulcers have evidence of arterial insufficiency, which has implications for treatment. This is why the accurate differential diagnosis of venous and arterial leg ulcers is so important and will now be described.

7.3 Patient assessment

7.3.1 Introduction

When a patient presents for the first time with a leg ulcer a general patient assessment is required to determine:

- The underlying **cause** of the ulcer.
- Any **local problems at the wound site** that may delay healing—such as infection, excess exudate, or necrotic tissue.
- Other general **medical conditions** that may delay healing.
- The patient's **social circumstances** and the optimum setting for care.

7.3.2 Assessing the underlying cause of the ulcer

Unless the underlying *cause* of the ulcer is determined and where possible corrected, delayed wound healing is inevitable. At worst, inappropriate treatment can lead to the necessity to amputate the limb!

Assessment of the patient's clinical signs and symptoms, medical history, and some simple investigations normally give sufficient information for the nurse to decide whether the patient is presenting with an ulcer as a result of:

- **Chronic venous hypertension** (70% of ulcers).
- **Arterial disease** (about 10% of ulcers).
- **A combination of chronic venous hypertension and arterial disease** (10–20% of ulcers).
- **Some other cause** (about 1% of ulcers).

If there is any doubt about the ulcer's aetiology, the nurse is strongly advised to refer the patient to a doctor, as soon as possible, to arrange for further tests.

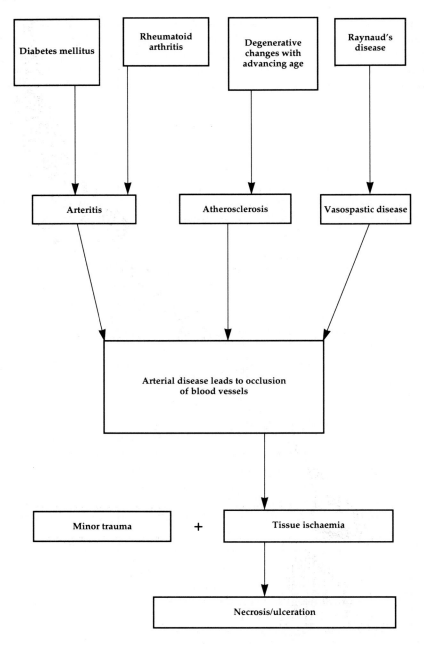

Figure 7.5. Arterial ulcers: pathophysiology.

Clinical signs and symptoms The clinical signs and symptoms of venous and arterial disorders in the lower limb are summarised in *Tables 7.5* and *7.6*, respectively. An explanation of the underlying patho-physiology which gives rise to these signs and symptoms was given in Section 7.2, which discussed the mechanisms leading to ulceration.

Table 7.5 Venous problems: clinical signs and symptoms

1. *Prominent superficial leg veins or symptoms of varicose veins*
   - *Aching* or *heaviness* in legs, generalized or localized.
   - Mild ankle *swelling*.
   - *Itching* over varices.
   - Symptoms due to thrombophlebitis, localized *pain, tenderness* and *redness*.

   Gentle exercise such as walking round the room or repeated heel raising helps to show distension of the veins.
2. *Skin surrounding the ulcer*
   - *Ankle flare* distension of the tiny veins on the medial aspect of the foot below the malleolus.
   - *Pigmentation* 'staining' of the skin around the ulcer due to breakdown products of haemoglobin from extravasated red blood cells.
   - *Lipodermatosclerosis* hardening of dermis and underlying subcutaneous fat.
   - *Stasis eczema.*
   - *Atrophe blanche* ivory white skin stippled with red 'dots' of dilated capillary loops.
3. *Site of ulcer*
   - Frequently near the medial malleolus, sometimes near the lateral malleolus.
4. *Characteristics of the ulcer*
   - *Depth and shape* usually shallow, with flat margins; often an elongated oval in shape.
   - *Pain* only painful if grossly infected and/or there is marked peripheral oedema.
   - *Changes over time* develop slowly if untreated unless seriously infected, e.g. with β-haemolytic streptococci.

Medical history *Table 7.7* summarises factors in a patient's medical history which may throw some light on the underlying vascular problems that led to the development of the ulcer.

Chronic venous hypertension is suggested by a history of varicose veins with valve incompetence, which may have been precipitated by any one or more of a number of thrombogenic events, e.g. leg fracture, post-surgery immobility, or during pregnancy.

Callam *et al.* (1987a) found that a history of stroke, transient ischaemic attacks, angina, or myocardial infarction increased the probability of

Table 7.6 Arterial problems: clinical signs and symptoms

1. *Whole leg/foot*
   Symptoms
   - *Intermittent claudication*: cramp-like pain in the muscles of the leg, brought on by walking a certain distance (depending partly on speed, gradient and patient's weight). The patient then has to stop and stand still to rest the ischaemic calf muscles.
   - *Ischaemic rest pain*: intractable constant ache felt in the foot, typically in the toes or heels overnight in bed. Usually relieved by dependency: hanging the leg over the bed or sleeping upright in a chair.

   Signs
   - Coldness of the foot (but not specific to ischaemia).
   - Loss of hair.
   - Atrophic, shiny skin.
   - Muscle wasting in calf or thigh.
   - Trophic changes in nails.
   - Poor tissue perfusion, e.g. colour takes more than 3 s to return after blanching of toe-nail bed by applying direct pressure.
   - Colour changes foot/toes dusky pink when dependent, turning pale when raised above the heart.
   - Gangrene of toes.
   - Loss of pedal pulses.
2. *Site of ulcer*
   - Usually on the foot or lateral aspect of the leg but may occur anywhere on the limb, including near the medial malleolus (most common site for venous ulcers).
3. *Characteristics of the ulcer*
   - *Depth and shape*: often deep with loss of tissue exposing muscle and tendons, especially if the patient has rheumatoid arthritis; often irregular in shape and may be multiple small lesions, e.g. in diabetic patients.
   - *Pain*: can be very painful.
   - *Changes over time*: rapid deterioration is characteristic.

arterial impairment in the lower limb, and a history of intermittent claudication was almost invariably associated with poor peripheral perfusion.

Simple vascular assessment In the past *the presence of palpable foot pulses* has been taken as a sign of unimpaired arterial circulation, and the *absence* of pulses as indicative of arterial impairment. This is not an entirely 'fail-safe' test. Oedema is a common problem in patients with venous ulcers and can make pulses hard to feel.

A simple vascular assessment technique, which can be readily carried out by nurses with a little training, is the *resting pressure index (RPI) test*.

Table 7.7 Past medical history

1. *Indicators of possible venous problems*
   - *Previous thrombogenic events*
     Has the patient ever suffered from one or more of the
     following:
       deep vein thrombosis
       thrombophlebitis
       leg or foot fracture
     in the affected limb?
   - *Varicose veins*
     Does the patient have prominent superficial leg veins, with
     signs of valve incompetence?
     Has the patient ever had any varicose vein surgery or
     sclerotherapy in the affected leg?
2. *Indicators of possible arterial problems*
   - *Generalized arterial disease*
     Are there any indicators of arterial disease such as:
       previous myocardial infarction
       angina
       transient ischaemic attacks
       intermittent claudication
       cerebrovascular accident
       diabetes mellitus
       rheumatoid arthritis?

This is a most important starting point in patient assessment and it requires little practice to become proficient at this technique.

The RPI test involves determining the ratio of ankle-to-brachial systolic pressures using a simple hand-held battery operated Doppler ultrasound probe in place of a stethoscope. The patient should sit with the legs elevated on a stool for at least 20 minutes before the ankle systolic pressure is measured, to overcome the effects of gravity. During this time the patient's history can be taken and the brachial systolic pulse taken in the usual way. To measure the ankle systolic pressure the cuff is sited just above the malleolar area (above the ulcer) and the pressure measured using either the posterior tibial or dorsalis pedis pulse (*Colour Plates* **65, 66**).

$$\text{Resting Pressure Index (RPI)} = \frac{\textbf{Ankle systolic pressure}}{\textbf{Brachial systolic pressure}}$$

The RPI allows for individual variations in blood pressure and should normally be greater than 1.0. Patients with a ratio of 0.9–0.95 probably have some degree of arterial disease. If the RPI is less than 0.8 there is significant impairment in the arterial blood supply, which means that compression bandaging is contraindicated. A ratio of 0.5–0.75 is often associated with intermittent claudication and <0.5 with ischaemic rest pain. A referral to a doctor is advisable if the index is below 0.75.

In diabetic patients a falsely high RPI will be obtained. *No graduated compression should be applied to a diabetic patient's leg, except under the closest medical supervision.* An RPI above 1.2 may also be pathological; for example, in a patient with medical calcinosis. If in any doubt about the significance of the RPI consult the doctor for further advice.

Table 7.8   Other simple investigations

1. *Urinalysis* particularly to detect undiagnosed diabetes, which is often associated with peripheral arterial problems.
2. *Blood tests* to test for rheumatoid and antinuclear factors which may indicate potential arteritis or autoimmune disorders; full blood count and estimation of haemoglobin levels.
3. *Patch testing for allergens*, e.g. lanolin and parabens, which are present in many commonly used wound care products.
4. *Tissue biopsy* if malignant changes are suspected.
5. *Wound swabs* to identify the causation and antibiotic sensitivity of any organisms causing clinical signs of infection.

Other investigations   Some further investigations (*Table 7.8*) can yield valuable results.

Further vascular assessment methods   The physician may decide to request a more detailed vascular assessment, especially if localised occlusion of a blood vessel is suspected which might be amenable to surgery. Options include:

- *Venography (ascending phlebography)*: Detects acute thrombosis, chronic occlusion of the deep veins with the development of collateral circulation, and incompetent perforators.
- *Arteriography*: Investigates the site and extent of arterial occlusion, which is essential before any arterial reconstruction can be considered.

Incompetent valves in the perforating veins, and saphenofemoral and saphenopopliteal reflux can be demonstrated using portable Doppler ultrasound equipment (Ruckley, 1988). Such assessment requires considerable experience and is generally the province of the vascular surgeon. Other non-invasive vascular laboratory assessment techniques include foot volumetry to assess the efficiency of the foot and calf muscle pumps; plethysmography to measure ambulatory venous pressure (Norris *et al.*, 1983); and ultrasound imaging, which allows direct imaging of the deep and superficial veins (Ruckley, 1988).

Mixed aetiology ulcers Of leg ulcers, 10–20% do not fall neatly into either the venous or arterial ulcer categories. A patient's leg may show all the classic signs of chronic venous hypertension but there may also be underlying arterial problems. The checklist in *Table 7.9* can be used to help to determine whether the ulcer is venous, arterial, or of mixed aetiology.

Only 1% of leg ulcers are not due to vascular problems (*Table 7.2*). If the wound has an unusual appearance, is refractory to healing, or if the patient has recently arrived in the United Kingdom from abroad a more unusual cause should be suspected. *If the nurse is unsure of the underlying cause of any ulcer, the patient should be referred to a doctor for further assessment.*

7.3.3 Assessing the ulcer itself

After assessing the underlying cause of the ulcer, assessment of the wound itself should be undertaken (Chapter 2), as this may determine the method of wound cleansing (Chapter 4) and the most appropriate primary wound contact dressing (Chapter 3).

To assess the effectiveness of treatment it is helpful to *trace* the ulcer using an acetate sheet or transparent sterile glove and a fine permanent marker pen (*Figure 2.2*). The tracing can be annotated with further information, such as the nature of the wound bed and wound margins, some indication of the depth of the wound, the date and the patient's name.

Charting the healing of leg ulcers (see *Figure 2.1*) is helpful in evaluating the effectiveness of local wound treatment. A leg ulcer may show no signs of healing because:

- The local problems at the wound site have not been dealt with appropriately.
- The underlying cause of the ulcer has not been identified and corrected.
- Some other patient factor is delaying healing.

7.3.4 Other factors that may affect healing

When taking patients' histories and carrying out assessments of their current general physical condition, it is worth noting any other factors that could delay wound healing (see *Figure 1.1*), such as

- Evidence of or suspected *malnutrition*.
- *Poor mobility*, whatever the cause, which may adversely affect the calf muscle pump and venous return.
- An *occupation* or activities that involve prolonged standing, especially in warm conditions.

Table 7.9 Differential diagnosis of venous and arterial leg ulcers: some points to consider when assessing patients (tick boxes that apply to the patient; the pattern of ticks should give some indication of the underlying aetiology of the ulcer)

Indicators of venous problems

1. *Past medical history*
   - Has the patient ever suffered from any of the following: deep vein thrombosis, thrombophlebitis or leg/foot fracture in the affected limb? ☐
   - Has the patient ever had any varicose vein surgery or sclerotherapy in the affected limb? ☐

2. *Clinical signs and symptoms in the leg*
   - Prominent superficial leg veins. ☐
   - Brown pigmentation of the skin around and just above the ankle. ☐
   - Distension of the tiny veins in the medial aspect of the foot. ☐
   - Lipodermatosclerosis (hard 'woody' induration of the lower leg). ☐
   - Stasis eczema. ☐
   - Atrophe blanche (skin thin, white and stippled with red dots). ☐

3. *The ulcer*
   - Ulcer shallow, flat margins. ☐
   - Ulcer not painful (unless clinically infected). ☐
   - Site of ulcer: near medial or lateral malleolus (but may be anywhere). ☐

4. *Simple vascular assessment/tests*
   - Pedal pulses present. ☐
   - Resting pressure index (RPI) >0.9. ☐

Indicators of arterial problems

1. *Past medical history*
   - Are there any indicators of generalized arterial disease, e.g. myocardial infarction, angina, transient ischaemic attacks, intermittent claudication, cerebrovascular accident, diabetes mellitus, rheumatoid arthritis? ☐

2. *Clinical signs and symptoms in the leg*
   - Intermittent claudication. ☐
   - Ischaemic rest pain. ☐
   - Pain relief when the leg is lowered below heart level. ☐
   - Foot dusky pink when dependent, turning pale when elevated above the heart. ☐
   - Poor tissue perfusion, e.g. colour takes more than 3 s to return after blanching of toe-nail bed by applying direct pressure. ☐
   - Loss of hair, atrophic shiny skin. ☐

3. *The ulcer*
   - Ulcer deep, with loss of tissue exposing muscle and tendon. ☐
   - Ulcer very painful. ☐
   - Site of ulcer: on foot or lateral aspect of the leg (but may be anywhere). ☐

4. *Simple vascular assessment/tests*
   - Pedal pulses absent or very faint indeed. ☐
   - Resting pressure index (RPI) <0.9. ☐

- *Decreased resistance to infection,* whatever the cause.
- Poor *social* circumstances.

The patient's occupation and social circumstances should also be considered when deciding on the *practical arrangements* for managing the ulcer. The effects of advancing age on the rate of wound healing, even in an otherwise healthy individual, should not be underestimated (see Section 1.6.3).

7.4 Treatment options

7.4.1 Priorities in leg ulcer management
Having assessed the patient, and identified the underlying cause of the ulcer, and any local problems at the wound site, the next step is to plan appropriate care. The main priorities are:

- *Correcting the underlying cause of the ulcer* (this normally means improving the patient's venous and/or arterial circulation in the affected limb).
- *Creating the optimum local environment at the wound site.*
- *Improving all the wider factors that might delay healing* (especially poor mobility, malnutrition, and psychosocial issues).
- *Preventing complications* (such as wound infection or tissue damage due to overtight bandaging).
- *Maintaining healed tissue.*

The principles behind the management of venous, arterial, and mixed aetiology ulcers will now be described, with the emphasis on correcting the underlying cause of the ulcer. Creating the optimum local environment for healing is discussed in Section 7.4.5 and ways of correcting or alleviating the effects of general patient factors that can delay healing are discussed in Section 7.4.6.

7.4.2 The management of venous ulcers
Introduction The main cause of venous ulceration is chronic venous hypertension, with very high pressures being exerted on the superficial system, usually due to incompetent valves in the deep or perforating veins (Section 7.2).

The primary aims of venous ulcer management are therefore:

- *Reducing the pressure in the superficial venous system*
- *Encouraging venous return of blood to the heart, by increasing the velocity of flow in the deep veins*
- *Discouraging oedema, by reducing the pressure difference between the capillaries and the tissues.*

The best way to do this is to apply *graduated compression*, from the base of the toes to the knee, with the highest pressure at the ankle, falling to 50% of this pressure at the knee. Methods of achieving graduated compression include:

- *Bandages*, e.g. Blue Line, Tensopress, Setopress, Veinopress, Elasto-crepe.
- *Shaped Elasticated tubular bandage*, e.g. Tubigrip.
- *Compression stockings*, e.g. Venosan, Sigvaris, Jobst, Medi (UK).

The advantages and disadvantages of each method are shown in *Table 7.10*.

The characteristics of compression bandages Compression bandages can be divided into those containing an *elastomer*, such as rubber or Lycra, as in Blue Line, Elset, and Tensopress, and those *without elastomer*, which rely on crimped cotton, wool, or rayon threads for their extensibility, such as Elastocrepe, and all types of crepe bandage.

The *elasticity* of the bandage determines the amount of tension needed to achieve the required pressure, the ability of the bandage to maintain this pressure, and the conformability of the bandage to the awkward contours of the foot, ankle, and leg.

Some of the factors affecting the *pressure* that can be achieved under a bandage are given in the following equation:

$$P \text{ is proportional to } \frac{N \times T}{C \times W}$$

where P is the pressure exerted by the bandage, N is the number of layers of bandage, T is the bandage tension, C is the circumference of the limb, and W is the bandage width. Thus, the *more layers* (N) that are applied to the leg, the higher the pressure (P).

The *bandage tension* (T) is proportional to the *elasticity* of the bandage, the amount the bandage is *stretched* when it is applied, the number of times the bandage has been *washed*, and the *length of time* the bandage has been in place.

The *circumference of the limb* (C) also affects sub-bandage pressure. As the pressure exerted by the bandage is *inversely* proportional to the circumference of the leg, the thinner the leg the higher the pressures obtainable. *Dangerously high pressures* can be achieved with very heavy compression bandages in frail elderly patients with thin legs, especially over bony prominences such as the malleolus and tibia, and over the tendonous prominences around the ankle (*Colour Plate* **67**). Conversely, it is difficult to achieve high compression on a wide diameter leg. When seeking to aid venous return, graduated compression is required, with the highest pressure at the ankle (30–40 mm Hg), gradually decreasing to about 50% of this pressure just below the knee. Since most legs are considerably narrower at the ankle than at the knee, graduated compression is *automatically* achieved if the bandage is applied at the *same tension* all the way up the leg.

The advantages and disadvantages of a range of compression bandages are given in *Table 7.11*. As new products are regularly being added to the Drug Tariff, for community use, it is advisable to check which bandages are currently available.

Applying the bandage   It is helpful to place the patient's leg on a stool, with the foot at a right angle, and at a height which is comfortable for the nurse to work at. All the materials required should be arranged so that they are within easy reach.

When applying any sort of compression to the lower leg it is important to include the *base of the toes* and to apply the bandage to just below the knee. Graduated compression can be obtained by applying the bandage *at the same tension* all the way up the leg, after suitably padding bony prominences. *Colour Plates* **68–73** show how the bandage should be applied, beginning with the base of the toes, incorporating the heel and filling in under the foot before spiralling up the leg. Extra pressure can be achieved at the ankle by beginning the bandaging with a locking turn. This is particularly important when applying the lighter compression bandages, such as Elastocrepe, if they are to maintain reasonable pressures for several days.

Multilayer bandaging can help to achieve good compression, even when only medium-to-low compression bandages are available. A layer of Velband (Johnson & Johnson) or Soffban (Smith & Nephew) is applied up to the knee, starting at the ankle to prevent excessive bulk over the foot. An Elastocrepe bandage is applied from the base of the toes to the knee, and this can be prevented from slipping by applying an outer layer of shaped Tubigrip. The size of the Tubigrip required should be determined by measuring the circumference of the ankle and calf *after* the other layers have been applied. Any surplus Tubigrip should be cut off at the knee to prevent a garter effect from hindering venous return.

Another effective multilayer regime, developed at Charing Cross Hospital, London, is Velband/Crepe/Elset/Coban. The Coban is a relatively inelastic cohesive bandage (*Table 7.11*) against which the calf muscle pump can act, aiding venous return.

Whichever bandaging regime is used, care should be taken to overlap bandages evenly to prevent tight bands over bony prominences. Where bandages overlap the pressure is higher than where there is a single layer of bandage. It is therefore important that each turn of the bandage overlaps its predecessor by half the bandage width to give an even pressure gradient. When the bandage is removed no deep grooves or

Table 7.10 Methods of achieving graduated compression

Method	Advantages	Disadvantages
1. Bandages	a. Can be left in situ for up to a week in the absence of excess exudate except for highest compression bandages, e.g. Blue Line. b. By varying the tension under which the bandage is applied the pressure can be varied to suit individual needs and tolerances. c. A range of bandages is available in the community. d. Relatively low initial cost.	a. Excessively high pressures can be obtained with the heavy compression bandages, especially on thin legs and over bony prominences. b. Not cosmetically acceptable to many, leading to low compliance. c. Uncomfortable in hot weather. d. May require patient to purchase a larger size of shoe to accommodate bandage. e. Some prone to slip, leading to tight bands.
2. Shaped elasticated tubular bandages	a. Two layers toe to knee useful in patients who cannot tolerate an elastic compression bandage. b. Can help to reduce bandage slippage when used over a medium–light compression bandage.	a. Not currently available in the community. b. Only slightly increases the pressures obtained when applied over a bandage; little sustained compression achieved when applied alone.
3. Elastic compression stockings	a. Pressure profiles of stockings are tested and known. b. A range of compression profiles is available to meet individual needs. c. Much safer than inappropriately applied heavy compression bandages. d. Cosmetically acceptable. e. Useful in preventing recurrence of ulceration.	a. Require proper fitting for length, ankle and calf size. b. Initial cost is high, but compares well with the cost of elastic compression bandages over 6 months. c. Difficult for patients with restricted movement to apply themselves. d. Compliance rate variable; high compression stockings often poorly tolerated by the elderly but well liked by younger patients who are more mobile.

indentations should be seen. Bandage damage can precipitate amputation, especially in ischaemic limbs where compression is contraindicated.

It is well worth practising bandaging technique on a friend, before practising on patients! One method that can be used to gain a feeling for the correct pressures is to inflate a sphygmomanometer cuff round the ankle to 40 mm Hg and then move it up to the upper calf and inflate it to 20 mm Hg. The cuff should feel pleasantly firm and supportive but not too tight.

Some bandages, e.g. Setopress, now include a simple visual guide to facilitate application of the bandage at the correct extension (*Colour Plates* **74**, **75**).

For some patients with chronic skin disorders a *paste* bandage may be indicated (*Table 7.12*). Several layers are applied over the ulcerated area and the paste bandage folded back over itself (*Colour Plate* **76**), over the bony prominences, to prevent excessive pressure here and to allow the leg room to expand should it become oedematous (as it may do in hot weather or if the patient stands in one place for too long).

A double layer of tube gauze can be applied over the paste bandage before continuing with the multilayer principle, e.g. Velband/Tensopress/shaped Tubigrip. Paste bandages are soothing and can rehydrate the skin surrounding the ulcer. Unfortunately they contain ointment bases and preservatives that lead to sensitivity reactions in some patients.

A very interesting alternative to paste bandages is the *hydrocolloid adhesive compression bandage (HACB)* made by Convatec. This medium–high compression bandage (*Table 7.11*) can be applied direct to the skin, with a hydrocolloid wafer dressing over the ulcer itself. The hydrocolloid in the bandage helps to rehydrate dry eczematous skin over the whole leg (Clay and Cherry, 1990) (*Colour Plates* **77**, **78**) and patients find it comfortable and conformable. There is minimum slippage of the bandage, which maintains good pressures for many days (Sockalingham *et al.*, 1990). The bandage is contraindicated, however, in patients with very fragile, paper thin skin.

Compression stockings Compression stockings have a number of advantages over bandages (*Table 7.10*): they are a safer alternative, so long as the patient has been properly measured for them, and they are more cosmetically acceptable to many people. They are not, however, particularly easy to put on; this problem can be overcome for many patients by supplying them with a dressing aid (*Colour Plates* **79**, **80**). Full-length stockings are required only in a few instances—when treating patients with severe post-phlebitic syndrome, or lymphoedema with swelling in the thigh. Generally, below-knee stockings are

Table 7.11 Advantages and disadvantages of a number of commonly used compression and support bandages

Type of bandage	Examples (Manufacturer)	Advantages	Disadvantages
1. *Non-adhesive extensible bandages* Very high compression	Blue Line (Seton); Elastoweb (Smith & Nephew)	a. High pressures obtainable, suitable for counteracting venous stasis in the lower limb for active patients with venous ulcers (RPI $\geq$ 0.9 and preferably $\geq$ 1.0). b. Can be washed and reused.	a. High risk of tissue necrosis over bony prominences if inexpertly applied, especially to a thin leg. b. Must be taken off at night and reapplied in the morning, therefore only suitable for patients who can apply the bandage themselves. c. Cosmetically unacceptable to some patients.
Medium–high compression	Tensopress (Smith & Nephew); Veinopress (Steriseal); Setopress (Seton)	a. Good compression, well sustained, suitable for patients with venous ulcers (RPI $\geq$ 0.9). b. Less risk of pressure necrosis than with very high compression bandages. c. Can be worn continuously for up to one week. d. Comfortable and conformable. e. Can be washed and reused.	a. High pressures can be obtained over thin legs, therefore potentially hazardous if inexpertly applied.
Light compression/light support	Elastocrepe (Smith & Nephew)	a. Useful over paste bandages; increasing pressure achieved and pressure maintained over time (RPI $\geq$ 0.8).	a. Low pressures obtained; used alone it only gives light support. b. A single wash reduces

		b. Performance improved when covered with shaped elasticated tubular bandage which helps to prevent bandage slippage.	pressures obtained by about 20%. c. Bandage slippage can occur.
Light support only	Crepe (Many manufacturers)	Only useful for: a. Holding dressings in place. b. As one of several layers in a multilayer bandage in treatment of venous ulcers. c. For light support of minor strains and sprains.	a. Pressures obtained are too low to be effective in management of venous ulcers. b. 40–60% of bandage tension (and hence pressure) lost in first 20 min after application.
2. *Cohesive extensible bandages* Cohesive bandages	Tensoplus forte (Smith & Nephew); Coban (3M); Secure forte (Johnson & Johnson); Lestreflex (Seton)	a. Adhere to themselves, preventing slippage, therefore useful over non-adhesive bandages such as Elastocrepe, and over paste bandages. b. Compression well sustained. Suitable for patients with an RPI ≥ 0.85–0.9.	a. Can be hazardous in inexperienced hands as can cause tight bands round ankle and damage to tendons if wrongly applied.
3. *Hydrocolloid adhesive compression bandages* Hydrocolloid compression bandage	Granuflex adhesive compression bandage (Convatec)	a. Good compression, well maintained (RPI > 0.8). b. Comfortable and conformable. c. Hydrocolloid can greatly improve condition of skin surrounding ulcers. d. Little slippage.	a. Not recommended for very fragile skin or where there is extensive wet eczema.

Table 7.12 Paste bandages

Principal constituents	Proprietary name	Manufacturer	Indications
1. Zinc paste	Viscopaste PB7 Zincaband	Smith & Nephew Seton	General purpose treatment for leg ulcers, venous stasis eczema and chronic dermatitis. Soothing. Sensitivity reactions relatively infrequent.
2. Zinc paste and calamine	Calaband	Seton	Emollient properties, soothing and hydrating for dry, scaly lesions surrounding leg ulcers. Can be applied over ulcer itself.
3. Zinc paste and ichthammol	Ichthopaste	Smith & Nephew	Wet ulcers surrounded by sensitive skin. Soothing and mildly keratolytic. Ichthammol has a milder action than coal tar and is useful in less acute forms of eczema.
4. Zinc paste and coal tar	Coltapaste Tarband	Smith & Nephew Seton	Dry, itchy eczema where the skin surface has not broken down. Coal tar relieves itching and has keratolytic properties.

all that is required, and being easier to apply than full-length hosiery, compliance is likely to be better.

Compression stockings give graduated compression, with the greatest compression exerted at the ankle, and are graded into three classes (Dale and Gibson, 1990):

Class I   Light compression: used to treat mild varicose veins.

| Class II | Medium compression: used to treat more severe varicosities and to prevent venous ulcers in patients with thin legs. |
| Class III | Heavy compression: used to treat severe chronic venous hypertension and severe varicose veins and to prevent ulcers in patients with large-diameter legs. |

Intermittent compression therapy Pneumatic intermittent compression therapy, which can be helpful in reducing oedema and aiding venous return in hospitalised patients, has been found to be less successful in patients living at home as many patients are wary of the apparatus and are disinclined to use it (Hazarika and Wright, 1981).

Precautions when applying compression Before any treatment is begun a full assessment of the patient should be done (Section 7.3) to eliminate the possibility that the patient also has an arterial problem in the affected leg with poor peripheral perfusion. Graduated compression should not be applied if the RPI is less than 0.8 or if the leg is oedematous. The oedema must *not* be reduced by applying a compression bandage, which could lead to extensive tissue damage. Limb elevation or bed rest may be required in severe cases (Section 7.4.6). **If in doubt consult the patient's doctor** *before* **applying compression**.

Local wound management is discussed in Section 7.4.5 and in Chapters 3–5.

7.4.3 The management of arterial ulcers

The prognosis for an elderly patient with an arterial ulcer is much less hopeful than for a patient with a venous ulcer, properly treated, unless the underlying arterial problem is relatively local and is amenable to surgery. Where there are generalised arterial problems, such as arteritis, associated with rheumatoid arthritis, or micro-angiopathy, associated with diabetes mellitus, the treatment will be the doctor's responsibility. Vasodilator drugs are of questionable benefit and even symptomatic relief of the effects of ischaemia is hard to achieve in some patients. The nurse's responsibility will be confined to symptom relief, local wound management (Section 7.4.5 and Chapters 3–5), and patient education.

Patients should be encouraged to mobilise to the limit of their capabilities, to avoid smoking, to keep warm, to reduce weight where this is a problem, and to eat a nutritious diet (see Section 7.5).

Compression bandaging should *not* be applied as severe damage to the leg can result (*Colour Plates* **67, 81**). For example, see Callam *et al.* (1987d).

7.4.4   The management of mixed aetiology ulcers

Where the underlying cause of the ulcer appears to be a *combination* of *chronic venous hypertension* and *poor peripheral arterial circulation*, it is the degree of *arterial* insufficiency that will determine whether or not it is safe to apply compression. If the RPI is *less than 0.8 no compression* should be applied. If the RPI is 0.8–0.9 the patient may tolerate only light compression, such as a double layer of shaped elasticated tubular bandage or a paste bandage plus a light support bandage (*Table 7.11*).

7.4.5   Creating the optimum local environment for healing

Introduction   Correcting the *underlying cause* of an ulcer, where possible, is the first principle of leg ulcer management, but at the same time it is important to create the optimum conditions at the *wound site* to promote healing.

Adverse local conditions at the wound site that can delay healing are summarised in *Figure 1.1*, and include clinical infection, necrotic tissue, excess slough, excess exudate, and dehydration. Priorities in wound management and selection of the most appropriate primary wound dressing to overcome these problems are discussed in this section (see also Chapter 3), which also contains a brief mention of the use of ultrasound to stimulate healing and a summary of the indications for skin grafting.

Creating the optimum local environment for healing begins with cleansing the whole leg.

Cleansing the leg   Before applying any kind of dressing to an ulcer it is important to render the whole of the lower leg 'socially clean'. One way to do this is to immerse the leg in a deep plastic bowl, lined with a disposable polythene bag, and half filled with lukewarm tap water. This helps to remove debris from the ulcer and the surrounding skin, and is comforting for the patient, especially if the leg has been encased in a multilayer bandage regimen for the previous week! The leg can be gently dried with soft disposable paper and the bowl surface disinfected as in the Health Board Infection Control Policy.

If the leg is known to be clinically infected by a virulent microorganism, reversion to an aseptic technique for wound toilet is desirable, in the short term, to reduce the risk of contaminating the physical environment and to reduce the risk of cross-infection.

After washing the whole leg, the ulcer can be traced (see *Figure 2.2*) before a dressing is applied.

Local wound management

Introduction   The principles behind the local management of leg ulcers are the same as for any open wound. Guidance in the selection of the most appropriate primary wound dressing to overcome local problems is given in Chapter 3, and guidance on the management of clinical wound infection is given in Chapter 5.

If a wound is producing *copious* volumes of exudate, attempting to mop this up with a dressing is not enough. The skin surrounding the ulcer quickly becomes macerated, especially at the lower border, and 'strike through' of exudate increases the risk of wound infection. The oedema should be reduced, as described in Section 7.4.6, and then the levels of exudate will lessen until a stage is reached when weekly dressing changes are sufficient. In the meantime, extra absorbent padding can be applied over the primary dressing and under the bandages.

Sensitivity to wound care products Sensitivity to components found in topical skin and wound preparations is a common phenomenon in patients with leg ulcers. Signs and symptoms of a sensitivity reaction include marked erythema of the skin (where the product has been in contact), aggravation of pre-existing eczematous conditions, and itching.

The commonest causes of a sensitivity reaction include:

- *Topical antibiotics*, e.g. neomycin or framycetin sulphate.
- *Bases of ointments*, e.g. lanolin.
- *Preservatives*, e.g. parabens (Fraki *et al.*, 1979).

Several proprietary antiseptics and antihistamine creams that patients buy and administer to themselves can also cause an adverse skin reaction in some patients.

The paste bandages (*Table 7.12*) can cause sensitivity reactions in some patients. The longer the ulcer has been open the more sensitive to skin and wound care products the patient is likely to be.

If a sensitivity reaction does occur, use of the sensitising agent should be discontinued at once, and the event clearly documented in the patient's notes. A 1% hydrocortisone cream may be prescribed by the doctor for application only to the skin surrounding the ulcer. Until the reaction has subsided, only the blandest of dressings should be applied to the wound itself, such as a non-medicated paraffin tulle dressing.

Patch testing can be used to identify allergens, but the results should be viewed with caution. Late positive reactions can occur (Paramsothy *et al.*, 1988), three weeks or more after the patch test, and the skin on the back, where patch testing is often performed, is less readily sensitised than the skin surrounding the ulcer. This is why some doctors suggest carrying out the patch test a little higher up on the same leg. In some centres, patients are routinely patch tested (Cameron, 1990) in order to prevent contact dermatitis, as far as possible.

Ultrasound Several studies have suggested that ultrasound can promote healing in chronic wounds, and results in healed wounds with greater strength and elasticity. Callam *et al.* (1987c) found that treatment with ultrasound once-a-week was effective when used as an adjunct to compression therapy.

Surgical intervention: skin grafting The healing of large venous ulcers may be rapidly accelerated by simple skin grafting methods using either pinch (*Colour Plate* **82**) or meshed split-skin. Although skin grafting can even be performed on outpatients taken as day cases, greater success is likely to be attained with inpatient care (Ruckley, 1988). Before grafting is carried out a period of bed rest is usually required to reduce oedema and promote the formation of healthy granulation tissue. The successful take of a graft requires a 'clean' wound bed, free from potential pathogens such as haemolytic streptococci and pseudomonads (see Section 1.5).

A successful skin graft can give a new lease of life to a patient who has suffered from chronic ulceration for many years (Moody, 1984), but in itself is no guarantee that ulceration will not recur.

7.4.6 Wider issues
The causes of delayed healing The main cause of delayed healing in leg ulcers is:

Failure to identify and treat the underlying cause of the ulcer

---

Other causes of delayed healing include local wound infection (Chapter 5), sensitivity to wound care products and a number of *general patient factors* (see *Figure 1.1*). Factors particularly significant for patients with leg ulcers—restricted mobility, oedema in the limb, malnutrition, and psychosocial problems—are now discussed in turn.

Restricted mobility Poor mobility is a common problem for elderly patients with leg ulcers, whether because of joint stiffness, neuromuscular disorders, obesity, or respiratory problems. Improving mobility in patients with any type of leg ulcer aids venous return by activating the calf muscle pump and reduces the risk of other problems associated with prolonged immobility, such as chest infections and deep vein thromboses.

Patients should be encouraged to mobilise to the limits of their ability. For a patient with advanced arterial disease the limit may be 100–200 metres, or even less. By contrast, many patients with venous ulcers are capable of walking 3–5 kilometres per day, and should be encouraged to do so. This is the ideal and may be unattainable for many elderly patients, especially if their poor mobility is accompanied by chronic respiratory problems.

The *physiotherapist* may need to be involved if the patient has restricted ankle movements or other musculoskeletal problems. Housebound patients can be encouraged to walk on the spot for a few minutes every hour. Prolonged standing in one place should be avoided. Washing up and ironing can be done sitting down if chairs of suitable height are available. Chairbound patients can be taught ankle extension, flexion, and rotation exercises by the physiotherapist or nurse.

Peripheral oedema There are many causes of peripheral oedema, including cardiac failure, liver disease, venous disease, and malnutrition. Peripheral oedema in a dependent limb can also be encountered in a patient with hemiparesis following a cerebrovascular accident. Identification by the doctor of the underlying cause of the oedema is important as this will in part determine treatment.

Whatever its cause, peripheral oedema in the lower limb delays healing by increasing the diffusion distance between blood capillaries and the tissues they serve, so that the tissues become starved of oxygen and nutrients and metabolic waste products build up.

No attempt should be made to reduce oedema by applying compression bandages—this can cause further ischaemia and breakdown of tissues, especially over bony prominences.

Improving mobility is one very important way of reducing oedema. For patients with venous ulcers, sitting with the legs elevated *above the level of the hips* (*Colour Plate* **83**) helps to reduce oedema by aiding venous return of blood to the heart. It is *not* sufficient to raise the legs a few inches above the ground by placing them on a low foot stool.

Most patients will benefit from sleeping with *the foot of the bed raised 9 inches,* as this aids venous return and can significantly reduce oedema overnight. However, sudden return of fluid to the heart caused by leg elevation can precipitate cardiac and/or respiratory failure in frail elderly patients. It is therefore advisable to check with the patient's physician that leg elevation is not contraindicated. It is unlikely to be tolerated in patients with poor arterial circulation who often find it necessary to lower the affected limb below the heart to reduce ischaemic rest pain. It is also worth enquiring whether the patient suffers from dyspepsia, as reflux oesophagitis is made worse by leg elevation.

Severe oedema can be alleviated by bed rest, but prolonged bed rest causes problems of its own. Patients may be less mobile when they get up, with stiffened ankle and knee joints. They may develop a chest infection, or a deep vein thrombosis that causes further damage to the valves in their veins.

Malnutrition   As with all wounds, delayed healing is inevitable if the patient's diet is deficient in protein, calories, vitamins, such as A and C, and minerals, such as iron, zinc, and copper.

Malnutrition is a common problem for the elderly for many reasons. Poverty, difficulty in getting to the shops and in preparing food, loss of interest in diet when living alone, and ill-fitting dentures are all implicated, as well as specific gastrointestinal disorders involving malabsorption problems.

If malnutrition is suspected a full patient assessment should be carried out by the *dietician* (Goodinson, 1986; Williams, 1986). Overweight patients can be just as 'malnourished' as the obviously underweight if their diet is deficient in vitamins and minerals. *The control of obesity can make a crucial contribution to ulcer healing* by reducing prolonged back-pressure in the venous system, caused by deep vein obstruction in the pelvic area (*Figure 7.4*), and by enabling increased mobility.

Where the causes of malnutrition are largely social the *health visitor* or *social worker* can help to arrange meals on wheels, lunch club activities, etc.

Psychosocial issues   Many patients with leg ulcers are elderly, poor, and alone. They welcome the visits of the community nurse who treats their ulcer, because of the social contact that it brings. Much has been written about the 'social' ulcer. There is no doubt that some patients do not have a vested interest in their ulcer healing, but the proportion of patients who actually *interfere* with the ulcer in an attempt to delay healing is unknown. Many patients who interfere with their bandages do so for very good reasons: the bandage may have been applied under *too much tension*, especially over the dorsum of the foot, causing considerable discomfort; the bandage may have *slipped*, causing a tight band of constriction, and pain over a bony prominence; a *bulky* bandage may be causing the patient problems with wearing ordinary footwear.

Prodding a knitting needle between the bandage and the leg may be the patient's solution to an intolerable itch rather than a wilful attempt at undoing the nurse's good work in attempting to heal the ulcer. The natural recurrence rate for leg ulceration is also high, especially if no measures are taken to prevent recurrence.

If, after exploring with the patient the reasons behind obvious tampering with bandages and dressings, a conscious attempt at self-inflicted injury is still suspected, the problem *must* be dealt with sympathetically.

If the problem is one of loneliness, ways of improving the patient's social contacts should be explored with the *health visitor* and the *Social*

Services' social worker. If the patient is finding it increasingly difficult to cope alone at home, some form of day-care may need to be considered.

7.5 Patient education

Where patients are truly partners with the health care team in planning their care and monitoring its progress, compliance with treatment and rapid reporting of adverse reactions are most likely (Chapter 12).

There are many strategies available for patient teaching, including:

- **Videos of bandaging techniques** for the able patient who is re-applying a heavy compression bandage daily.
- **Group discussions** for alert patients attending outpatient clinics.
- **Information leaflets** on care of legs and other self-help measures for leg ulcer patients and/or their carers. The Appendix shows an information leaflet suitable for patients with a venous ulcer, or for their carers.

An individualised health education programme should be devised that takes account of the patient's cognitive abilities and learning needs. Patient education is an *ongoing process* and should include, where appropriate:

- **A simple explanation of the underlying cause of the ulcer**
- **Advice on:**
  exercise
  reducing oedema
  leg care
  nutrition

It is important, however, that patients receive certain *key information* at their *first visit*:

- **The nurse's name and workplace.**
- **A contact phone number.**
- **The simple signs and symptoms that suggest that treatment may require to be changed quickly, such as increased pain, redness, itching, or loss of sensation in the leg.**

THIS ADVICE SHOULD BE WRITTEN DOWN AND LEFT WITH THE PATIENT IN A PROMINENT PLACE, OR HANDED TO THE PRINCIPAL CARE GIVER.

7.6 Preventing recurrence of leg ulceration

The recurrence rate for leg ulceration is very high (*Table 7.1*). If the patient can be encouraged to follow the self-help advice on improving mobility, reducing oedema, and improving nutrition given in Section 7.4.6 this should go some way to improving the local conditions in the lower leg. Patient education and methods of encouraging compliance with treatment and self-help advice are discussed in the previous section and in more depth in Chapter 12.

For patients with venous ulcers, wearing compression hosiery (*Colour Plate* **84**), even after the ulcer has healed (Dale and Gibson, 1990), is an important way of preventing recurrence. For some patients surgery to correct the underlying vascular disorder may be beneficial (Negus and Friegood, 1983).

APPENDIX

A typical leaflet for patients with venous ulcers, and their carers, is shown.

How to care for your legs

How long must I keep the dressing and bandage (or stocking) in place?

Wear the support bandages or elastic support stockings as advised by the doctor and nurse. They will make arrangements for your next dressing change.

Do not be tempted to look under the bandage or disturb the dressing in the meantime as this may delay healing. It is particularly important not to scratch the skin around the ulcer as this skin is easily damaged.

Ask for help AT ONCE if:

- Your leg is more itchy, hot, or painful than usual.
- You feel that the bandage is too tight anywhere.
- You lose sensation in your toes, or they turn cold or blue.
- You need any other advice.

Contact person:
Contact telephone number:

Can I exercise?

Yes. Exercise is good for your circulation and your general health. If possible, take a gentle walk every day. Even indoors you can bend and stretch your toes while sitting, and bend, flex, and circle your ankles to prevent them from becoming stiff. It is important not to stand still for too long. It is a good idea to do the dishes and the ironing sitting down, if you can obtain a chair of the correct height.

Should I sit with my legs up?

Yes. Sitting with your legs hanging down is almost as bad as standing in one place for too long. You should sit with your legs supported on a stool, on a cushion or pillow, that is above the level of your hips. It is also helpful to raise the foot of your bed 9 inches, as this aids return of blood from the legs to the heart overnight.

Do I need a special diet?

You do not need a special diet, but try to eat a balanced one that includes protein (meat, fish, eggs), fresh fruit, and vegetables. Being overweight does not help the circulation in your legs. Ask the doctor for advice on weight loss if this is a problem for you.

Are there any other ways I can help my legs?

Yes:

- Avoid knocks to your legs, as this could lead to another ulcer.
- Keep your legs warm, but do not sit too close to the fire as this can damage the skin.
- Do not wear anything tight round the tops of your legs, such as garters or girdles, as your circulation will be hindered.
- Stop smoking.

Further reading

Compression bandages and hosiery

Cornwall, J.V., Dore, C.J. and Lewis, J.D. (1987), Graduated compression and its relation to venous refilling time. *Br. Med. J.*, **295** , 1087–1090.

Dale, J.D. and Gibson, B. (1990), Back-up for the venous pump: compression hosiery. *Professional Nurse*, 5(9), 481–486.

Fentem, P.H. (1990), Defining the compression provided by hosiery and bandages. *Care: Science and Practice*, 8(2), 53–55.

Thomas, S. (1990), Bandages and bandaging. *Nurs. Stand.*, 4(39), supplement, 4–6.

The ischaemic leg

Orr, M.M. and McAvoy, B.R. (1987), The ischaemic leg. In Fry, J. and Berry, H.E. (eds), *Surgical Problems in Clinical Practice*, pp. 123–135. Edward Arnold, London.

The surgical management of venous disease

Ruckley, C.V. (1988), *A Colour Atlas of Surgical Management of Venous Disease*. Wolfe Medical Publications, London.

References

Browse, N.L. and Burnand, K.G. (1982), The cause of venous ulceration. *Lancet*, **2**, 243–245.

Callam, M.J., Harper, D.R., Dale, J.J. *et al.* (1987a), Arterial disease in chronic leg ulceration: an under-estimated hazard? Lothian and Forth Valley Leg Ulcer Study. *Br. Med. J.*, **294**, 929–931.

Callam, M.J., Harper, D.R., Dale, J.J. *et al.* (1987b), Chronic ulcer of the leg: clinical history. *Br. Med. J.*, **294**, 1389–1391.

Callam, M.J., Harper, D.R., Dale, J.J. *et al.* (1987c), A controlled trial of weekly ultrasound therapy in chronic leg ulceration. *Lancet*, **2**, 204–205.

Callam, M.J., Ruckley, C.V., Dale, J.J. *et al.* (1987d), Hazards of compression treatment of the leg: an estimate from Scottish surgeons. *Br. Med. J.*, **295**, 1382.

Cameron, J. (1990), Patch testing for leg ulcer patients. *Nurs. Times*, **86**(25), 63–64.

Clay, C.S. and Cherry, G.W. (1990), Improvement in skin quality using Granuflex Adhesive Compression Bandage. *Care: Science and Practice*, **8**(2), 84–87.

Cornwall, J., Dore, C.J. and Lewis, J.D. (1986), Leg ulcers: epidemiology and aetiology. *Br. J. Surg.* **73**, 693–696.

Dale, J. and Gibson, B. (1986), The epidemiology of leg ulcers. *Professional Nurse*, **1**(8), 215–216.

Dale, J.D. and Gibson, B. (1990), Back-up for the venous pump: compression hosiery. *Professional Nurse*, **5**(9), 481–486.

Fraki, J.E., Peltonen, L. and Hopsu-Havu, V.K. (1979), Allergy to various components of topical preparations in stasis dermatitis and leg ulcer. *Contact Dermatitis*, **5**, 97–100.

Gardner, A.M.N. and Fox, R.H. (1986), The return of blood to the heart against the force of gravity. In Negus, D. and Jantet, G. (eds), *Phlebology '85*, 65–67. Libbey, London.

Goodinson, S.M. (1986), Assessment of nutritional status. *Nursing*, **3**(7), 252–257.

Hazarika, E.Z. and Wright, D.E. (1981), Chronic leg ulcers: the effect of pneumatic intermittent compression. *Practitioner*, **225**, 189–192.

Moody, M. (1984), A new lease of life. *Nurs. Times* (July 4), 46.

Negus, D. and Friegood, A. (1983), The effective management of venous ulceration. *Br. J. Surg.*, **70**, 623–627.

Norris, C.S., Beyreau, I. and Barnes, R.W. (1983), Quantitative photoplethysmography in chronic venous insufficiency: a new method of non-invasive estimation of ambulatory venous pressure. *Surgery*, **94**, 758–764.

Orr, M.M. and McAvoy, B.R. (1987), Varicose veins and their effects. In Fry, J. and Berry, H.E. (eds), *Surgical Problems in Clinical Practice*, pp. 111–122. Edward Arnold, London.

Paramsothy, Y., Collins, M. and Smith, G.M. (1988), Contact dermatitis in patients with leg ulcers: the prevalence of late positive reactions. *Contact Dermatitis*, **18**, 30–36.

Ruckley, C.V. (1988), *A Colour Atlas of Surgical Management of Venous Disease*, p. 30. Wolfe Medical Publications, London.

Sockalingham, S., Barbenel, J.C. and Queen, D. (1990), Ambulatory monitoring of the pressures beneath compression bandages. *Care: Science and Practice*, **8**(2), 75–79.

Williams, C.M. (1986), Wound healing: a nutritional perspective. *Nursing*, **3**(7), 249–251.

8   Other Chronic Open Wounds

8.1   Introduction

Pressure sores (Chapter 6) and leg ulcers (Chapter 7) are the most commonly encountered chronic open wounds in the United Kingdom and the responsibility for their management is often delegated to nurses. Other types of open wound include diabetic foot ulcers, malignant wounds, sinuses, and fistulae. Open wounds associated with an underlying pathophysiological problem, such as diabetes or malignancy, can be particularly resistant to healing; for very debilitated patients, healing may be an unrealistic goal.

Responsibility for the management of these wounds is usually shared between several health care professionals. For a patient with a diabetic foot ulcer the nurse may liaise with the physician, chiropodist, and specialist diabetic sister when planning, delivering, and evaluating care. In hospital, the management of sinuses and fistulae is usually initiated by the physician or surgeon, with the nurse responsible for day-to-day care. In the community, responsibility for the conservative management of intractable open wounds is often delegated to the nurse.

The principles of management are the same as for any wound. The patient should first be assessed to determine the immediate cause of the wound, any underlying pathology (which may delay healing and make recurrence more likely), any local problems at the wound site, and the possible psychological and social consequences of the wound for the individual (Chapter 2). Care can then be planned in accordance with the needs of the patients and their families and will be aimed at:

- Correcting, where possible, the immediate cause of the wound and any underlying pathology.
- Correcting any more general patient factors, such as malnutrition, that could contribute to delayed healing (see *Figure 1.1*).
- Creating the optimum local environment for healing, by appropriate cleansing (Chapter 4) and dressing (Chapter 3).

- Preventing complications, especially clinical wound infection (Chapter 5).
- Relieving pain and discomfort.

Chapter 8 briefly summarises the special problems associated with these wounds and indicates some solutions. *Figure 3.1* should be consulted for further guidance on the appropriate choice of dressing.

8.2   Diabetic foot ulcers

Foot ulcers are a common complication for patients with diabetes mellitus (Robertson *et al.*, 1986). Delayed wound healing and increased vulnerability to infection (Joseph and Axler, 1990) are likely, gangrene may develop, and there is a high risk of the need for lower-limb amputation. In the USA it has been estimated that 50% of all non-traumatic amputations occur in diabetic patients, with the elderly at particular risk, and men at significantly higher risk than women, of requiring an amputation. Furthermore, the prognosis for the contra-lateral leg is poor, 42% of patients requiring a second amputation within 1–3 years and 56% within 3–5 years. It has been suggested that 50–75% of these amputations are preventable, but the long-term management of diabetic patients and the prevention of complications is challenging. It requires a co-ordinated multidisciplinary team approach, which involves the physician, specialist diabetic nurse, chiropodist, and orthotist, and in some cases the vascular and orthopaedic surgeon; but above all, it requires informed patient co-operation.

Diabetic foot ulcers usually result from the triad of:

- Peripheral neuropathy (the insensate foot).
- Peripheral vascular insufficiency (ischaemia).
- Infection.

For patients with peripheral neuropathy, a reduced or absent pain sensation in the feet can result in unnoticed trauma from ill-fitting shoes and misshapen toe nails. Foot deformity is common, with atrophy of the small muscles of the foot, clawing of the toes, and prominent metatarsal heads. Repeated trauma, especially prolonged pressure, can cause ulceration on the sole of the foot, especially under the head of the first metatarsal bone, over enlarged bunions, and on the bony prominences of the toes (*Colour Plate* 85).

According to Levin (1988), management of diabetic foot ulcers requires aggressive treatment. In the short term this involves:

- Radical local débridement to healthy tissue.
- Systemic antibiotic therapy to combat infection, following antibiotic sensitivity testing.
- Diabetic control, to optimise efficiency of the immune system.

- Non-weight bearing for plantar ulcers.

Appropriate wound dressing selection (Chapter 3) is important, but is merely an adjunct to the above therapies. Having stated this, the application of inappropriate topical agents can considerably worsen an already dire situation. In addition, feet should be kept dry. Soaking the feet causes maceration between the toes and increases the risk of infection. Attention should also be given to rehydrating dry skin around the ulcer and over the lower leg. If an ulcer is refractory to all treatment, the physician may request an X-ray to exclude the possibilities of osteomyelitis or a retained foreign body that the patient does not feel.

For some patients it is possible to improve the peripheral circulation through vascular by-pass surgery, percutaneous angioplasty, laser treatment, and the use of haemorrheologic agents, such as oxpentifylline (Trental) which improves red cell flexibility and blood flow. The combination of endovascular revascularisation, growth factor therapy, and comprehensive wound-care protocols can lead to very high limb-salvage rates in specialist centres (Bild *et al.*, 1989; Knighton *et al.*, 1990). However, prevention is infinitely preferable to cure. Some risk factors for peripheral vascular disease in diabetic patients are not treatable, such as age and the duration of the diabetes, but many risk factors are treatable, such as smoking, hypertension, hyperlipidaemia, hyperglycaemia, and obesity. Encouraging a diabetic patient to give up smoking and comply with dietary advice can significantly reduce many long-term complications. The nurse has a special part to play in reinforcing the advice given to patients, as well as in local wound management.

Patient education is, in fact, the key to preventing foot ulceration. All patients should receive special instruction in foot care (see Appendix), and their feet should be inspected at every routine outpatient visit, when this instruction should be reinforced. They should be encouraged to report foot problems as soon as they occur.

Patients should be reassessed regularly by the chiropodist, especially in terms of the need for special footwear to reduce pressure over bony prominences. Extra-depth shoes can be designed to accommodate clawed toes, and insoles can be made to reduce plantar pressures. The chiropodist should trim the patient's toe nails, and treat calluses and other local foot problems. Local remedies applied by the patient are often the forerunners to serious foot problems.

There are many conditions besides diabetes mellitus that can lead to poor peripheral arterial circulation in the legs and feet, including rheumatoid arthritis, Buerger's disease, Raynaud's disease, and atherosclerosis. Further guidance on the assessment and management of arterial ulcers of the foot and leg is given in Chapter 7.

8.3   Malignant wounds

The management of patients with open malignant wounds is particularly challenging and requires a holistic approach; i.e. one which takes account of the patient's psychological and social as well as physical needs. Selecting a dressing regimen that reduces pain, controls odour, is cosmetically acceptable, and allows maximum independence can have important psychological benefits and can improve considerably the patient's quality of life. The local management of fungating breast carcinomas will be described in some detail, but similar principles can be applied to most cutaneous malignant wounds, including wounds to the face, neck, groin, and axilla.

Nearly all cancers of the breast are adenocarcinomas, originating either in the epithelium of the mammary ducts or in the glands of the breast lobules. Most invasive carcinomas excite a strong fibrous reaction in nearby breast tissue, which is largely responsible for the mass becoming palpable. The rate of progress of the disease is very variable and treatment methods vary widely from one hospital to another.

In advanced breast cancer palliation is the only realistic objective. Radiation therapy or chemotherapy may be employed with varying degrees of success, but may delay local wound healing. In very advanced stages of the disease the local tumour may spread into overlying skin, and the chest wall and can give rise to a fungating mass of fragile tissue (*Colour Plate* **86**). This tissue bleeds easily, is often malodorous, producing large volumes of exudate, and can cause the patient considerable discomfort. The physical appearance of the ulcer is a visual reminder of the underlying malignancy and can therefore cause considerable psychological as well as physical distress.

Accurate patient assessment is particularly important:

- What are the local problems at the wound site (see Section 2.4)?
- Is the patient in pain? What is the patient's perception of its severity and what has been found, so far, to relieve it (see Section 2.2.3)?
- What are the social and emotional consequences of the wound for the individual? Common problems include altered body image, low self-esteem, difficulties in social relationships, and sexual problems (see Section 2.5).
- Where is the best environment for giving care, and how self-caring can the patient be?
- How much does the patient know about the cause of the wound and its prognosis, and how much does she want to know (see Chapter 12)?

The aims of local wound management are to:

- Promote patient comfort.
- Control and prevent bleeding of friable tissue.

- Prevent or manage clinical infection.
- Control odour.
- Contain exudate.

The algorithm given in *Figure 3.1* is a particularly useful aid to dressing selection. All other considerations being equal, the dressing that is chosen should be the most convenient, comfortable, and cosmetically acceptable to the patient. If evaluation of the treatment regimen selected shows that the quality of the patient's life has not improved, alternatives should be sought rapidly. The difficulty is that a dressing which successfully controls a problem in one patient may be less effective or inappropriate for another. The best methods for locally managing malignant ulceration are as yet not well-established, and few products have been systematically evaluated in clinical trials in this client group. An exception to this is Silastic Foam. Bale and Harding (1987) found this dressing to be non-adherent, absorbent, soft, and comfortable, as well as allowing patients considerable independence. It can be fashioned into a simple prosthesis using an appropriately sized pudding basin and can be held in place with Netelast or with the patient's own close-fitting underwear. The twice-daily disinfection of the dressing with a 0.5% Hibitane solution can often be managed at home by the patient or the carer, and the dressing is re-usable for about a week.

The successful use of Silastic Foam dressings has also been reported in the management of excised carcinoma of the cheek (Shukla, 1982). With the dressing in place, patients were able to drink fluids, eat, and speak normally, which helped to raise their morale while awaiting reconstructive surgery.

When securing any dressing it is important to avoid the use of skin tapes, especially if the patient has had recent radiotherapy. Following radiotherapy, specialist advice should be sought from the Radiotherapy Department as to the management of dry skin and the control of itchiness.

Despite the poor prognosis of most malignant wounds, the nurse's attitude to the patient and the care taken with dressing the wound can do a great deal to improve the patient's quality of life and ability to cope.

8.4 Sinuses

A sinus is a blind-ended track, lined with granulation tissue, which extends from a free surface, such as skin, into the tissues. It often ends in an abscess cavity (*Figure 8.1*) and fails to heal because the cavity contains some foreign material. The foreign material may be iatrogenic, such as a buried non-absorbable suture or retained gauze packing material. It could be a retained splinter of metal or glass, following a

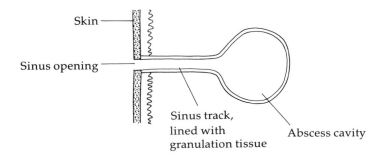

Figure 8.1. A sinus.

traumatic injury (Chapter 11). In the case of a pilonidal sinus, the foreign material is hair, which slowly works its way into the upper end of the natal cleft between the buttocks and excites an inflammatory reaction, which leads to an abscess if the cavity becomes secondarily infected. Sinuses associated with chronic osteomyelitis fail to heal because of the presence of necrotic bone.

Management of the sinus will depend upon its cause. The extent of a sinus and its ramifications may first need to be established by sinography. If the foreign body is a superficial, non-absorbable suture, it may be possible to locate and remove it at the outpatient clinic but exploration under general anaesthetic is usually required.

Pilonidal sinuses may be radically excised and the defect created surgically closed or allowed to heal by secondary intention (Chapter 10). Alternatively, the sinus may be deroofed, with curettage of granulation tissue, or the sinus network may be curetted and filled with liquefied phenol for a short time to encourage fibrosis. Unfortunately, pilonidal sinuses commonly recur, especially in hirsute men who sit for prolonged periods while driving, e.g. bus, truck, and tractor drivers.

A sinus may persist because of inadequate drainage of an abscess. This can happen if a narrow sinus is tightly plugged with ribbon gauze or with any dressing at its point of exit to the skin surface, preventing the underlying cavity from draining adequately. The retained material becomes infected and purulent and the cavity beneath enlarges. Very deep narrow sinuses, such as those associated with a pleural empyema cavity, may need to be drained with a tube drain, which is progressively withdrawn as the sinus closes.

8.5 Fistulae

A fistula is an abnormal track between two epithelial surfaces that connects one viscus to another or a viscus to the skin (*Figure 8.2*). There

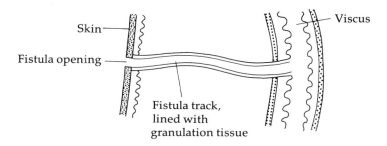

Figure 8.2. A fistula between the skin and a viscus.

are many causes of fistulae (*Table 8.1*). They may be associated with specific diseases, caused by traumatic injury, iatrogenic, or even planned. Only fistulae opening onto the surface of the skin are considered here.

The nature and volume of the fluid leaking from the fistula gives a very good indication of its origin. Fluid from a gastric fistula is acidic and contains any fluid the patient has recently taken in by mouth. It can be compared with aspirate from a nasogastric tube, and tested for acidity using litmus paper. Bile-stained fluid may have come from the biliary tree, stomach, or duodenum. Pancreatic fluid is colourless and causes rapid excoriation of the surrounding skin because of the proteolytic enzymes it contains. So, too, does fluid from a small bowel fistula, which is usually yellow-orange in colour. Brown faecal fluid, preceded by a purulent discharge, is characteristic of a large bowel fistula. Large volumes of serosanguineous fluid suggest deep wound disruption from the abdominal or thoracic cavities.

A number of radiological procedures are available to establish the site and extent of the fistula. Most fistulae close spontaneously if there is adequate distal drainage, the patient is given adequate nutritional support (Soeters *et al.*, 1979), and any sepsis is controlled; healing is unlikely, however, if there is carcinoma at the site of the fistula, if a foreign body is still present, and for some patients with advanced Crohn's disease.

Care of the skin surrounding the fistula is very important to prevent excoriation (*Colour Plate* **87**). Responsibility for this is often left to the nurse. The methods used will depend on the nature and volume of the fluid being drained and the site of the fistula.

An open thoracic fistula in a terminally ill patient can leak 2 litres or more of serosanguineous fluid in 24 hours. This may be collected in a drainable stoma bag to keep the patient comfortable and to protect the surrounding skin. The volume must be accurately measured to allow adequate fluid replacement. Since protein and electrolyte losses may be

Table 8.1 Some causes of fistulae

Inflammatory bowel disease
e.g. Crohn's disease

Abscess formation and inadequate drainage
e.g. perianal abscess leading to an anal fistula

Malignancy

Iatrogenic
e.g. breakdown of an anastomosis following surgery, or damage to a viscus
from a drain

Traumatic
e.g. penetrating stab wound injury

Planned therapeutic surgical procedure
e.g. ileostomy, colostomy, and nephrostomy

substantial, the patient's nutritional status and electrolyte levels should be carefully monitored.

A fistula arising from a dehisced wound can be managed with a wound irrigation device (see *Colour Plate* **99**) held in place by Stomahesive if the wound is reasonably small. This method overcomes the need for frequent dressing changes and prevents excoriation of the surrounding skin. If there is extensive wound breakdown an alternative method of draining the fistula fluid away from the wound may need to be sought, such as a sump drain (Everett, 1985), with care taken to protect the surrounding skin from excoriation. It may be appropriate to cover the whole wound with a film dressing to prevent exogenous contamination.

APPENDIX

A typical leaflet for diabetic patients who require foot care is shown.

Advice to diabetic patients on foot care

Do:

- Wash feet daily.
- Dry feet well, especially between the toes.
- Check your feet at least once a day for early signs of redness, blisters, or any other minor damage; always check between the toes and the soles of the feet (a mirror may help with this). If your vision is impaired, ask a friend to do this for you.
- Consult the doctor at once for even minor foot injuries.
- Change socks and/or stockings daily.

- Before putting shoes on, check the insides for small stones or other foreign bodies.
- Consult a chiropodist about care of toe nails, calluses, and any other foot problems, and tell the chiropodist that you are diabetic.
- Have new shoes fitted by a trained fitter—your chiropodist will advise whether or not you need special shoes and how to obtain them.
- Avoid extremes of temperature—use a bath thermometer to check that the water temperature does not exceed 43°C, and avoid extreme cold, as chilblains can lead to ulcers. It is useful to wear fleecy lined boots in winter.

Do not:

- Attempt your own chiropody or use chemicals to remove corns or calluses or to treat an infection.
- Wear socks or stockings with bulky seams.
- Wear shoes with poorly finished seams or other potential pressure points.
- Wear shoes without socks or stockings.
- Wear anything that restricts blood circulation in the legs and feet, such as garters or tight corsets.
- Walk barefoot, especially on hot surfaces such as a sandy beach.
- Sit too close to the fire (instead, use extra socks and fleecy lined slippers to keep your feet warm).
- Put your feet on a hot water bottle.
- Soak your feet for prolonged periods.
- Smoke.

Further reading

Diabetic foot ulcers

Edmonds, M.E. (1986), The diabetic foot: pathophysiology and treatment. *Clin. Endocrinol. Metab.*, **15**(4), 889–916.

Harrelson, J.M. (1989), Management of the diabetic foot. *Orthop. Clin. North Am.*, **20**(4), 605–619.

Levin, M.E. (1988), The diabetic foot: pathophysiology, evaluation and treatment. In Levin, M.E. and O'Neal, L.W. (eds), *The Diabetic Foot* (4th edn). C.V. Mosby, St Louis.

Fungating and ulcerating malignant lesions

Ivetic, O. and Lyne, P.A. (1990), Fungating and ulcerating malignant lesions: a review of the literature. *J. Adv. Nursing*, **15**, 83–88.

References

Bale, S. and Harding, K. (1987), Fungating breast wounds. *Journal of District Nursing*, June, 4–5.

Bild, D.E., Selby, J.V., Sinnock, P., *et al.* (1989), Lower extremity amputation in people with diabetes: epidemiology and prevention. *Diab. Care*, **12**, 24–31.

Everett, W.G. (1985), Wound sinus or fistula? In Westaby, S. (ed.), *Wound Care*. Heinemann, London.

Joseph, W.S. and Axler, D.A. (1990), Microbiology and antimicrobial therapy of diabetic foot infections. *Clin. Podiatr. Med. Surg.*, **7**(3), 467–481.

Knighton, D.R., Fylling, C.P., Fiegel, V.D., *et al.* (1990), Amputation prevention in an independently reviewed at-risk diabetic population using a comprehensive wound care protocol. *Am. J. Surg.*, **160**, 466–472.

Levin, M.E. (1988), The diabetic foot: pathophysiology, evaluation and treatment. In Levin, M.E. and O'Neal, L.W. (eds), *The Diabetic Foot* (4th edn). C.V. Mosby, St Louis.

Robertson, J.C., Daunt, S. O'N. and Nur, M. (1986), Tissue viability—wound healing and the diabetic. *Practical Diabetes*, **3**, 14–19.

Shukla, H.S. (1982), Cosmetic and functional advantages of foam elastomer dressing in the management of epidermoid cancer of the cheek. *Br. J. Surg.*, **69**, 435–436.

Soeters, P.B., Ebeid, A.M. and Fischer, J.E. (1979), Review of 404 patients with gastro intestinal fistulas. Impact of parenteral nutrition, *Annals of Surgery*, **190**, 189–202.

COLOUR PLATES

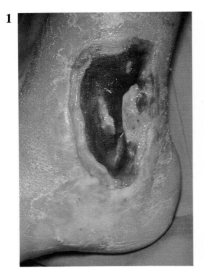

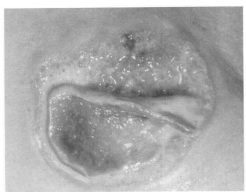

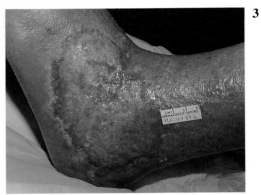

Colour Plates 1–4. Local problems at the wound site: 1 necrotic tissue in a leg ulcer; 2 necrotic sloughy tissue in a pressure sore; 3 thick slough covering a foot ulcer; 4 a grossly infected pressure sore.

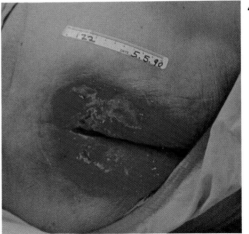

5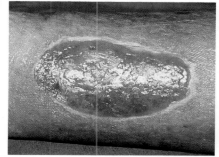

6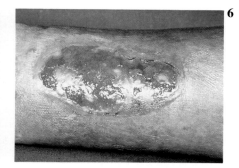

Colour Plates 5–7. Healthy wounds: **5** *healthy granulation tissue,* **6** *epithelialisation is apparent from the wound margins and from islands of epithelial cells,* **7** *epithelialisation is almost complete and the wound has started to contract.*

7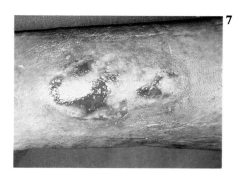

8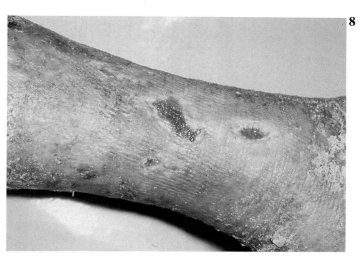

Colour Plate **8.** *Leg ulcers surrounded by dry eczema.*

9

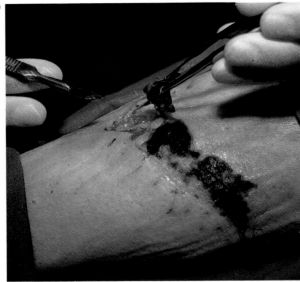

*Colour Plate **9.** Surgical débridement of necrotic tissue: having been debrided, the wound was closed with a skin graft.*

10

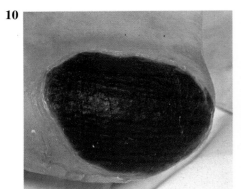

11

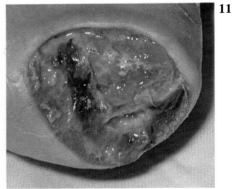

12

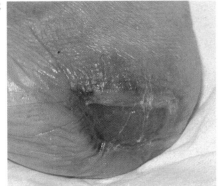

*Colour Plates **10–12.** A black necrotic heel in an 89-year-old patient: **10** before treatment; **11** during treatment; the necrotic tissue is being gently removed with Varidase; **12** following débridement, the wound bed is clean and an enzymatic preparation is not required. The wound has already contracted considerably.*

13

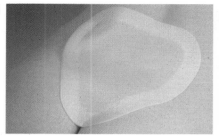

Colour Plate **13.** *Granuflex E bordered dressing on sacrum.*

Colour Plate **14.** *Scherisorb gel being applied to a necrotic wound.*

14

15

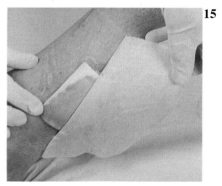

Colour Plate **15.** *Debrisan absorbent pad being removed from a sloughy cavity wound.*

16

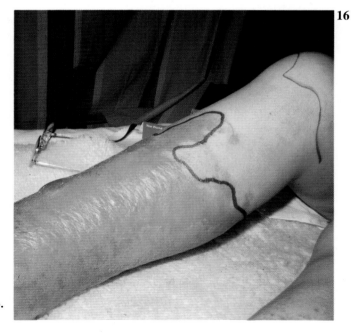

Colour Plate **16.** *Cellulitis.*

17

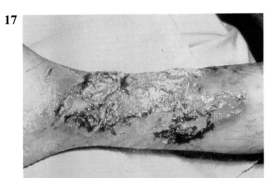

Colour Plates **17, 18.** A grossly infected leg ulcer: **17** with extensive necrotic tissue; **18** after treatment of the patient with a systemic antibiotic and the local application of Iodosorb ointment.

Colour Plate **19.** Applying Inadine to a superficial infected wound.

18

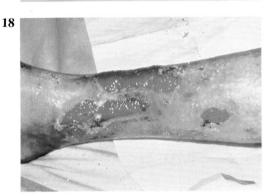

 **19**

20

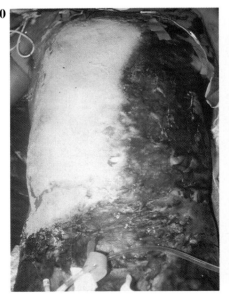

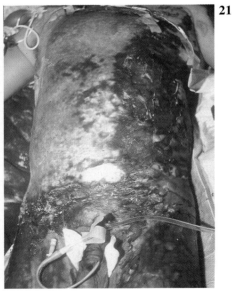 **21**

Colour Plates **20, 21. 20** Secondary infection on the torso, by a pin mould, following major trauma to the skin from a landmine explosion; **21** following local treatment of the infection with Debrisan dressings.

Colour Plate **22.** *An activated charcoal dressing, Actisorb Plus, being applied to a heavily infected superficial leg ulcer.*

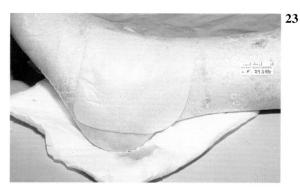

Colour Plates **23, 24.** *Granuflex E hydrocolloid dressing on removal from a moderately exuding ulcer. Minimum handling of the wound bed is necessary, as it is healthily granulating.*

Colour Plates **25, 26.** *A leg ulcer before (**25**) and during (**26**) treatment with Comfeel. The hydrocolloid dressing is particularly effective at rehydrating the dry eczema surrounding the ulcer, as well as promoting ulcer healing.*

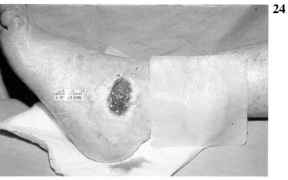

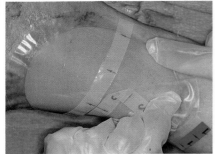
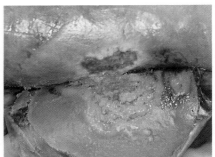

*Colour Plates **27**, **28**. Applying Tegasorb hydrocolloid dressing, **27**; easy removal of the dressing **28**.*

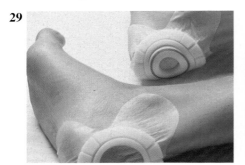
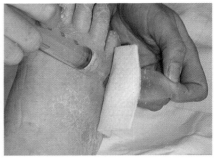

*Colour Plate **29**. Comfeel pressure-relieving hydrocolloid dressing is particularly suitable for dressing heels.*

*Colour Plate **30**. Irrigation easily removes Sorbsan Plus from a moderate exudate wound.*

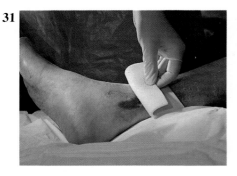
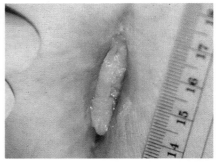

*Colour Plate **31**. A polyurethane foam sheet, Allevyn, being applied to a clean, high-exudate ulcer.*

*Colour Plate **32**. Tegagel alginate dressing used to pack a clean, moderate-exudate wound.*

33

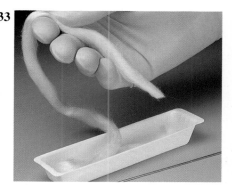

Colour Plate 33. Sorbsan alginate ribbon is useful for packing narrow, moderate-to high-exudate wounds.

34

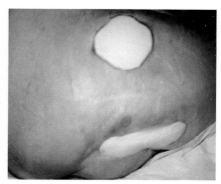

Colour Plate 34. Allevyn cavity wound dressings, applied to saucer-shaped cavity wounds, are comfortable, absorb exudate, and are very easy to remove.

35

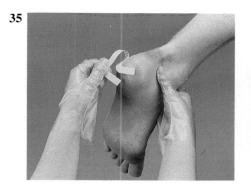

Colour Plate 35. Tegaderm film dressing, applied to a superficial abrasion, conforms well to this awkwardly shaped area.

36

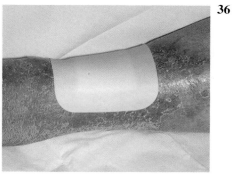

Colour Plate 36. An alginate island dressing, such as Sorbsan SA, maintains a moist environment in a low-exudate open wound.

37

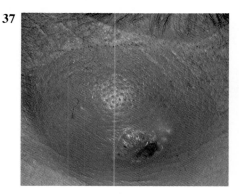

Colour Plate 37. An infected sebaceous gland cyst. The area is tender, red, indurated, and warm.

38

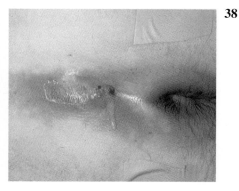

Colour Plate 38. A painful pilonidal abscess with spreading erythema and discharging purulent material.

39

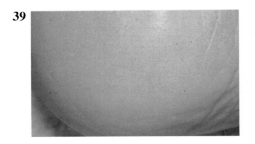

40

41

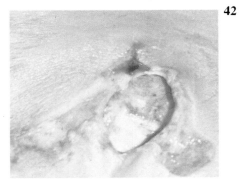

42

43

Colour Plates **39–43**. The five stages of pressure sores: **39** Stage I, blanching hyperaemia; **40** Stage II, superficial damage to the epithelium; **41** Stage III, ulceration progresses through the dermis. **42** Stage IV, the ulcer extends into the subcutaneous fat; **43** Stage V, extensive necrosis, which involves muscle destruction.

*Colour Plate **44**. The patient is being rotated from supine to a 30° lateral tilt position, on a bead pillow support system (Paraglide; see also Colour Plate **53**).*

*Colour Plates **45–48**. Some examples of pressure-relieving beds: **45** Clinitron air-fluidised bed (Support Systems International) in use in an Intensive Care Unit; **46** Mediscus Monarch low air-loss bed (Mediscus); **47** Beaufort–Winchester flotation bed (Paraglide), 1986 static model; the physiotherapist is rotating the patient by gently pulling the membrane; **48** A net suspension bed, Mecabed (Arjo-Mecanaids).*

44

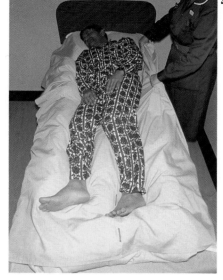

45

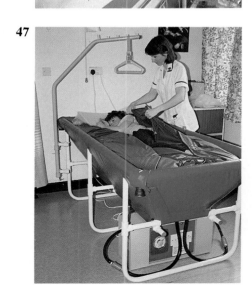

46

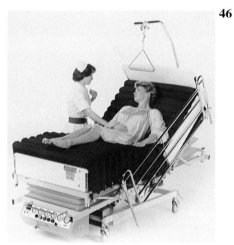

47

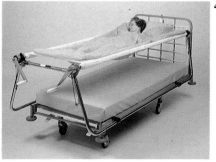

48

49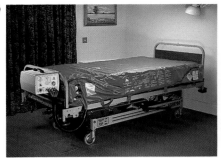

50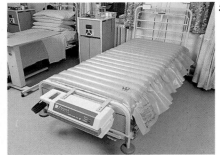

51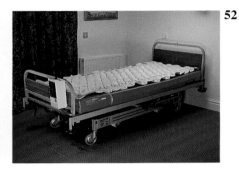

52

53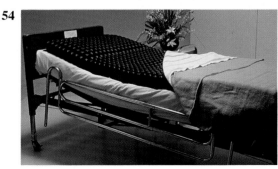

54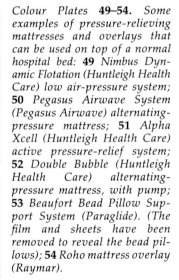

Colour Plates **49–54.** Some examples of pressure-relieving mattresses and overlays that can be used on top of a normal hospital bed: **49** Nimbus Dynamic Flotation (Huntleigh Health Care) low air-pressure system; **50** Pegasus Airwave System (Pegasus Airwave) alternating-pressure mattress; **51** Alpha Xcell (Huntleigh Health Care) active pressure-relief system; **52** Double Bubble (Huntleigh Health Care) alternating-pressure mattress, with pump; **53** Beaufort Bead Pillow Support System (Paraglide). (The film and sheets have been removed to reveal the bead pillows); **54** Roho mattress overlay (Raymar).

Colour Plates **55–57.** *Some examples of pressure-relieving cushions:* **55** *A range of Roho cushions (Raymar)—the high-profile cushion is particularly suitable for patients with existing pressure sores;* **56** *Omega 5000 cushion (Spenco Medical);* **57** *Superdown wheelchair set (Huntleigh Health Care), comprising a seat cushion, back support, and side pads (which can be removed for transfers).*

55

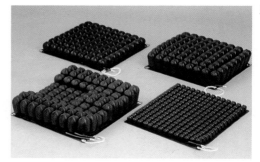

56

57

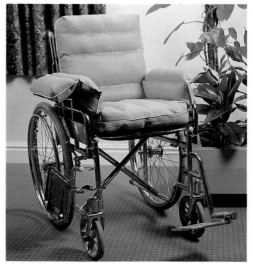

58

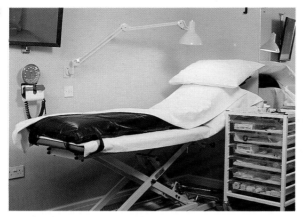

*Colour Plate **58**. A pressure-relieving mattress, such as the Trolley Topper (Huntleigh Health Care), is suitable for use on hospital trolleys, in the Accident and Emergency and X-ray departments, on stretchers, and on treatment couches, and can protect high-risk patients while they are on some of the hardest support surfaces in the hospital.*

59 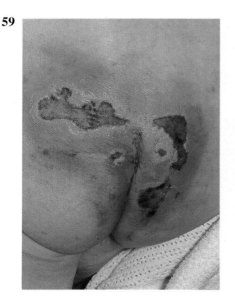 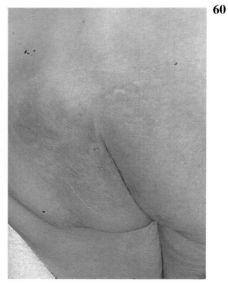 **60**

*Colour Plates **59, 60**. Pressure relief aids healing: **59** Relief of the pressure, shearing, and frictional forces that led to the development of this pressure sore is essential before healing can begin; **60** healing was facilitated using a Clinitron air-fluidised bed to provide pressure relief.*

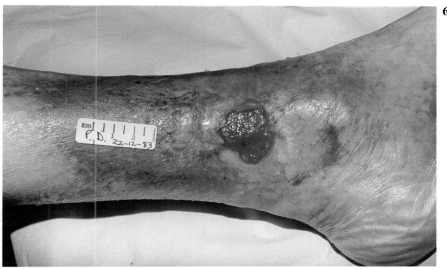

61

Colour Plate **61.** *A venous ulcer.*

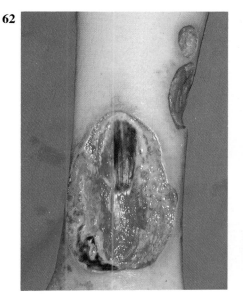

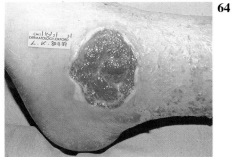

Colour Plate **62.** *A deep arterial ulcer in a patient with rheumatoid arthritis, with exposed tendon and necrotic tissue visible. The underlying vascular problem is arteritis.*

Colour Plate **63.** *Superficial multiple ulcers in a diabetic patient.*

Colour Plate **64.** *An arterial ulcer on the lateral malleolus.*

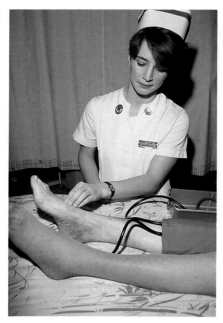

Colour Plate **65.** *Finding the dorsalis pedis pulse by palpatation.*

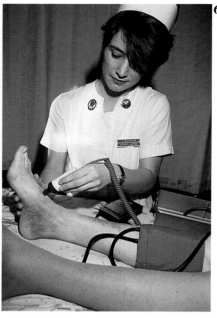

Colour Plate **66.** *The use of doppler ultrasound to measure the ankle systolic pressure.*

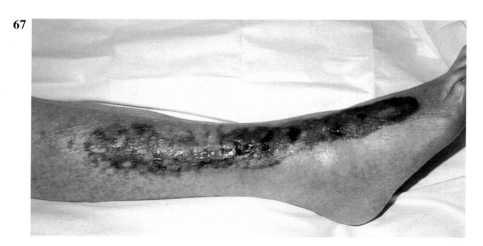

67

Colour Plate **67.** *A bandage-induced ulcer, which led to amputation.*

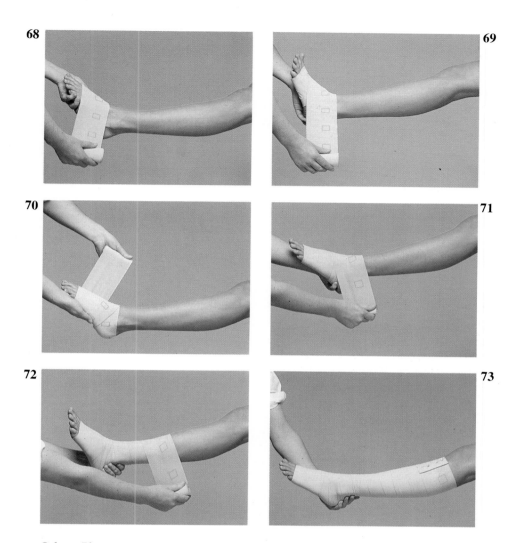

Colour Plates **68–73.** *Applying a compression bandage. (Follow manufacturer's instructions on the precise method of application and the bandage tension required.)*

74

75

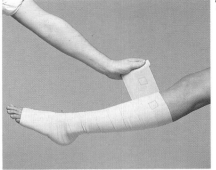

76

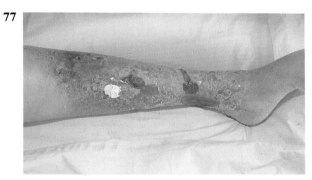

Colour Plate **74.** *A simple visual guide to correct extension. The yellow rectangles become squares when the correct extension is reached.*

Colour Plate **75.** *The squares are covered by the overlapping bandage.*

Colour Plate **76.** *A paste bandage being applied.*

77

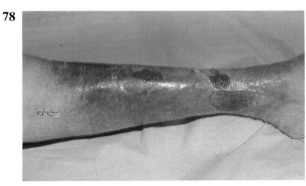

Colour Plate **77.** *Dry eczematous skin surrounding an ulcer.*

78

Colour Plate **78.** *Rehydration of skin surrounding an ulcer after treatment with a hydrocolloid adhesive compression bandage.*

79

80

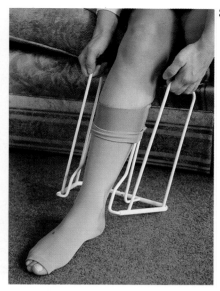

*Colour Plates **79, 80**. A dressing aid, such as Valet (Medi), can solve the often difficult problem of putting on a compression stocking.*

81

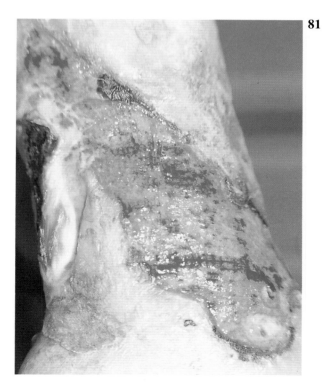

*Colour Plate **81**. A deep arterial ulcer, with exposure of the Achilles tendon, which developed from a minor skin lesion, following application of an elastic bandage.*

82

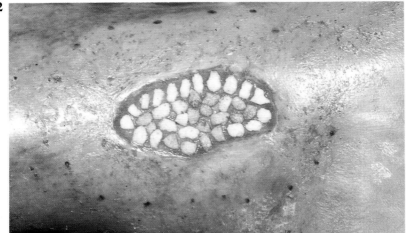

83

Colour Plate **82.** *Pinch skin grafting.*

Colour Plate **83.** *Elevation of the legs at rest, above the level of the hips.*

84

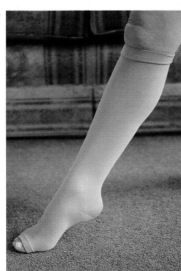

Colour Plate **84.** *A class 2 compression stocking.*

85

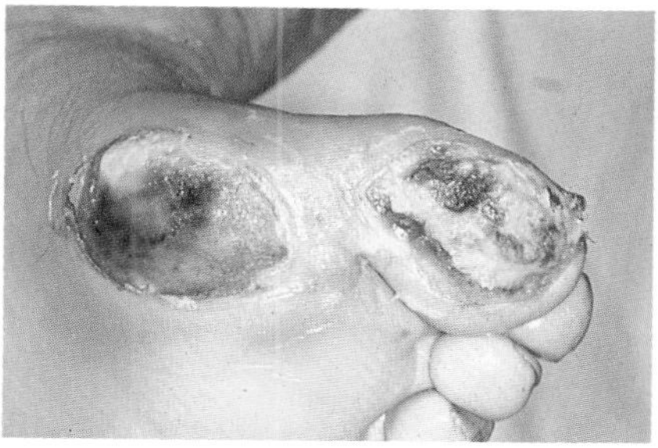

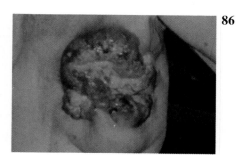

Colour Plate 85. Diabetic foot ulceration.

86

Colour Plate 86. A fungating breast carcinoma.

87

Colour Plate 87. The skin surrounding this fistula is being protected from excoriation by a hydrocolloid sheet dressing.

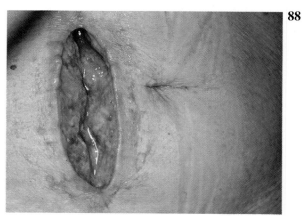

88

Colour Plate 88. An obese patient with a dehisced abdominal wound.

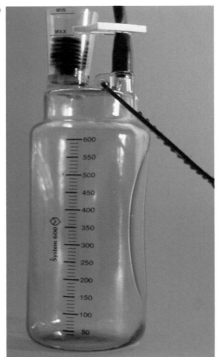

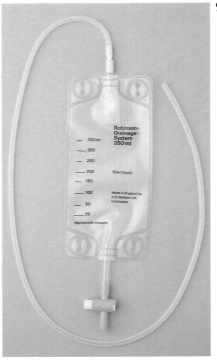

90

Colour Plate **89.** A disposable pre-vacuumed lightweight drainage system with vacuum indicator and Luer lock safety feature for disconnecting bottles, System 600 (Summit Medical).

Colour Plate **90** The Wallace–Robinson passive drainage system (Medical-Assist) with pre-connected bag and integral non-return valve.

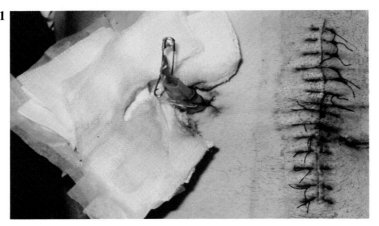

91

Colour Plate **91.** A 'traditional' open drain with the drainage fluid collected on a keyhole gauze dressing held in place with tape. The drain is shortened and can be prevented from re-entering the wound with a safety pin.

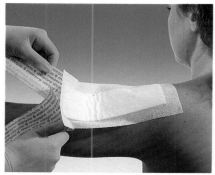
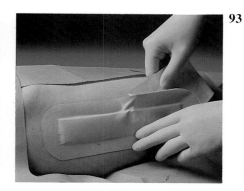

*Colour Plates **92, 93**. Simple island theatre dressings: **92** Mepore; **93** Airstrip.*

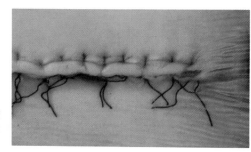

*Colour Plate **94**. A clean, closed surgical wound covered with a film dressing, Bioclusive.*

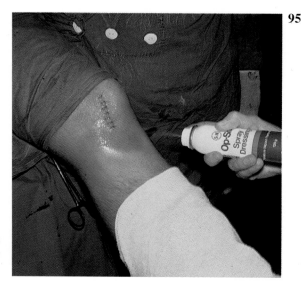

*Colour Plate **95**. Opsite spray in use as a post-operative dressing.*

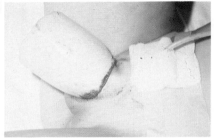

97

*Colour Plate **96**. Silastic Foam dressing used here to immobilise and protect the penis, to prevent excessive swelling, and to allow early mobility in a young patient following hypospadias surgery.*

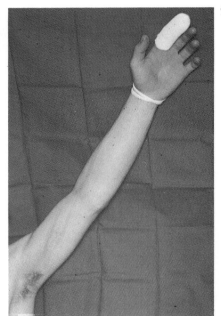

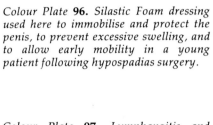

*Colour Plate **97**. Lymphangitis and lymphadenitis in the arm and axilla arising from a focus of infection in the hand.*

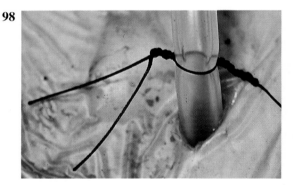

*Colour Plate **98**. A drain held in place with suture material.*

*Colour Plate **99**. A wound irrigation device.*

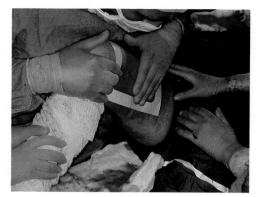

100

*Colour Plate **100**. A split-skin graft donor site being covered with a film dressing, Tedaderm.*

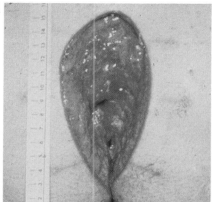

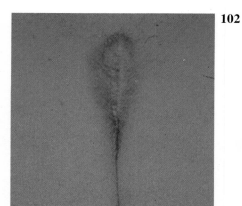

*Colour Plates **101–103**. Treatment of a pilonidal sinus with Silastic Foam: **101** surgically excised; **102** after packing with Silastic Foam dressings for 129 days the wound is fully healed; **103** a collection of the foam 'stents', changed weekly, from this patient.*

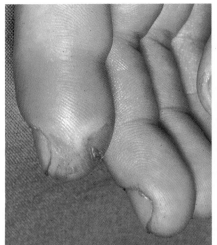
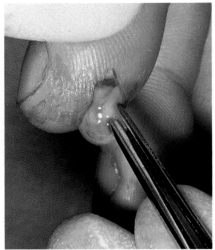

103

*Colour Plates **104, 105**. **104** A distal pulp space abscess; **105** being drained of purulent material.*

*Colour Plate **106** A thoracotomy wound left to heal by secondary intention. This clean wound is being dressed with Silastic Foam.*

Colour Plate **107.** *It is important to cleanse this dirty, superficial abrasion of all contaminants, in order to prevent the tattooing effect caused by retained dirt, which can cause permanent disfigurement.*

107

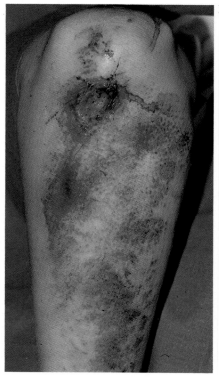

108

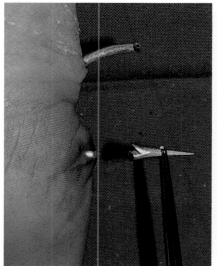

109

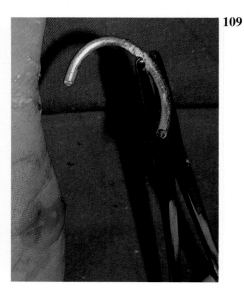

Colour Plates **108, 109.** **108** *Under a local anaesthetic the fishhook is pushed forward until the barb has emerged; it is then cut off;* **109** *the cut end of the fishhook is pulled back through the wound.*

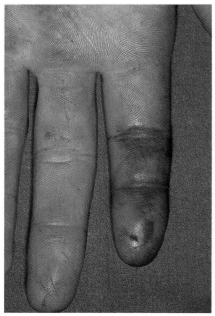 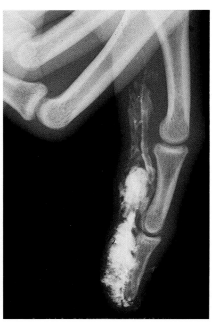

Colour Plate **110.** *(a) This apparently superficial penetrating wound was caused by a high-pressure spray gun; (b) An X-ray reveals the extent of penetration of the paint from the spray gun; it is important to remove as much paint as possible to prevent tissue necrosis and infection.*

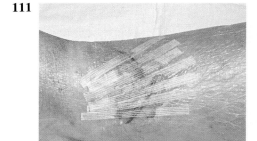

Colour Plate **111.** *A clean superficial laceration closed with Steristrips.*

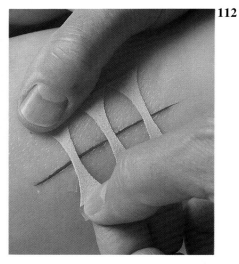

Colour Plate **112.** *Non-stitch dumbbell sutures used to hold the opposing edges of a laceration firmly together.*

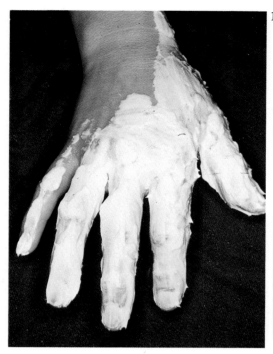

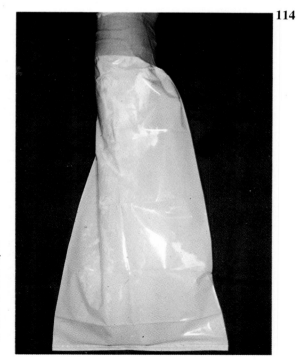

Colour Plates 113, 114. 113 A burn covered in a thick layer of silver sulphadiazine cream to reduce the risk of infection; 114 the hand is placed into a burn bag, anchored at the wrist, to maintain a moist environment and allow full mobility of the hand.

115

Colour Plates **115, 116.** *Applying a traditional sling.*

116

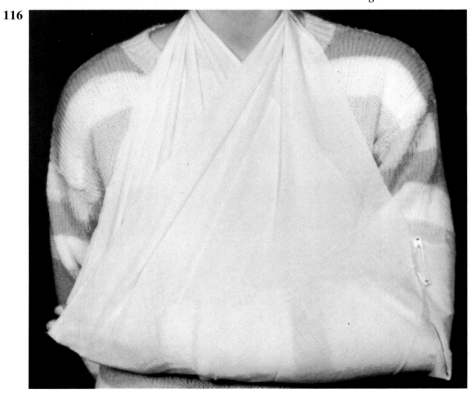

117

118

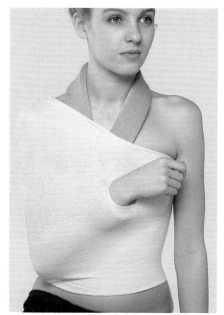

119

*Colour Plates **117–119**. Some uses of collar 'n' cuff: **117** to provide wrist support; **118** to immobilise the arm and shoulder; **119** to support the arm in a balanced position.*

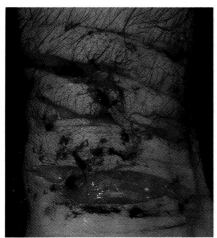

Colour Plate **120**. *Self-inflicted lacerations to the wrist.*

Colour Plates **121, 122**. **121** *An abused child covered in haematoma of different ages; a hand mark is visible (bottom left);* **122** *cigarette burns to the buttocks.*

121

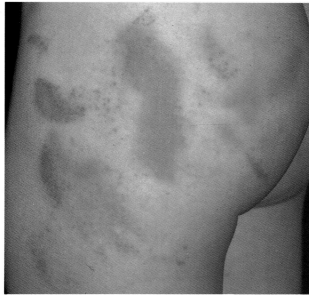

122

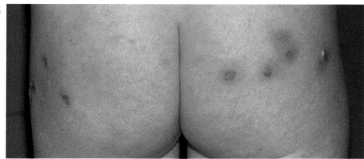

9 Surgically Closed Wounds

9.1 Introduction

This chapter focuses on the nurse's role in the *local* assessment and management of general surgical wounds. Detailed accounts of the assessment and care of patients with wounds in special sites, such as eyes, ears, nose, and throat, newly made gastrointestinal stoma, major thoracic wounds, and specialised wounds encountered in orthopaedics and neurosurgery can be found in the references given in the Further reading section of this chapter but the general principles of the procedures are given in the body of Chapter 9.

The nurse's wider role in pre-operative patient assessment, psychological support, immediate post-operative care, and preparation of the patient for discharge from hospital is the subject of many excellent nursing textbooks, some of which are also given in the Further reading section; it is outside the scope of this book.

Most surgeons take considerably more interest in the management of the wounds that they have created than in the management of chronic open wounds, such as leg ulcers and pressure sores (*Lancet* editorial, 1990), and will normally prescribe their care. Most wound complications arise from events or findings in theatre, which are totally outside the nurse's control. The nurse's role is not, however, confined to managing drains, changing dressings, and removing sutures and staples. Augmenting a general role in pre-operative patient preparation and post-operative patient care, which can both directly and indirectly affect wound healing, the nurse's *observational* skills are of crucial importance in the early detection of wound complications postoperatively.

In addition to the general principles of wound care outlined in Chapters 1–5, an understanding of the influence of the site of a surgical incision on wound healing, and the pre- and peri-operative factors that increase the risk of post-operative wound infection is fundamental to understanding the principles of local surgical wound management. These factors will be discussed first.

9.2 The influence of the site of a surgical incision on wound healing

The principal factors taken into account by surgeons when planning the site and length of a surgical incision are

- *Ease of access to the site of the operation.*
- *Effect on function of underlying structures.*
- *Long-term cosmetic effect.*

Ease of access to the operation site is of overriding importance to the surgeon. Ideally, the best access is achieved by siting the incision directly over the organ or structure to be operated on, with the possibility of extending the incision in either direction should this be necessary.

The orientation of the incision relative to the body's ·natural skin creases has important consequences for wound healing. Professor Langer described the natural lines of skin cleavage, which generally correspond to the orientation of subcutaneous bundles of collagen fibres. They are now known as Langer's lines. Incisions made parallel to these lines tend to fall together naturally and therefore heal more rapidly and with a better cosmetic result than incisions made at right angles to them, which tend to gape apart.

The effect of the site of a surgical incision on the function of underlying structures can best be illustrated with reference to limb incisions. Incisions are never normally made across the flexor surface of a joint because of the risk of contracture, deformity and loss of function. Incisions over subcutaneous bone are also avoided wherever possible, as such wounds are generally slow to heal and the excessive scar tissue formed may become tethered to the bone.

The principal sites of abdominal and some thoracic incisions are illustrated in *Figure 9.1*. Common surgical incisions and the organs to

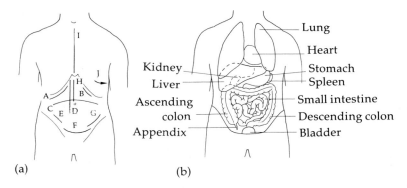

Figure 9.1. (a) Principal sites of abdominal and thoracic incisions; (b) the organs to which access can be gained.

Table 9.1 Principal sites for abdominal and thoracic incisions
(see *Figure 9.1*)

Incision	Organs to which access can be gained
A. Right subcostal (Kocher's)	Gall bladder and common bile duct, hepatic flexure of colon, portal venous system
B. Left subcostal (Kocher's)	Spleen, stomach, splenic flexure of colon
C. Transverse epigastric[a]	Spleen, stomach, gastro-oesophageal junction, portal venous system
D. Right paramedian	Both upper and lower abdominal structures depending on how much the incision is extended
E. Gridiron (McBurney's)	Appendix
F. Transverse suprapubic (Pfannenstiel)	Prostate gland, bladder, uterus
G. Left inferior oblique (Rutherford Morrison)	Descending colon, ureters and iliac vessels
H. Midline epigastric[b]	Stomach[c], duodenum
I. Midline sternotomy	Heart (open surgery)
J. Thoracotomy (anterior or posterolateral)	Lungs, pleura, oesophagus, heart and thoracic blood vessels

Notes:
[a] For a liver transplant, a transverse epigastric incision (C) may be combined with a midline epigastric incision (H).
[b] A long midline incision, extending below the umbilicus, may be used for colorectal surgery.
[c] A thoraco-abdominal incision may be used for a total gastrectomy.

which access is gained are summarised in *Table 9.1*. Vertical incisions that cut across the natural lines of skin cleavage are not ideal from the point of view of wound healing, especially in obese patients where the possibility of abdominal wound dehiscence is greatly increased (*Colour Plate* **88**). Nevertheless, laparotomies are generally performed through vertical incisions, as these can most easily be extended to gain access to any intra- or retroperitoneal structure.

The principal sites of thoracic incisions are illustrated in *Figures 9.1* and *9.2*. Access to the lungs, pleura, oesophagus, and heart (for closed

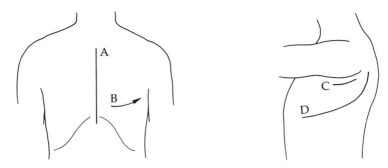

Figure 9.2. Principal sites of thoracic incisions: A, midline sternotomy; B, anterior thoracotomy incision; C, axillary incision; D, posterolateral thoracotomy incision (Westaby, 1985, p. 25).

procedures) is generally gained through an incision between two ribs. Posterolateral thoracotomies are more common than anterolateral thoracotomies as the ribs can be detracted to a greater extent posteriorly, facilitating access. They generally heal rapidly. Open heart operations are carried out through a vertical midline sternotomy. This incision is unsatisfactory from many points of view. The sternum lies subcutaneously and must be repaired with a strong material, such as stainless steel wire, which can lead to a wound sinus formation and at worst osteomyelitis. A thick, unsightly scar is almost inevitable. As a midline sternotomy is the only satisfactory way to gain access for open heart surgery, this example illustrates the principle that *access* is the prime consideration in determining the site of an incision and can override all other considerations.

Common sites for head and neck incisions are illustrated in *Figure 9.3*. Cosmetic considerations are of obvious importance here. In neck wounds it is usually possible to achieve a good long-term cosmetic

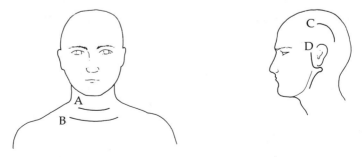

Figure 9.3. Common sites for head and neck incisions: A, tracheostomy incision; B, thryroidectomy incision; C, craniotomy incision; D, parotidectomy incision (Westaby, 1985, p. 26).

result by raising a flap of skin and subcutaneous tissue and incising beneath this, thus partly concealing the incision. Neurosurgical procedures are generally performed through incisions behind the hairline. In the short term the repair can be very unsightly, depending upon how much of the head has to be shaved. Head and neck incisions are generally, however, quick to heal because of the rich blood supply to these areas.

A number of operations that required large incisional wounds are now being replaced in some centres by endoscopic procedures or are performed via a small laparoscopic incision, including laparoscopic cholecystectomy and appendicectomy.

Less invasive procedures are usually much more desirable from the patient's perspective and can dramatically reduce the length of postoperative stay: as techniques are perfected, large surgically made incisions may well become less common.

Many factors, apart from the site of the incision, affect the probability of uncomplicated wound healing. General pathophysiological factors that can delay healing, such as malnutrition, cardiovascular disorders, and chronic infection, including cytotoxic drugs and radiotherapy, were discussed in Chapter 1. The influence of pre- and peri-operative factors on the healing of surgical wounds is now discussed.

9.3 The influence of pre- and peri-operative factors on surgical wound infection and wound breakdown

A number of factors that affect infection rates in surgical wounds were identified in a much-quoted 10-year prospective study commenced by Cruse and Foord in 1967, at the Foothills Hospital, Calgary, in which almost 63,000 wounds were eventually followed up. A wound was defined as 'infected' if it discharged pus, and 'possibly infected' if it developed signs of inflammation or a serous discharge. In the latter case, the wounds were followed up daily until they resolved into a non-infected or infected category.

Table 9.2 The effect of length of pre-operative stay on surgical wound infection rate (Cruse and Foord, 1980)

Duration of pre-operative stay (days)	Infection rate (%)
1	1.2
7	2.1
14+	3.4

Factors that can influence the risk of wound infection are summarised in *Figure 9.4*, and include the duration of pre-operative hospitalisation, pre-operative skin preparation, trauma during the operative procedure and, especially today, the prophylactic use of antibiotics.

9.3.1 Duration of pre-operative stay

The longer patients stay in hospital before operations, the more susceptible they become to wound infection (*Table 9.2*). The precise reasons for this are not known. It could be that the patient's skin becomes colonised with multiple antibiotic-resistant micro-organisms from the hospital environment, which act as a source of endogenous contamination when the skin is breached by surgery, or it could be that hospitalisation reduces the patient's general physical fitness! It could be that the efficiency of the patient's immune system is depressed because of the anxiety generated by the stress of being in hospital (Cohen and Lazarus, 1979; Maier and Laudenslager, 1985), or it could be any combination of these possible mechanisms.

9.3.2 Pre-operative showering and bathing

Some form of total body washing seems to be part of the standard 'routine' when a patient is admitted to hospital, but a number of studies have shown that showering or bathing with non-medicated soap does not reduce the incidence of post-operative wound infection (see, for example, Cruse and Foord, 1980) and indeed may lead to the transfer of bacteria from areas of high colonisation, such as the perineum, nose, and axilla, to skin surfaces that harbour few micro-organisms (Brandberg and Andersson, 1979). However, whole-body disinfection with an *antiseptic* solution is a valuable adjunct to pre-operative skin cleansing in theatre, and helps reduce hospital-acquired infections caused by organisms derived from the patient's own skin (Bruun, 1970).

Hibiscrub, a pink detergent solution containing 4% w/v chlorhexidine gluconate, is increasingly popular as a pre-operative skin cleanser for patients undergoing elective surgery, and a number of studies have confirmed its effectiveness. In a preliminary study of 888 patients, van Diemen (1985) demonstrated a reduction in the level of hospital-acquired infection from 21.5%, when patients bathed well with unmedicated soap, to 9.8%, when they bathed with Hibiscrub. The period of post-operative hospitalisation was also found to be reduced in the Hibiscrub group. A survey involving 2,015 patients at Torbay Hospital showed the overall infection rate was 9.0% for Hibiscrub, 12.7% for bar soap, and 11.7% for a placebo (Hayek *et al.*, 1987). Staphylococcal infections were found to be 2.6%, 5.3%, and 4.0%, respectively. Two whole-body pre-operative washes with Hibiscrub, usually the night before and on the day of the operation, would therefore seem to be beneficial for patients.

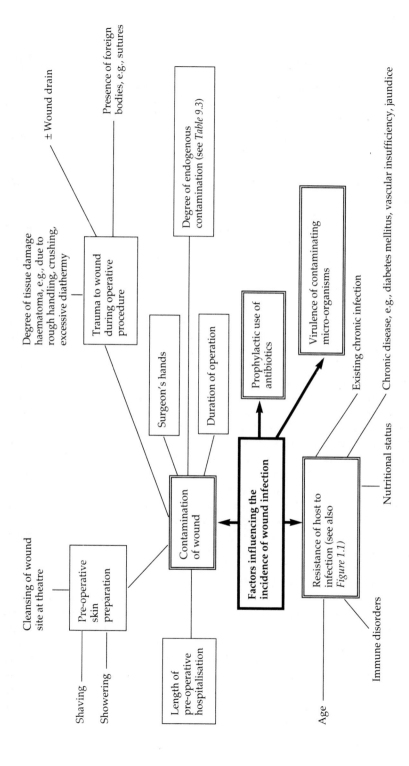

Figure 9.4. *Factors that influence the incidence of wound infection in surgically made wounds (Cruse and Foord, 1980; Westaby, 1985).*

9.3.3 Shaving the operation site

There is now considerable evidence that pre-operative shaving of the operation site *increases* the risk of infection in clean surgical wounds. Cruse and Foord (1980) found the infection rate was 2.5% in patients who were shaved with a safety razor, 1.7% in those who were not shaved but had their pubic hair clipped, 1.4% where an electric razor was used, and 0.9% in those who were neither shaved nor clipped. Using a scanning electron microscope to examine skin prepared with a safety razor, an electric clipper or a depilatory cream, Hamilton *et al.* (1977) demonstrated that safety razors produced gross cuts in the skin; the clipper tended to nip the skin creases while depilatory creams caused no visible injury. The damaged skin provides entry points for micro-organisms, which can become foci of infection prior to surgery. Depilatory creams are not expensive when compared with the cost of prolonged hospitalisation associated with surgical wound infections, and their use should be considered. They save nurses' time and are preferred to shaving by many patients (Winfield, 1986). However, if nurses (and surgeons) are resistant to them, shaving should be performed just prior to surgery, in the anaesthetic room, to reduce the time for bacterial growth, or electric clippers should be used (Pettersson, 1986).

9.3.4 Bowel preparation

The colon naturally contains very large numbers of micro-organisms, some of which are potential pathogens. Any operation involving surgery to the colon therefore carries a high risk of subsequent infection, including the risk of peritonitis, which can be life-threatening for debilitated patients, especially if it is not diagnosed quickly. For elective surgery to the colon, some form of bowel preparation is mandatory. Methods vary and depend on the nature of the surgery, the patient's immediate presenting problems, and general physical condition. Suppositories or an evacuant enema may be used, but their use is contraindicated in cases of paralytic ileus, colonic obstruction, or recent gastrointestinal surgery. Rectal lavage may be requested prior to major abdominal surgery but is contraindicated in patients with some forms of inflammatory bowel disease, large tumours in the rectum or sigmoid colon, a suspected internal fistula, or where the patient suffers from congestive cardiac failure or impaired renal function. Further guidance on the selection and administration of enemas and suppositories and the procedure for rectal lavage is given in Jamieson *et al.* (1988) and in Pritchard and David (1988). If any doubt persists the surgeon should be consulted about the precise requirements in each case. A stimulant laxative, such as Picolax, may be prescribed. A low or non-residue diet may also be prescribed pre-operatively.

Table 9.3 The relationship between the degree of contamination at the time of operation and post-operative wound infection rates (based on data from Cruse and Foord, 1980)

□ No   ◧ Yes or no   ■ Yes

Category of wound	Basis for inclusion of wound in category						Infection rate (%)
	Gut or respiratory tract entered	Inflammation	Pus	Gross spillage of organ contents	Major break in aseptic technique	Perforated viscus	
a) Clean	□[a]	□	□	□	□	□	1.5
b) Clean, contaminated	■	□	□	□	□	□	7.7
c) Contaminated[b]	◧	■	□	or ■	or ■	□	15.2
d) Dirty[c]	◧	■	■			or ■	40.0

Notes:

[a] But cholecystectomy, appendicectomy in passing, and hysterectomy are included in this category if no acute inflammation is present.

[b] Or a traumatic wound less than 4 hours old.

[c] Or a traumatic wound more than 4 hours old.

This table defines the degree of contamination of a wound in summary form. For example, a 'clean' wound is a wound where (with the exceptions given) the gut and respiratory tract are not entered, where no inflammation or pus is encountered, and where there is no major break in aseptic technique. A 'clean, contaminated' wound differs from a 'clean' wound in that the gut or respiratory tract is entered, and so on. The categories of wound can then be compared with the likely infection rate. Infection rates will, however, be affected by the prophylactic use of antibiotics.

9.3.5 Prophylactic use of antibiotics

Cruse and Foord's 1980 study showed unequivocally the significance of endogenous contamination at the time of operation on subsequent wound infection. For 'clean' wounds the infection rate was 1.5%; when pus was encountered the rate of infection was 25 times higher (*Table 9.3*).

Nowadays, the prophylactic use of antibiotics enables almost all wounds to be surgically closed, with the risk of subsequent infection reduced by 75% when a high degree of contamination is encountered at theatre (Burkitt *et al.*, 1990). Where antibiotics have been given prior to surgery in lower risk cases, such as 'clean, contaminated' wounds (*Table 9.3*), the infection rate may actually be lower than for clean wounds where no antibiotic prophylaxis is administered.

The antibiotic, which is chosen to match the potentially pathogenic organisms that are anticipated to be in the area of the operation, is generally administered either an hour before surgery or during the induction of anaesthesia to ensure that high levels are achieved in the blood during the operation, when contamination is most likely to occur. A single pre-operative dose of antibiotic may be sufficient, but short-term post-operative antibiotic therapy may be indicated for high-risk surgery, in high-risk patients, or in low-risk surgery where the consequences of infection would nevertheless be catastrophic.

9.3.6 Peri-operative factors

The duration of the operation, the degree of trauma inflicted on the tissues during the operative procedure, and the insertion of 'foreign bodies', such as sutures and drains, all influence the probability of wound infection and the possibility of subsequent wound breakdown, as does the degree of contamination encountered at theatre (*Figure 9.4*).

Cleansing the operation site   During the first five years of Cruse and Foord's (1980) study, skin was prepared in the operating room with green soap and an alcohol rinse. This took 10 minutes and the infection rate was 2%. In the second five years, povidone–iodine or chlorhexidine was used and the rate of clean wound infection dropped to 1.6%. Povidone–iodine and chlorhexidine skin cleansing preparations are now widely used in theatre.

Draping the patient   After skin cleansing all but the immediate field of operation is usually covered with sterile cotton drapes. Sterile, impermeable paper sheets may be placed beneath the drapes to prevent the patient's skin flora from wicking up through drapes which may become soaked with blood or body fluids. For operations where the risk or consequences of infection are particularly severe, such as joint replacement, plastic drapes with adhesive borders may be used to minimise contamination of the wound site by the patient's skin flora. Clark (1989) and Campbell (1989) reviewed the advantages and disadvantages of reusable theatre linen and single-use drapes.

Management of endogenous contamination   The action taken by the surgeon when dealing with a 'contaminated' or 'dirty' wound (*Table 9.3*) in theatre will depend on the nature of the contaminant, the site of contamination, and the patient's general physical condition. Irrigation and drainage may be employed.

Methods of wound closure
Sutures and suturing   The aim of wound closure is restoration of the physical integrity and functioning of the injured tissues, with the minimum of long-term scarring and deformity.

The wound edges can be brought together and held in place with sutures, staples, clips, or skin tapes, depending on the site and depth of the wound. This is referred to as *primary closure* and healing is said to occur by *primary intention*. The mechanisms involved in healing by primary intention were outlined in Chapter 1. In summary, although it will take many months before the tissues regain anything like their former tensile strength, epithelialisation is normally complete within 10–14 days. The physical integrity of the injured tissue is restored and the mechanical barrier provided by intact skin protects the underlying tissues from infection and dehydration while connective tissue reorganisation is taking place.

Poor suture techniques can lead to a wound with diminished tensile strength which is more prone to dehiscence. Significant factors include

- *Tightness of the suture*: Overtight suturing leads to tissue necrosis and weaker wounds.
- *Size of the tissue bite*: In general, larger bites of tissue within the suture result in stronger wounds than small bites.
- *Distance between sutures*: There is an optimum distance between sutures for different wound types and sites; reducing the distance between sutures can actually weaken the wound.
- *Continuous versus interrupted suturing*: Wounds closed with continuous suture are significantly weaker than wounds closed with interrupted sutures (*Figure 9.5*).
- *Choice of suture material*: There is a bewildering variety of suture materials available and a number of ways of classifying them (*Table 9.4*). Each type of suture material has advantages and disadvantages, as summarised in *Tables 9.5* and *9.6*. The appropriateness of the choice in a specific anatomical area in specific clinical circumstances can be very important in determining the tensile strength of the wound, risk of infection, risk of breakdown, and the long-term

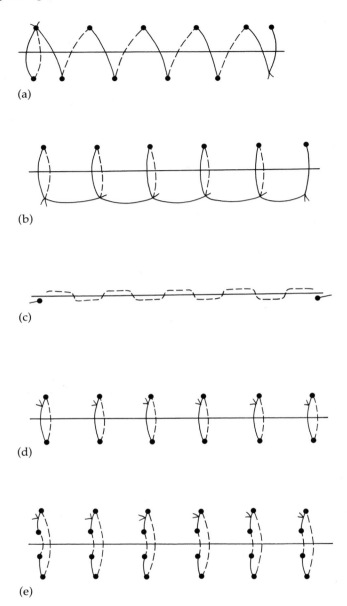

(a)

(b)

(c)

(d)

(e)

Figure 9.5. Methods of suturing: (a) continuous, over-and-over; (b) continuous, blanket; (c) continuous, subcuticular; (d) interrupted, simple; (e) interrupted, vertical mattress.

Table 9.4 Principal types of suture material and some methods of classifying them

(● Yes   ○ No)

Suture material	Non-absorbable	Absorbable	Man-made	Biological
Polyester, e.g. Mersilene*, Ticron*	●	○	●	○
Polyamide (nylon), e.g. Ethilon*	●	○	●	○
Polypropylene, e.g. Prolene*	●	○	●	○
Polyethylene, e.g. Goretex*	●	○	●	○
Stainless steel wire	●	○	●	○
Silk, e.g. Mersilk*	●	○	○	●
Cotton	●	○	○	●
Linen	●	○	○	●
Catgut, plain or chromic	○	●	○	●
Collagen, plain or chromic	○	●	○	●
Homopolymer of glycolide, e.g. Dexon*	○	●	●	○
Copolymers of glycolide and lactide, e.g. Vicryl*	○	●	●	○
Homopolymer of polydioxanane, e.g. PDS*	○	●	●	○

*Trademark

Table 9.5 Relative strengths of different suture materials

Weakest ⟶	Intermediate ⟶	Strongest
Biological materials, e.g. silk, catgut	Synthetic materials, e.g. polyester, polyamide, polypropylene	Metallic materials, e.g. steel

Table 9.6 Graded tissue reactions to the main types of suture material

Weakest ⟶	Intermediate ⟶	Strongest
Synthetic materials, e.g. polypropylene,	Metallic materials, e.g. steel	Biological materials, e.g. cotton, linen, silk

cosmetic result. Choice of suture material, however, is generally second in importance to surgical technique.

A review of the properties and uses of suture materials is given by Capperauld (1989).

Skin tapes For superficial wounds in areas of the body that do not produce copious secretions and that are not over movable joints, wound closure with skin tapes can be a very effective alternative to suturing; there is a lower risk of wound infection. The use of skin tapes in the

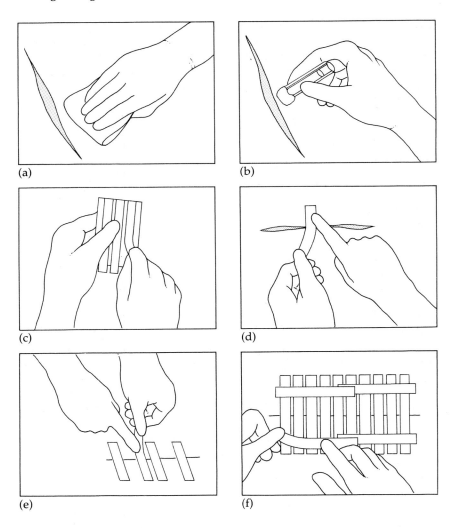

Figure 9.6. Method of applying Steristrip Skin Closures: (a) clean and dry area of skin within 5cm of the wound; (b) a skin tackifier (e.g., Tincture of Benzoin Compound), may be applied to increase the tape-closure adhesion; (c) peel open the envelope and remove the card (to prevent curling, remove the strip carefully at a 45° angle to the card); (d) at mid-portion of the wound apply one-half of the first closure up to one wound margin and press firmly into place; appose the skin edges exactly, using fingers or forceps; press the free half of the closure firmly into place; (e) complete the wound apposition with additional closures spaced approximately 2–3mm apart to allow for drainage; if the skin has parted under the first strip or two, due to the initial stress, remove these closures and re-approximate the wound edges with fresh closures; (f) continue to apply closures until the wound is fully closed; to redistribute tension, additional closures may be applied parallel to the wound.

closure of superficial skin wounds is illustrated in *Figure 9.6* and considered in more detail in Chapter 11. Skin tapes applied between sutures give additional wound support, better alignment of skin edges, and a more even distribution of tension across the wound. They can also be used in combination with absorbable and non-absorbable sub-cuticular sutures to ensure that both dermal and epidermal layers are held firmly in apposition to give a better cosmetic result.

Clips and staples   Closure of skin wounds with clips and staples (*Figure 9.7*) is a more rapid procedure than suturing but has been shown to produce wounds with diminished tensile strength, which are more susceptible to infection in some cases.

The nurse's role in the removal of sutures, skin tapes, clips, and staples is described in Section 9.4.4.

Wound drainage   Surgeons differ widely in their use of wound drains for prophylactic and therapeutic purposes. In the pre-antibiotic era drainage tubes were commonly employed to conduct purulent material away from the abdominal and thoracic cavities. They may be used today to facilitate the therapeutic drainage of post-operative clinically infected wounds and in a prophylactic capacity to abolish dead space or to drain any physiological fluid expected to collect after a surgical procedure; for example, if haemostasis has been difficult to achieve and there is a high risk of haematoma. Drainage may also be used to deflect temporarily natural body fluids away from a new suture line, as in T-tube drainage of the common bile duct. Chest drainage may be

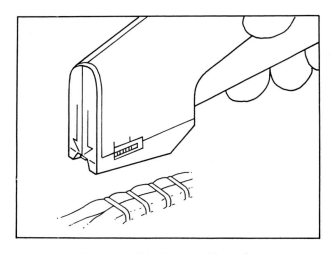

Figure 9.7. Skin closure with staples.

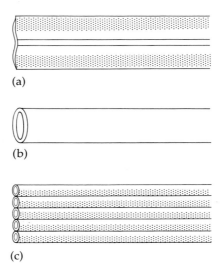

(a)

(b)

(c)

Figure 9.8. Examples of passive open drains: (a) corrugated drain; (b) Penrose drain, with wick; (c) Yeats drain.

required to remove air, blood, or pus from the pleural cavity, to prevent compression of the lungs, or to allow them to re-expand.

Wound drainage systems can be subdivided into active suction systems and passive systems. Active suction systems are closed systems, which may provide high-pressure suction, with re-usable autoclavable drainage bottles, or low-pressure suction, with disposable, compressible plastic bellows, bulbs, or bottles (*Colour Plate* **89**). Passive drainage systems may be open or closed. Closed passive systems, such as the Wallace–Robinson system (*Colour Plate* **90**) rely on gravity. Material drains via pre-connected tubing into a calibrated bag. A number of open passive drains are illustrated in *Figure 9.8*.

The main disadvantages of drains are that:

- They can act as *retrograde conduits* through which skin contaminants can gain access to the deep layers of the wound.
- They are foreign bodies, and as such their presence *reduces the resistance of tissues to infection.*
- They can cause pressure necrosis to internal organs and blood vessels, leading to the formation of *fistulae* or to *secondary haemorrhage.*

The risk of infection is significantly less when a closed active or passive drainage system is used rather than an open passive drainage system (*Colour Plate* **91**). In a closed system the incorporation of non-return valves abolishes the risk posed by reflux of the contents of a contaminated reservoir. The correct siting of drains and the use of soft, inert materials reduces the risk of pressure necrosis to internal organs. The prompt removal of a drain, once it has performed its function, is particularly important in minimising drain-related complications.

A review of the advantages and disadvantages of prophylactic and therapeutic drainage is given in Westaby (1985), Harland and Irving (1988), and Nightingale (1989). Robinson's (1986) historical view of methods of wound drainage is interesting not only because it explains the evolution of and principles behind the use of wicks, tube drains, and sump drains, but also because it highlights the controversy that has surrounded this aspect of surgery since records began. The nurse's role in the management of wound drains is described in Section 9.4.3.

The rest of Chapter 9 is concerned with the nursing management of primarily closed surgically made wounds. The management of surgical wounds left to heal by secondary intention is discusssed in Chapter 10.

9.4   The nurse's role in the post-operative management of closed surgical wounds

9.4.1   The wound dressing

The purpose of the wound dressing applied in theatre is to absorb exudate and to protect the wound from exogenous contamination until the incision line is sealed.

A secondary benefit of the dressing is that it prevents sutures from catching on clothing and bedding. If the dressing is opaque it conceals the wound from the patient in the short term, which may be helpful in an anxious patient in the immediate post-operative period.

In most cases a simple island dressing that incorporates an absorbent pad is sufficient (*Colour Plates* **92, 93**). If the level of exudate is very low it may be possible to apply a semipermeable film dressing, such as Opsite, Tegaderm, or Bioclusive in theatre (*Colour Plate* **94**). Some surgeons prefer an Opsite spray dressing (*Colour Plate* **95**). Sites which are particularly vulnerable to trauma, such as amputation sites, may be padded with Gamgee or an equivalent thick absorbent dressing as a secondary dressing. An absorbent secondary dressing may also be required in a heavily exuding wound or beneath pressure bandages. Where a wound in a difficult site would benefit from protection and immobilisation, a Silastic Foam dressing may be appropriate (*Colour Plate* **96**).

So long as no exudate strikes through the dressing, the patient remains afebrile, and there are no other indicators of wound complications (Sections 9.4.2 and 9.4.5), the dressing can be left undisturbed. The surgeon will generally specify when the dressing is to be removed and whether it is to be replaced or the wound left exposed.

9.4.2 Wound observation and patient assessment

Because of their contact with patients over the whole 24-hour period, nurses are in a particularly good position to detect wound complications at an early stage, *if they know what to look for*.

The importance of accurate and ongoing wound assessment was emphasised in Chapter 2. A wound assessment chart to facilitate the accurate recording of the nurse's observations of the wound site is given in *Figure 9.9*. Nurses are encouraged to identify and note down any general patient factors that may delay healing, as well as details of the wound itself, to alert the nurses on the next shift to potential as well as to any actual problems.

Unless a transparent theatre dressing is used, direct wound observation is difficult in the immediate post-operative period. The theatre dressing should only be removed if exudate strikes through or there are any signs or symptoms of infection. The first indications of infection may be spreading erythema of the skin surrounding the incision line, with local pain and oedema. This must be differentiated from the initial inflammatory response to injury (see *Table 1.1*), which is part of the normal healing process.

A malodorous wound is always a cause for concern. The nature and colour of any abnormal exudate should be noted and reported promptly. A wound swab should be taken and sent to the Bacteriology Department for culture and antibiotic-sensitivity testing.

If the wound is clinically infected the patient's body temperature may be raised. If the infection is deep seated, pyrexia may precede local signs of infection by some time. Knowledge of the nature of the operation and the degree of contamination encountered peri-operatively helps the surgeon to assess the probability that pyrexia is due to a deep-seated infection. Fever in the absence of any other signs should not be taken as an absolute indicator of wound infection. There may be another cause, such as a urinary tract or chest infection.

In the very young and the very elderly the classic signs of wound infection, described so far, may not be seen due to immature or impaired host responses to infection. Lethargy, refusal of feeds, and thrombocytopenia may be the only indications of a life-threatening post-operative infection in a young baby. In the very elderly the first evidence of infection may be generalised septicaemia, accompanied perhaps by a subnormal temperature.

The way in which a clinical infection presents will also depend on the nature of the pathogen. The infection may remain localised and give rise to a discrete abscess, or it may spread via the lymphatic system causing lymphangitis and lymphadenitis (*Colour Plate* 97), with perhaps abscesses in distant sites. Alternatively, infection may spread by direct extension through subcutaneous tissues and along fascial planes. When bacteria spread from a focus of infection in the general circula-

ASSESSMENT CHART FOR SURGICALLY CLOSED WOUNDS

Nature of operation ....
Wound site .... **Date of operation** ....
Method of closure ....
Drains: (a) type .... (b) site ....
SPECIAL INSTRUCTIONS FROM SURGEON ....
....

General patient factors which may delay healing (e.g., obese, chronic chest infection) ....
....

Allergies to wound care products ....
Chart the following factors at *every* dressing change. If there is marked erythema trace this, and note if erythema spreads.

Wound factors/Date									

1. **EXUDATE**
   a. amount: heavy/moderate/
      minimal/none
   b. type
   c. colour									

2. **ERYTHEMA OF SURROUNDING SKIN**
   a. around stitches only
   b. extending beyond a
   c. max. distance from wound edge (mm)									

3. **OEDEMA** Severe/moderate/minimal/none									
4. **HAEMATOMA** Severe/moderate/minimal/none									

5. **PAIN (SITE)**
   a. at wound itself
   b. elsewhere (specify)									

6. **PAIN (FREQUENCY)**
   Continuous/intermittent/only at
   dressing changes/none									

7. **PAIN (SEVERITY)** Patient's score (0–10)									
8. **ODOUR** Offensive/some/none									

9. **INFECTION**
   a. suspected
   b. wound swab sent
   c. confirmed (specify organism)									

WOUND ASSESSED BY:

Figure 9.9. Assessment chart for surgically closed wounds.

165

tion, septicaemia may result; this is usually accompanied by pyrexia and is confirmed by a positive blood culture.

The principles behind the management of infected wounds and the signs and symptoms of other wound complications are described in Section 9.4.5.

9.4.3 The management of drains

A brief review of the methods of prophylactic and therapeutic wound drainage is given in Section 9.3.6. Of course, the manufacturers' guidelines on drain management should always be consulted. Detailed procedures for managing drains, including changing drainage bottles, methods of shortening drains, and the procedure for drain removal, are normally specified in hospital nursing procedure manuals or policy documents. The surgeon may also give special instructions for drain management in individual cases and will decide if and when a drain is to be shortened and when it should be removed. As there is considerable variation in drainage system design, hospital policies on drain management, and surgeons' preferences, it is possible here only to outline some general principles of drain management.

Observe the drain and drainage fluid on the patient's immediate return to the ward from theatre and thereafter   (1) Document the volume and nature of the drainage fluid on arrival at the ward and continue to monitor this at regular intervals, according to ward policy; (2) ensure that all drainage tubing is unclamped (unless there is a specific instruction to allow only intermittent drainage), that the drainage tubing is not blocked, and that the drain is properly secured and not dragging or kinked.

Explain the function and care of the drain to the patient   At the least, drains are inconvenient for patients; they can be uncomfortable, depending on where they are sited, and can lead to anxiety. Patients are often afraid of dislodging the drain and may be afraid to move, even in bed. Reassurance and explanation at an early stage minimises anxiety and encourages patients to live and move safely with their drain(s) for as long as they are required.

Change drainage bottles or bags   Following the manufacturer's instructions, take precautions to avoid reflux of fluid and to minimise the risk of infection. Record the volume of fluid on the patient's fluid balance chart.

Observe the drain site   Check for leakage and signs of local infection.

Change the drain dressing   Do this before exudate strikes through, using a strict aseptic technique. Some form of 'keyhole' dressing is usually employed. A stoma bag may be fitted to collect the exudate from open drains.

Shorten drains Follow the surgeon's instructions. One method for shortening a passive drain, using a sterile safety pin, is illustrated in *Colour Plate* **91**. The safety pin prevents the drain from re-entering the body.

Remove the drain Follow the surgeon's instructions, and use an aseptic technique. The drain is often held in place by a suture (*Colour Plate* **98**), which should be removed using the same precautions as when removing any suture material (Section 9.4.4). A sterile absorbent dry dressing is normally all that is required to cover the drain site. The volume and nature of any fluid that continues to drain out should be documented and reported to the surgeon.

9.4.4 Removal of sutures, clips, staples, and tapes

The purpose of sutures, clips, staples, and tapes is to approximate the edges of a surgical incision so that they heal rapidly and leave a minimal scar. They are 'foreign bodies' and as such can set up an inflammatory tissue response (*Table 9.6*). It is therefore important that they are removed as soon as the wound is strong enough to remain intact without their support.

The surgeon will usually decide when sutures are to be removed. In uncomplicated cases sutures to abdominal wounds are generally removed on about the seventh post-operative day. If the patient is obese, on steroid therapy, or liable to delayed wound healing for any other reason (see *Figure 1.1*), it may be decided first to remove alternate sutures or to leave all the sutures in place for a little longer. In sites such as the head and neck, which have a particularly good blood supply, sutures can normally be removed after 4–5 days. The earlier the sutures are removed the better the cosmetic effect. The timing of the removal of clips and staples will be governed by similar factors and will generally be decided by the surgeon.

The removal of non-absorbable sutures, staples, and clips should be regarded as an aseptic procedure that should be carried out according to hospital policy. Methods of suture removal are illustrated in *Figure 9.10*. The stitch cutter or scissors should be held in the dominant hand while the forceps in the other hand gently lift the knot of the stitch. The suture should be cut close to the skin and removed so that *no part of the suture material which was above the skin surface is pulled through the tissues, and no suture material is left in the wound*. Retained suture material can lead to a wound sinus (Chapter 8). Pulling surface suture material through the tissues draws micro-organisms beneath the skin surface, which can lead to local infection. The removal of staples is illustrated in *Figure 9.11*.

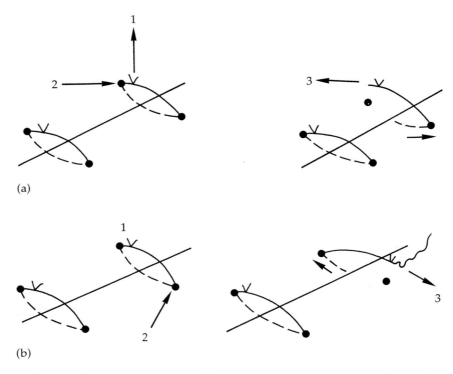

(a)

(b)

Figure 9.10. Methods of suture removal: (a) with scissors, (1) lift knot with forceps, (2) cut suture next to the skin with fine, sharp scissors, (3) pull out suture towards the wound; (b) with a stitch cutting blade, (1) hold knot with forceps, (2) cut suture, with the stitch cutting blade next to the skin, (3) pull suture towards the wound.

Removal of skin closure tapes requires a different technique. The tapes should be gently released from the outside towards the line of the incision from both directions. If the tape was used to hold a flap of tissue in place, particular care should be taken not to pull the tape in such a way that it will re-open the wound.

If, after removing one or two closures, the wound begins to gape, a swab should be taken of any exudate which leaks out and the wound covered with a sterile dry dressing until a decision is made as to whether or not to continue with closure removal.

After removal of the sutures, clips, or tapes the wound can be cleansed of any remaining surface debris. It may be left exposed, covered with a sterile non-adherent dry dressing, or sprayed with a waterproof plastic film dressing, such as Opsite, depending on the surgeon's instructions.

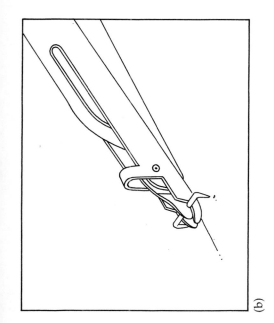

(a)

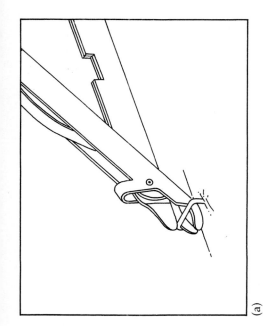

(b)

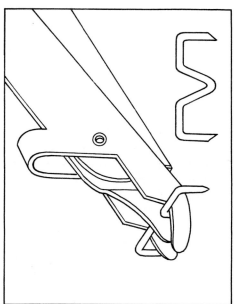

(c)

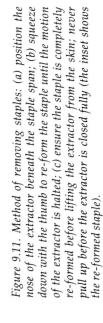

Figure 9.11. Method of removing staples: (a) position the nose of the extractor beneath the staple span; (b) squeeze down with the thumb to re-form the staple until the motion of the extractor is halted; (c) ensure the staple is completely re-formed before lifting the extractor from the skin; never pull up before the extractor is closed fully (the inset shows the re-formed staple).

9.4.5 Wound complications

The majority of surgical wounds heal without major complications. The complications that can occur after surgical wound closure include

- Primary and secondary haemorrhage.
- Wound infection.
- Wound dehiscence.
- Sinus formation.
- Fistula formation.
- Incisional hernia.

Both local and systemic factors can contribute to these complications. Local factors include suture technique (see Section 9.3.6) and the degree of contamination encountered at the time of operation. Systemic factors include any medical conditions that delay wound healing (see *Table 1.2*), such as diabetes, hepatic failure, and malignant disease. Patients who are malnourished, for whatever reason, are also more prone to wound complications.

Primary and secondary haemorrhage   Primary haemorrhage, that is haemorrhage encountered during an operation, is normally controlled by the surgeon before the operation is completed.

Haemorrhage during the immediate post-operative period is, in general, a form of primary haemorrhage in that it is usually due to inadequate peri-operative haemostasis, or a technical problem, such as a slipped ligature or unrecognised damage to a blood vessel. Early post-operative haemorrhage is a particular risk in operations involving highly vascular tissues, such as the liver and spleen, and in arterial surgery, especially in heparinised patients. A central venous pressure (CVP) catheter may be inserted to allow accurate estimation of the patient's blood volume and a clotting screen obtained. If the haemorrhage is substantial the patient may need to return to theatre for re-exploration of the source of bleeding and for haemostasis.

Secondary haemorrhage usually occurs several days after an operation and may be due to erosion of a blood vessel or vessels secondary to infection, or due to pressure necrosis caused by a badly sited wound drain. Treatment involves managing the infection. Very occasionally the patient may need to be returned to theatre to ligate vessels.

The management of infected wounds   There are a number of adverse consequences of wound infection. Infecting organisms compete with the cells in healing tissues for available nutrients and oxygen, healing is delayed, and where bacterial toxins are produced these may have adverse local or systemic effects (Chapter 5).

The signs and symptoms of wound infection were described in Section 9.4.2. When infection is suspected or confirmed the management of the wound will be decided by the surgeon. The principles of treating an infected surgical wound are

Facilitate wound drainage It may be necessary to re-open the wound along the length of the infected part and position the patient to encourage reliable dependent drainage. The management of superficial abscesses is considered in Chapter 10. A deep-seated abscess may be kept open by a drain. The wound may be allowed to heal by secondary intention (Chapter 10). Re-suturing at the time of drainage is to be avoided, but delayed primary closure may be possible in some cases.

Cleanse the wound of organic debris Clear away pus and slough, mechanically or by irrigation (*Colour Plate* **99**).

Use systemic antibiotics These may be prescribed if there is evidence of cellulitis, septicaemia, or the infection progresses in spite of all attempts at drainage.

Consider surgical excision of dead and devitalised tissue Along with aggressive chemotherapy, radical excision may be required in cases of severe infection, such as necrotising fasciitis and synergistic gangrene.

Use a simple non-adherent dressing Change the dressing before exudate strikes through. An occlusive dressing should be avoided unless the wound is under strict medical supervision.

The nurse's observations of the problems at the wound site should be charted at each dressing change (*Figure 9.9*) and any further deterioration in the wound or the patient's general physical condition reported promptly to the surgeon. In some hospitals it is the policy for all cases of wound infection to inform the infection control nurse or hospital bacteriologist, who advises on any special precautions required to prevent cross-infection of other patients (*Table 5.3*).

A patient with a wound infection may be pyrexial, is likely to be suffering from a general feeling of malaise, is prone to dehydration, may have a depressed appetite, and may well be feeling anxious about the unexpected complication. High-quality nursing care can improve the patient's physical and psychological well-being, which in turn will promote more rapid wound healing. Psychological support, maintenance of an adequate dietary intake, especially during the catabolic phase of healing, and avoidance of dehydration are particularly important.

Wound dehiscence Wound dehiscence is the breakdown of a wound along part or all of its length and may or may not be associated with wound infection. Exacerbating factors, which include malnutrition, anaemia, concurrent malignant disease, and jaundice, adversely affect wound healing through a number of mechanisms (Section 1.6).

Dehiscence is most frequently seen following abdominal surgery, especially in elderly obese patients who develop a post-operative chest infection (*Colour Plate* **88**). Dehiscence results when the sutures are unable to hold the wound edges together—usually at a time of raised intra-abdominal pressure due, for instance, to coughing or vomiting.

Total breakdown of an abdominal wound to reveal coils of bowel is sometimes referred to as a 'burst abdomen'. It is an uncommon phenomenon but is alarming both to patients and to nurses and junior doctors. The immediate management is to cover the wound with sterile swabs soaked in saline and to reassure the patient. The patient is generally returned to theatre within a few hours for surgical repair. In a few cases, if evisceration has not occurred, the surgeon may decide to manage the wound conservatively, especially if the patient is a very poor anaesthetic risk and the dehiscence is associated with gross wound infection and peritonitis. The peak incidence of burst abdomen is 7–10 days after surgery, just before the skin sutures are normally removed. It is often preceded by the discharge of serosanguineous fluid.

Sinus formation   A wound sinus is generally a late infective complication of surgery. It is a blind-ended track, usually ending in an abscess cavity, which fails to heal because the cavity contains foreign material, such as a buried non-absorbable suture or retained packing material. The foreign material must normally be removed before healing can take place. The management of chronic discharging sinuses is described in Section 8.4.

Fistulae   A fistula is an abnormal track between two epithelial surfaces that connects one viscus to another or a viscus to the skin (see *Figure 8.2*). There are many causes of fistulae (see *Table 8.1*). Fistula formation can be iatrogenic, due to breakdown of an anastomosis following surgery, or to damage caused by a badly positioned wound drain. The management of fistulae is described in Section 8.5.

If a bowel fistula is associated with intra-abdominal sepsis the patient will require intensive therapy and the mortality rate is high.

Incisional hernia   An incisional hernia is generally a late complication of abdominal surgery caused by breakdown of the repair to the muscle and fascial layers while the overlying skin remains intact. It usually presents as a bulge in the abdominal wall near the incision scar. An incisional hernia can develop as late as 5 years post-surgery for many complex reasons, both local and systemic, but normally becomes apparent within the first post-operative year. It may be asymptomatic but tends to enlarge over time. Repair is indicated for strangulation, pain, or inconvenience to the patient, for instance with clothing.

9.4.6   The meaning of pain at dressing changes

The change of the theatre dressing may be a painful procedure, even for a surgically closed wound, because the wound site will still be very tender and exudate may have soaked into the dressing and dried out, leading to adherence. The procedure should be explained to the patient beforehand and any prescribed analgesia given, in sufficient time to have reached peak effectiveness at the time of the dressing change. If the patient becomes unexpectedly distressed during the procedure, then Entonox may be indicated. However, if painful dressing changes become the *normal* experience for a particular patient, then the nurse should ask herself certain questions:

- *Is the wound infected?* The classical signs of infection may not be obvious at first, especially if the infection is deep seated (Section 9.4.2).
- *Is the dressing being changed too infrequently?* Even 'non-adherent' dressings may adhere if left in place too long, especially in a wound where the exudate strikes through the dressing and dries out.
- *Are any topical agents, dressings or tapes being used which could be producing an irritant response?*
- *Does the patient feel the nurse is lacking in empathy?* Is the nurse minimising the psychological and social significance of the wound to the individual? It might be timely to discuss the meaning of the wound with the patient, as well as the treatment plan and likely prognosis, if this has not already been done.

Other causes of pain at the wound site and at dressing changes are given in *Table 2.2*. Some wider issues to consider when assessing pain are described in Section 2.2.3.

9.4.7   Patient education

Surgery can pose threats not only to a patient's physical well-being, but also to the patient's self-image, social, and occupational functioning and emotional equilibrium (Cohen and Lazarus, 1979). The individual's perception of the consequences of the wound and ability to cope with it will depend upon many factors, including the site and type of wound, whether or not the surgery was planned, the degree of anticipated long-term functional disability, the visibility and extent of scarring, the availability of social support, the individual's personality, and the accuracy of the individual's appraisal of the long-term prognosis (*Figure 1.5* and Section 2.5).

The nurse has a very important role in supporting patients through the potentially stressful events associated with surgery, including pre-surgery diagnostic procedures, preparation for theatre, immediate post-operative recovery, and preparation for discharge from hospital. Providing patients with information both pre- and post-operatively has been shown to be very important in aiding recovery (Hayward, 1975; Boore, 1978; Horsley, 1981; Wade, 1989). Before discharge all patients will require basic information on how to manage their wound at home. Teaching patients or their carers how to manage a colostomy, ileostomy, or tracheostomy is often undertaken by a stoma care specialist nurse but the teaching should be reinforced by ward-based nursing staff. Successful patient education motivates patients to take responsibility for their health to the limits of their ability. The role of the nurse as an educator is discussed in more detail in Chapter 12.

Further reading

General surgery
Burkitt, H.G., Quick, C.R.G. and Gatt, D. (1990), *Essential Surgery: Problems, Diagnosis and Management*. Churchill Livingstone, Edinburgh.

General surgical nursing
Brunner, L.S. and Suddarth, D.S. (1990), *The Lippincott Manual of Medical – Surgical Nursing* (2nd edn). Harper and Row, London.
Game, C., Anderson, R.E. and Kidd, J.R. (eds) (1989), *Medical – Surgical Nursing: a Core Text*. Churchill Livingstone, Melbourne.
Luckmann, J. and Sorensen, K.C. (1987), *Medical – Surgical Nursing: a Psychophysiologic Approach* (3rd edn). W.B. Saunders, Philadelphia.
Watson, J.E. and Royce, J.A. (1988), *Watson's Medical – Surgical Nursing and Related Physiology* (3rd edn). Baillière Tindall, London.

Clinical nursing procedures
Jamieson, E.M., McCall, J.M., Blythe, R. and Logan, W.W. (1988), *Guidelines for Clinical Nursing Practices*. Churchill Livingstone, Edinburgh.
Pritchard, A.P. and David, J.A. (eds) (1988), *The Royal Marsden Hospital: Manual of Clinical Nursing Procedures* (2nd edn). Harper and Row, London.

Nursing care of patients with wounds in special sites
EYES
Kirkton, M. and Richardson (1987), *Ophthalmic Nursing*. Current Nursing Practice Series, Baillière Tindall, London.
Perry, J.P. and Tullo, A.B. (eds) (1990), *Care of the Ophthalmic Patient: a Guide for Nurses and Health Professionals*. Chapman and Hall, London.
Stollery, R. (1987), *Ophthalmic Nursing*. Blackwell Scientific Publications, Oxford.

EAR, NOSE AND THROAT
Serra, A.M., Bailey, C.M. and Jackson, P. (1986), *Ear, Nose and Throat Nursing*. Blackwell Scientific Publications, Oxford.
Stalker, A.E. (1988), *Ear, Nose and Throat Nursing* (6th edn). Current Nursing Practice Series, Baillière Tindall, London.

NEUROSURGERY
Hickey, J.V. (1986), *The Clinical Practice of Neurological and Neurosurgical Nursing* (2nd edn). J.P. Lippincott, Philadelphia.

ORTHOPAEDICS
Farrell, J. (1986), *Illustrated Guide to Orthopaedic Nursing* (3rd edn). J.P. Lippincott, Philadelphia.

THORACIC SURGERY
Foss, M.A. (1989), *Thoracic Surgery*. Clinical Skills Series, The Professional Nurse, London.

GASTROINTESTINAL STOMA
Elcoat, C. (1986), *Stoma Care Nursing*. Current Nursing Practice Series, Bailliere Tindall, London.
Wade, B. (1989), *A Stoma is for Life*. Daphne Heald Research Unit, RCN, UK.

PLASTIC SURGERY
McCarthy, J.G. (1990), *Plastic Surgery*. W.B. Saunders, London.
McGregor, I.A. (1989), *Fundamental Techniques of Plastic Surgery and Their Surgical Applications* (8th edn). Churchill Livingstone, Edinburgh.

References

Boore, J. (1978), *Prescription for Recovery*. Royal College of Nursing, London.
Brandberg, A. and Andersson, I. (1979), Whole body disinfection by shower-bath with chlorhexidine soap. In *Problems in the Control of Hospital Infection*, pp. 65–70. Royal Society of Medicine International Congress and Symposium Series No. 23, Academic Press, London.
Bruun, J.N. (1970), Postoperative wound infection—predisposing factors and the effect of a reduction in the dissemination of staphylococci. *Acta Medica Scandinavica*, **188** (supplement 514), 1–89.
Burkitt, H.G. *et al.* (1990), *Essential Surgery: Problems, Diagnosis and Management*. Churchill Livingstone, Edinburgh.
Campbell, L. (1989), Single use drapes. *British Journal of Theatre Nursing*, **26**(1), 13–15.
Capperauld, I. (1989), Suture materials: a review. *Clinical Materials*, **4**, 3–12.
Clark, C. (1989), Reusable or disposable theatre linen: which is best? *Professional Nurse*, 4(4), 183–185.
Cohen, F. and Lazarus, R.S. (1979), Coping with the stresses of illness. In Stone, G.C. *et al.* (eds) *Health Psychology – a handbook*. Jossey-Bass, San Francisco.
Cruse, P.J.E. and Foord, R. (1980), The epidemiology of wound infection – a 10 year prospective study of 62,939 wounds. *Surg. Clin. North America*, **60**(1), 27–40.
Hamilton, H.W. *et al.* (1977), Preoperative hair removal. *Canadian J. Surg.*, **2**, 269.
Harland, R.N.L. and Irving, M. (1988), Surgical drains. *Surgery*, 1360–1362.
Hayek, L.J. *et al.* (1987), A placebo-controlled trial of the effect of two pre-operative baths or showers with chlorhexidine detergent on post-operative wound infection rates. *J. Hosp. Infect.*, **10**, 165–172.
Hayward, J. (1975), *Information: a Prescription against Pain*. Royal College of Nursing, London.
Horsley, J.A. (1981), *Structured Pre-operative Teaching* (Curn Project). Grune and Stratton, New York.

Jamieson, E.M., MacCall, J.M., Blythe, R. and Logan, W.W. (1988), *Guidelines for Clinical Nursing Practices*. Churchill Livingstone, Edinburgh.

Lancet editorial (1990), Preventing pressure sores. *Lancet*, **335**, 1311–1312.

Maier, S.F. and Laudenslager M. (1985), Stress and health: exploring the links. *Psychology Today*, **19** (8), 44–49.

Nightingale, K. (1989), Wound drainage. *Nursing Times*, **85**(27), 40–42.

Pettersson, E. (1986), A cut above the rest? *Nursing Times* (March 5), 68–70.

Pritchard, A.P. and David, J.A. (eds) (1988), *The Royal Marsden Hospital: Manual of Clinical Nursing Procedures* (2nd edn). Harper and Row, London.

Robinson, J.O. (1986), Surgical drainage: an historical perspective. *Br. J. Surg.*, **73**, 422–426.

van Diemen, A.H. (1985), Prevention of postoperative infection by using chlorhexidine soap. *Zickenhuis Hygiene en Infektiepreventie*, **4**, 123–127.

Wade, B. (1989), *A Stoma is for Life*. Royal College of Nursing, London.

Westaby, S. (1985), Wound closure and drainage. In Westaby, S. (ed.) *Wound Care*, pp. 32–46. Heinemann, London.

Winfield, V. (1986), Too close a shave? *Nursing Times* (March 5), 64–68.

10   Open Surgical Wounds

10.1   Introduction

Where there is little tissue loss, as in a surgically closed wound (Chapter 9) or a minor laceration whose edges are held together with Steristrips (Chapter 11) healing occurs by *primary intention*; that is, by the union of the two closely opposing wound edges (*Figure 1.3*). Very little granulation tissue is produced and within 10–14 days re-epithelialisation is normally complete.

In open wounds where there is significant tissue loss and the wounds are not surgically closed, healing is said to occur by *secondary intention*. Granulation tissue develops in the base of the wound (*Figure 1.4*) and epithelial cells migrate towards the centre of the wound from the margins. If the wound is superficial and the dermis is not entirely lost, epithelial cells can also migrate from islands of epithelial tissue associated with hair follicles, sebaceous glands, and sweat glands. The wound edges are brought together by wound contraction through the action of specialised fibroblasts (*Table 1.1*).

Where there is tissue loss, filling in of the defect with new tissue takes much longer than when wounds heal by primary intention, and the outcome is generally much less satisfactory cosmetically, and occasionally, functionally. It is for this reason that major skin defects are often repaired surgically using skin grafts or flaps (Section 1.5). There are, however, some surgical wounds which are deliberately left open (*Table 10.1*), for a variety of reasons.

Some open surgical wounds are initially clean. When a split-skin graft is taken to cover the defect caused by a burn, for example, a clean superficial wound is created at the donor site; this should heal quite satisfactorily within 10–14 days if appropriately managed. A radically excised pilonidal sinus will give rise to a clean deep wound.

Other surgically made open wounds are left to heal by secondary intention because the risk of them breaking down from infection is too high if they were to be surgically closed. Examples include newly

Table 10.1   Surgically made wounds which may be left to heal by secondary intention

A. *Clean superficial wounds*
Split-skin graft donor sites.

B. *Clean deep wounds*
Chronically inflamed tissue, excised to leave a clean deep wound bed, e.g. excised pilonidal sinus, axillary hidradenitis suppurativa.

C. *Contaminated wounds*
Drained abscesses, where there is still a high risk of infection, e.g. perianal abscesses, carbuncles, furuncles, osteomyelitic abscess, distal pulp space infection in the digits.
Surgical wounds where a very high level of contamination is discovered at theatre, e.g. gross faecal contamination.
Very heavily contaminated battle wounds, where there has been delay in treatment.

drained abscesses and surgically made wounds where a very high level of contamination is encountered at theatre.

The emphasis in managing all these open wounds is to create the optimum local environment for healing (Chapter 3), and ensure good drainage in the deeper wounds.

10.2   Clean superficial wounds

The harvesting of a whole or split-skin graft to repair a primary defect elsewhere in the body creates a clean superficial wound at the donor site. Most whole skin graft donor sites are either directly sutured or covered by a split-skin graft. Split-skin graft donor sites are normally left to heal by secondary intention. A comparison of whole and split-skin grafts and donor site repair is given in *Table 10.2*.

The management of a split-skin donor site, left to heal by secondary intention, is normally specified by the surgeon who created the wound. The main practical problem associated with donor site dressings is that the more traditional regimes, involving gauze and/or simple low adherent dressings, have a tendency to dry out, to become hard, and to adhere to the wound bed. Removal of the dressing frequently causes trauma and bleeding, as some of the regenerating epithelium is torn off with the dressing, and the first dressing change can be very painful. A number of the more modern dressings have been reported to reduce pain when the dressing is changed and to reduce healing times, with good cosmetic results.

The first priority in donor site management is haemostasis, but this is generally not a problem. A haemostatic agent, such as Kaltostat, has been found to accelerate donor site healing when compared with a more

Table 10.2 A comparison of whole and split-skin grafting and donor site repair

	Whole skin graft	Split-skin graft
Donor sites	Postauricular skin, upper eyelid, supraclavicular skin, thigh and abdomen.	Torso, thigh and upper arm, flexor aspect of forearm.
	Many factors affect choice of donor site, including nature of recipient site; amount of tissue required; whether a good colour and texture match is needed; the need for hairless skin, etc; ease of repair/healing of donor site; vascularity of tissue.	
Method of harvesting tissue	Graft is cut with a scalpel.	Graft is cut to a pre-determined thickness with a Humby knife, or electric or drum dermatome.
Size of recipient site	Restricted to small defects.	Extensive defects can be grafted.
Probability of graft 'take'	Except for grafts to the head and neck, where the blood supply of the recipient site is excellent, whole grafts take less readily than split-skin grafts because the number of cut capillary ends is smaller in the thicker grafts and revascularisation is slower.	
Donor site repair	No epidermal structures remain; small donor areas are directly sutured, while larger areas are covered by a split-skin graft.	Islands of epithelial tissue with pilosebaceous follicles and sweat glands act as foci for re-epithelialisation; healing is by secondary intention; the thinnest split-skin grafts, with many epithelial islands, heal within 7 days; the thicker split-skin grafts, where only islands of epithelium associated with sweat glands remain, may take 10–14 days to re-epithelialise.

traditional paraffin tulle dressing, and to give a healed wound with a better cosmetic result. Alternatively, a film dressing, such as Opsite or Tegaderm, could be used (James and Watson, 1975; Dinner *et al.*, 1979; Barnett *et al.*, 1983). Film dressings offer a number of advantages over more traditional dressings: they are highly conformable and non-bulky and do not require a secondary dressing (*Colour Plate* **100**). However, they are not particularly suitable where exudate levels are high.

Significant reductions in healing time have been reported when donor sites are dressed with a hydrocolloid wafer, such as Granuflex, compared with gauze or paraffin tulle dressings (Biltz *et al.*, 1985; Madden *et al.*, 1985; and Doherty *et al.*, 1986). As well as reducing pain at the wound site by maintaining a moist environment, Granuflex has been shown to produce good long-term cosmetic results. The healed donor site skin is soft and supple and has been considered to be ready for re-harvesting more quickly than skin healed under a paraffin tulle dressing. This is particularly important in a patient with large surface area burns, where the area of potential donor site skin is limited.

10.3   Clean deep wounds

The management of chronic sinuses, including pilonidal sinuses, was described in Chapter 8. One treatment option is radical excision of the sinus network, which creates a clean, deep wound bed that may be surgically closed or left to heal by secondary intention.

Another condition involving chronic inflammation that may require radical excision of the affected tissue is hidradenitis suppurativa. Hidradenitis, a bacterial infection of the apocrine sweat glands in the axilla and anogenital regions, occurs more frequently in women than in men. The discharge from the multiple abscesses is thick, purulent and may be blood stained. If treated early the infection may respond to high-dose antibiotics but, if the infection has been present for more than 8–10 weeks, a systemic antibiotic is much less likely to be effective since, by this time, fibrotic tissue has walled off the organisms, containing them within the deeply seated coils of the apocrine glands. It is at this stage that radical excision of affected tissues may be required. The resulting large surface area wound may be closed by grafting, but good results may be obtained in the axillary region by leaving the wound to heal by secondary intention so long as a suitable dressing is used.

Silastic Foam 'stents' have been found to be particularly suitable for managing clean, deep wounds (*Colour Plates* **101–103**) (Wood and Hughes, 1975; Morgan *et al.*, 1980; Cook and Devlin, 1985) and in the management of laid open anal fistulae. The dressing comes as two liquids, a foam base and a catalyst, which are mixed in the ratio of 100:6

for 15 seconds before being poured into the wound. The mixture expands to give a foam stent that is about four times the initial volume of the mixture. The stent follows the contours of the wound closely. It requires twice-daily disinfection with a 0.5% Hibitane solution and this can often be managed at home by patients or their carers. The stent is reusable for about a week, at which time the wound can be reassessed and a new stent made. The foam maintains a moist environment at the wound site, is thermally insulating, and prevents early bridging-over of deeper wounds by epithelium, which could impede wound drainage. Furthermore, many younger patients, who are otherwise perfectly fit, find this dressing enables an early return to work and resumption of normal activities, without the need to attend a health centre for daily dressing changes.

An alternative approach for the management of more superficial wounds, such as the wound created by wide excision of hidradenitis suppurativa, is to use a hydrocolloid dressing (Michel, 1985); this stimulates angiogenesis, reduces pain, and is waterproof, allowing the patient to shower.

Although the unit cost of the more modern dressings, such as Silastic Foam and the hydrocolloids, is higher than the cost of gauze, overall treatment costs can compare very favourably as healing is generally significantly faster and the newer dressings require to be changed less frequently. Silastic Foam and the hydrocolloids are generally more cosmetically acceptable to patients than traditional dressings; they conform well to difficult wound sites and are easy and convenient to manage.

10.4   Contaminated wounds

10.4.1   Drained abscesses

An abscess is a localised collection of pus produced as a result of infection involving pyogenic organisms (*Colour Plates* **104, 105**). The pus is a mixture of necrotic tissue, bacteria, and dead white blood cells, liquefied by autolytic enzymes. As the pressure within the cavity increases the pus takes the line of least resistance and may discharge through the skin or into an internal body cavity or viscus.

Abscesses can be classified according to their site and the tissues involved. The management of abscesses in the peritoneum, lung, liver, bone, oral cavity, and brain is outside the scope of this book. The principles behind the management of skin and subcutaneous abscesses (*Table 10.3*) are now described.

Furuncles or boils generally heal spontaneously once the pus has discharged and the necrotic tissue is removed. More deep-seated abscesses, e.g. perianal and ischiorectal abscesses, often require to be laid open surgically and drained. Wherever possible, an abscess should

Table 10.3 Common sites for abscess formation, involving skin and subcutaneous tissues

Type	Nature and sites of tissue damage	Principal treatment options
SKIN (GENERAL) *Furuncle* (boil)	An abscess originating in a hair follicle or sebaceous gland, usually due to *Staphylococcus aureus*. Develops into a painful indurated swelling. The centre may soften after 2–3 days, with discharge of thick, creamy pus, or it may subside without suppuration. Common on the back of the neck and in hirsute areas, such as the back of the trunk and lower limbs. Axillary furuncles occur most commonly in middle-aged women and tend to recur. An infection in an eyelash follicle gives rise to a sty (hordeolum).	Often discharges pus spontaneously. Drainage may be encouraged with a kaolin poultice or magnesium sulphate paste (not for use near the eye).
Carbuncle	A honeycomb mass of staphylococcal abscesses in the subcutaneous tissues. Tissues become erythematous, tender, and indurated. Purulent material is discharged onto the surface of the skin through multiple sinuses. Commonly occurs on the nape of the neck, especially in diabetic men.	Early antibiotic therapy can minimise pus formation, necrosis, and tissue loss. Once pus has formed, thorough desloughing and drainage of the abscess is needed.
Hidradenitis	Abscesses develop in deeply seated apocrine sweat glands in the axilla, the anogenital region, and under the breasts in women, causing chronic inflammation of the tissues. The discharge is thick and purulent and may be bloodstained. It may subside for a short time, only to recur.	Early treatment with antibiotics may be effective. Once the infection is deeply established, antibiotics are rarely effective because fibrosis has walled off the organism into inaccessible deep-seated coils of the apocrine glands. The whole mass of inflamed tissue then needs to be surgically excised.

PERIANAL *Perianal*	The abscess is due to an acute infection of the anal glands, which lie between the internal and external anal sphincters. The infection spreads laterally through the external sphincter into the tissue beneath the perianal skin. The patient presents with perianal pain, erythema, and swelling.	If diagnosed early, oral antibiotic therapy may control the infection. Established abscesses require excision and drainage.
Ischiorectal	Usually develops in the loose fibro–fatty tissue of the ischiorectal fossa from a neglected or inadequately drained perianal abscess. The patient presents with severe and constant perianal pain and swelling.	Surgical excision and drainage, with antibiotic cover.
Pilonidal	A sinus, or series of ramifying sinuses, develops as a result of hair slowly working its way into the upper end of the natal cleft between the buttocks. A chronic inflammatory reaction results which can lead to an abscess or abscesses if the cavity becomes secondarily infected. The area affected can be very painful and swollen with chronic or intermittent purulent discharge. Generally occurs in hirsute men who sit for prolonged periods while driving. Commonly recurs.	Occasionally drain spontaneously but rarely heal completely without treatment. Treatment options for acute exacerbations include radical excision of the inflamed tissue, if tissue damage is extensive; deroofing with curettage of granulation tissue or of the sinus network; and treatment with liquefied phenol to encourage fibrosis.
HAND AND FINGER *Distal pulp space*	The infection is usually secondary to a minor pinprick injury. The patient complains of a throbbing pain. The overlying skin is erythematous and swollen.	Surgical incision over the most tender region, allowing drainage of the infected material.
Paronychia	Infection of the skin fold surrounding the dorsum of the nail leads to a collection of pus.	Deroofing the subcutaneous blister of pus and exploration of the base of the nail to ensure that all pus is released. The proximal portion of the nail may need to be cut away.
Web space	Infection generally results from a puncture injury and often leads to a dumbbell-type abscess with tenderness and swelling, which pushes the adjacent digits apart.	Surgical incision and drainage.

be drained while it is still localised. Abscesses are usually too heavily contaminated with micro-organisms to be surgically closed, as the risk of recurrent infection is high, and are normally left open, to heal by secondary intention.

Traditionally, drained abscesses have been packed with ribbon gauze, often soaked in antiseptic solutions, such as Eusol. The advantages and disadvantages of a number of commonly used antiseptic solutions, including the hypochlorites, are reviewed in Chapter 4. There are a number of options now available. If there is a high risk of recurrent infection, a bead dressing, such as Iodosorb, which contains povidone–iodine, may be considered for short-term wound management. The ointment formulation is particularly easy to apply. After 2–3 days, when the wound is healing and beginning to granulate, an antiseptic is no longer required. A summary of dressing options to meet the needs of the wound at various stages of healing is given in *Figure 3.1*.

10.4.2 Other surgical wounds left to heal by secondary intention

Dirty traumatic wounds and surgically made wounds where a very high level of contamination is discovered in theatre may occasionally be left to heal by secondary intention (*Colour Plate* **106**) because the risk of the wound breaking down, if closed, is too high.

Local wound management will normally be decided upon by the surgeon and will depend upon the nature, site, and size of the wound and any locally encountered problems (Chapter 3). If the wound remains clean and there are no signs that the tissues are devitalised, the surgeon may decide to suture the wound loosely some days later. This is known as delayed primary closure.

Further reading

Burkitt, H.G., Quick, C.R.G. and Gatt, D. (1990), *Essential Surgery: Problems, Diagnosis and Management*. Churchill Livingstone, Edinburgh.

McGregor, I.A. (1989), *Fundamental Techniques of Plastic Surgery and Their Surgical Applications*. Churchill Livingstone, Edinburgh.

References

Barnett, A. *et al.* (1983), Comparison of synthetic adhesive moisture vapour permeable and fine mesh gauze dressings for split-thickness skin graft donor sites. *Am. J. Surg.*, **145**, 379–381.

Biltz, H. *et al.* (1985), Comparison of hydrocolloid dressing and saline gauze in the treatment of skin graft donor sites. In Ryan, T.J. (ed.) *An Environment for Healing: the Role of Occlusion*, pp. 125–128. International Congress and Symposium Series No. 8, Royal Society of Medicine, London.

Cook, P.J. and Devlin, H.B. (1985), Boils, carbuncles and hidradenitis suppurativa. *Surgery*, **19**, 440–442.

Dinner, M.I. *et al.* (1979), Use of semipermeable polyurethane membrane as a dressing for split-skin graft donor sites. *Plast. Reconstr. Surg.*, **64**, 112–114.

Doherty, C. *et al.* (1986), Granuflex hydrocolloid as a donor site dressing, *Care: Crit. Ill.*, **2**, 193–194.

James, J.H. and Watson, A.C.H. (1975), The use of Opsite, a vapour permeable dressing on skin graft donor sites. *Br. J. Plast. Surg.*, **28**, 107–110.

Madden, M.R. *et al.* (1985), Optimal healing of donor site wounds with hydrocolloid dressings. In Ryan, T.J. (ed.) *An Environment for Healing: the Role of Occlusion*, pp. 131–139. International Congress and Symposium Series No. 8, Royal Society of Medicine, London.

Michel, L. (1985), Use of hydrocolloid dressing following wide excision of perianal hidradenitis suppurativa. In Ryan, T.J. (ed.) *An Environment for Healing: the Role of Occlusion*, pp. 143–148. International Congress and Symposium Series No. 8, Royal Society of Medicine, London.

Morgan, W.P. *et al.* (1980), The use of Silastic Foam dressing in the treatment of advanced hidradenitis suppurativa. *Br. J. Surg.*, **67**, 277–280.

Wood, R.A.B. and Hughes, L.E. (1975), Silicone Foam Sponge for pilonidal sinus: a new technique for dressing open granulating wounds. *Br. Med. J.*, **3**, 131–133.

11 Traumatic Wounds

11.1 Introduction

People with a wide variety of problems find their way into the Accident and Emergency Department: the victims of road traffic accidents and assaults; cases of attempted suicide; people who have sustained accidental injury at work, during recreation, or at home; and people with minor medical ailments, who should instead have attended their general practitioner. The types of commonly encountered traumatic wounds are indicated in *Table 11.1*.

Many textbooks have been written on the management of patients with traumatic injury. Some texts of particular relevance to nurses are given in the Further reading section at the end of this chapter. While a detailed account of the management of the seriously injured patient is outside the scope of this book, the general principles behind the reception, prioritisation, and management of patients with traumatic wounds will be outlined, with the emphasis on the role of the nurse in creating a therapeutic environment, in patient assessment, and in managing minor wounds.

The general principles of local traumatic wound management include many of the basic principles of wound care outlined in Chapters 2–5.

11.2 Deciding on priorities for treatment

Triage has been defined by Westaby (1985a, p. 99) as 'the assessment of priorities in a busy situation'. The term is normally used in the context of prioritising multiple casualties following a major accident. People with minor injuries or irrecoverable major ones are afforded a lower priority than patients with major injuries where immediate and active intervention has a high probability of saving life.

The keys to ensuring the best possible outcome for a patient with major traumatic wounds are, first, accurate and rapid assessment of the patient's condition and its underlying pathology; and secondly, gaining

Table 11.1 Types of traumatic wounds that involve damage to the skin

Abrasions
Superficial, partial thickness injuries of the skin that often result from tangential shearing and/or friction of the skin surface relative to a harder or rougher surface, e.g. superficial injuries to the knees, face, or hands of a pedestrian or cyclist involved in a road traffic accident; these wounds are commonly contaminated with gravel, dirt, or glass.

Simple lacerations
Incised injuries that involve the full thickness of the skin and a variable depth of the underlying tissues and result from contact with a sharp object, e.g. a knife, piece of metal, or glass.

Lacerations with tissue loss
Incised wounds with tissue loss, e.g. traumatic amputations.

Penetrating wounds
Incised wounds that penetrate to deep tissue and are caused by a sharp object, such as a nail or knife.

High-pressure injection
Accidents with high-pressure devices used in industry, such as grease guns, diesel fuel injectors, and spray guns, can lead to penetrating injuries and contamination of deep tissues with organic fluids, such as lubricants and paint.

Contusions
Wounds with devitalised tissue that result from crushing injuries and range in severity from minor bruising or swelling of subcutaneous tissues to massive tissue destruction caused by impact with a moving vehicle. These wounds are often accompanied by lacerations and abrasions. Crush injuries can mask serious internal injury.

Burns
Tissue damage caused by heat, corrosive chemicals, electricity, or radiation range in severity from superficial wounds that involve damage to the epidermis to full-thickness burns in which all the elements of the skin are destroyed.

Bites
Penetrating, often ragged wounds, which may also be contused, caused by animals or humans.

Compound fractures
Bone penetrates the skin from within and creates soft-tissue damage and a track which may lead to deep infection, including osteomyelitis.

the fastest possible access for the patient to any specialist facilities and treatments required. In this situation patients are prioritised by senior members of the medical team.

A modified form of triage can be applied by the casualty officer or a very experienced nurse in a busy A&E Department on an ordinary day. Minor problems are afforded a low priority. Of the remaining patients

Table 11.2 Wounds that require specialist assessment and management (Westaby, 1985a, p. 99)

1. Penetrating wounds of the chest and abdomen
2. Penetrating wounds of the brain and spinal cord
3. Lacerations with damage to major blood vessels, nerves, or tendons
4. Compound fractures
5. Burns, other than very minor
6. Facial wounds involving fractures or significant disfigurement
7. Wounds to the eye
8. Wounds of potential legal or forensic importance, including suspected non-accidental injury to children
9. Wounds with foreign bodies that cannot be safely removed under local anaesthetic
10. Wounds associated with internal injuries

the doctor must decide which ones to treat himself and which to refer on rapidly for specialist assessment (*Table 11.2*).

Prioritising patients, even those with apparently minor injuries, should not be left to the receptionist, who has little medical knowledge. Wherever possible, patients who are assessed as being of low priority should be kept informed of the reasons for delay in their being attended to. A board indicating estimated waiting times for non-urgent cases can be helpful in this respect.

11.3 Patient reception, immediate assessment, and emergency management

11.3.1 *Airway, breathing, and circulation (primary survey)*
Assessment should begin the moment that the patient enters or is brought through the door of the A&E Department. The nurse is often the first person to see the patient and should rapidly ask herself a number of questions (*Figure 11.1*).

11.3.2 *Major haemorrhage*
Overt arterial haemorrhage requires very urgent management that is second only in importance to maintenance of the airway. Direct pressure and elevation of the affected part is often all that is required to arrest bleeding in the short term. Further management of wounds involving major blood vessels is the doctor's responsibility and the principles are described by Evans (1979) and Mansfield and Bradley (1985).

It is worth carefully examining clothes and temporary dressings to gain some idea of external blood loss. The size of a wound may bear little relationship to its seriousness. Penetrating wounds made with a stiletto-type instrument and having a small external opening can cause

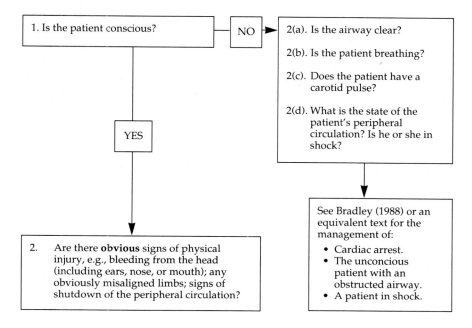

1. Is the patient conscious? — NO → 2(a). Is the airway clear?

2(b). Is the patient breathing?

2(c). Does the patient have a carotid pulse?

2(d). What is the state of the patient's peripheral circulation? Is he or she in shock?

YES

See Bradley (1988) or an equivalent text for the management of:
- Cardiac arrest.
- The unconcious patient with an obstructed airway.
- A patient in shock.

2. Are there **obvious** signs of physical injury, e.g., bleeding from the head (including ears, nose, or mouth); any obviously misaligned limbs; signs of shutdown of the peripheral circulation?

Figure 11.1. Immediate assessment on seeing a patient for the first time.

major internal blood vessel damage. A patient with internal bleeding can be in at least as life-threatening a state as a patient where trauma is obvious, in part because the problem may not be immediately recognised.

Pulse and blood pressure measurements can be very poor indicators of the severity of a haemorrhage as blood pressure is maintained as a very high priority by various autonomic mechanisms. By the time peripheral shutdown of the circulation is obvious, the position may be irrecoverable. Readings from a central venous pressure (CVP) line give a much more accurate estimate of the patient's blood volume than pulse and blood pressure measurements, and the line is ideal for giving rapid transfusions. In cases of less severe injury it is still very worthwhile to site an intravenous cannula, such as Venflon, before the veins collapse.

11.3.3 Multiple injuries
A discussion of the priorities in the management of the patient with multiple injuries is outside the scope of this book, but several relevant concise and readable reviews are given in the Further reading section of this chapter.

11.3.4   Severe burns

Early access to *specialist* assessment and management is imperative for all but the most minor burns, to minimise avoidable complications and long-term disfigurement. Clinical assessment of the depth of a burn (*Table 11.3*) is far from straightforward, although the skin's macroscopic appearance, sensitivity to pain, and an accurate history of the incident can give valuable clues.

In adults with burns involving more than 15% of their surface area, and children with more than 10% burns, hypovolaemia is a real possibility and can lead to hypovolaemic shock unless fluid replacement is instigated promptly.

A review of the management of severe burns and burns to special sites, such as the face, neck and hands, is outside the scope of this book. An authoritative account of the advantages and disadvantages of the main treatment options is given by Muir *et al.* (1987). In summary, the immediate priorities are:

- *Maintaining the airway*: In cases of severe oedema to the face or neck, intubation or tracheotomy may be required.
- *Breathing*: Oxygen may be required if smoke has been inhaled.
- *Fluid replacement*: Use a recognised regime and carefully monitor fluid balance, especially urinary output.
- *Pain relief*: Entonox or intravenous morphine may be needed; sedation may also be required.
- *Débridement of the wound*: Remove gross contaminants and devitalised soft tissue, often under a general anaesthetic.
- *Prevention of infection.*
- *Psychological support.*

The factors that determine the severity of a burn and the likely outcome for the individual are summarised in *Figure 11.2*. A superficial partial thickness burn, involving 10% of the body's surface area, has potentially far more serious short- and long-term consequences for a young child, or for a very elderly person who has a number of other concurrent medical problems, than for an otherwise fit young adult. The consequences of inhalation of smoke or hot gases are far more serious for a patient with pre-existing chronic respiratory problems than for an adult without these problems. Severe burns in an already malnourished, underweight patient are more life-threatening than for a patient who is well nourished and has reserves on which to draw during the early catabolic phases of the body's response to trauma.

11.3.5   Psychological support

It is important at a very early stage to develop a good relationship with the patient and any accompanying relatives. They should be given a calm, friendly, and reassuring reception and every allowance should be

Table 11.3 Depth of a burn and its implications for treatment and healing

Type of burn	Tissues involved	Implications for treatment and healing
Superficial: partial thickness	The epidermis is largely destroyed but the hair follicles, sebaceous glands, and sweat glands are not; the damage does not extend at any point through the dermis–subcutaneous tissue interface.	Can be painful, especially if extensive, as nerve endings are intact. Usually heal rapidly with conservative treatment with no permanent scarring or loss of function.
Deep: partial thickness	The epidermis and a substantial part of the dermis are lost, but islands of deep epidermal cells associated with hair follicles and sweat glands survive; some damage to subcutaneous tissue occurs at high points where it pushes into the dermis.	Nerve endings often intact, making these wounds very painful. Re-epithelialisation is slower than with superficial partial thickness burns as there are fewer surviving islands of epithelium. Healed skin may be imperfect and show some hypertrophic scarring. Skin grafting not normally required, except for cosmetic reasons.
Full thickness	The full thickness of the skin has been destroyed and there are no surviving epithelial elements.	Obliteration of nerve endings means that the patient may feel no pain. With conservative treatment granulation tissue develops beneath the slough of dead tissue, fibrotic scar tissue forms, and the tissues contract under tremendous force, leading to unsightly inelastic tissue with contractures. For cosmetic and functional reasons, full-thickness burns are normally surgically debrided and will be skin grafted.

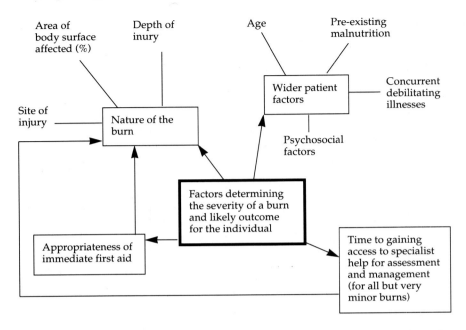

Figure 11.2. Factors that determine the severity of a burn, and the likely outcome, for the individual.

made for inappropriate or aggressive behaviour. Depending on the severity of the injury and the circumstances in which it occurred, patients and those accompanying them may be very anxious and distressed and may well behave in a manner which seems inappropriate. Parents accompanying a child scalded or burned in a domestic accident at home may be blaming themselves for the accident, but may redirect their negative feelings towards staff. A young person whose actions have led to the serious injury of a friend in a motoring accident may be overcome with remorse and in no need of censure from nursing or medical staff, whether verbal or non-verbal. Walsh (1989) gives an excellent account of psychology as it applies to patients, accompanying relatives and staff in an A&E Department, including the management of patients with behavioural problems who may have sustained a traumatic injury while under the influence of alcohol or drugs, and patients who are psychiatrically disturbed.

11.4 Further assessment of the conscious patient

11.4.1 Nursing assessment

For conscious patients with suspected traumatic injury awaiting the arrival of the casualty officer, the nurse should:

- *Give the patient nothing by mouth* until the casualty officer has assessed the patient and decided on treatment.
- *Ascertain the patient's name and date of birth* and place an identity bracelet on the patient at the first opportunity, unless the injury is very minor.
- *Obtain a brief history of the accident from the patient*—if the patient is unable to give this information the ambulancemen should be consulted before they depart, and information should also be obtained from accompanying friends or relatives.
- *Ask about and record allergies, current medication, and any serious medical conditions.*
- *Carry out baseline observations,* including pulse, blood pressure, respirations, and, in the case of head injury, level of consciousness and pupil reactions.
- *Obtain the name and address of next of kin.*
- *Check whether the patient is covered for tetanus.*

11.4.2 Casualty officer's preliminary assessment

The casualty officer will carry out a rapid head-to-toe examination or 'secondary survey'.

Head Looking and feeling for lumps, lacerations, and abrasions; observing for bleeding from the ears, nose, mouth, scalp, or face; looking for facial asymmetry; testing pupil reactions to light and observing pupil diameter; assessing neck pain on movement.

Chest Observing for signs of trauma, including flail chest (chest wall overlying serious rib fractures moves in the opposite direction to the rest of the chest wall), respiratory distress, etc., signs of impact with seat belt, steering wheel, etc.

Abdomen Looking for signs of trauma, including swelling, tenderness, and bruising.

Limbs Comparing both limbs and looking at their alignment, and looking for bruising, lacerations, abrasions, and swelling; testing for power in the limbs and sensation.

While doing the rapid physical examination the doctor will also be assessing the patient's conscious state. The Glasgow Coma Scale is a valuable tool for rapidly recording these assessments in a patient with impaired consciousness. The nurse can continue the assessments to aid in the identification of any change in mental state.

11.4.3   Preparing a patient for transfer

When the decision is made to transfer the patient to another hospital or to a specialist unit within the same hospital, a suitably qualified escort must be arranged. A temporary protective dressing should be applied to wound sites to prevent further contamination, especially where deep tissues are exposed. The patient should be observed for signs of further deterioration in physical and mental condition while awaiting transport and vital signs should be charted at appropriate time intervals.

Arrangements should be made to transport the medical notes, X-rays, any ECGs and emergency laboratory results, observation charts, and personal possessions with the patient.

Any accompanying relatives should be treated with compassion and kept informed of events and the patient's destination. Allowing close relatives to see the patient is important so long as the patient's (and the relatives') condition allows this.

11.4.4   Documentation

Accurate documentation of the history of the injury and of examinations, investigations, diagnoses, and treatment will be completed by the examining doctor. The nurse will record observations and any treatment that he or she has carried out. Documentary evidence may need to be produced in cases of criminal prosecution, industrial compensation, or where patients or their relatives file a complaint alleging negligence by medical or nursing staff with the health authority.

The rest of this chapter is devoted to the *nursing* management of *minor* traumatic wounds, such as minor lacerations, abrasions, burns and bites, where the possibility of underlying fracture, undetected foreign bodies, or other complications has already been excluded by the doctor.

11.5   The nursing management of minor traumatic wounds

After an initial assessment by the doctor, the management of many minor traumatic wounds is delegated to the nurse.

Mismanagement of minor wounds, such as inappropriate closure of a dirty, superficial laceration or failure to remove all gross contaminants from a superficial abrasion, can result in serious consequences for the patient, leading to:

- Wound infection, which delays healing and can cause systemic infection.
- Avoidable pain and discomfort.
- Inconvenience, and perhaps economic hardship if a person has to stay off work.
- More pronounced scarring.

Adherence to the principles of wound cleansing and dressing as out-lined below should help to prevent avoidable complications.

11.5.1 Haemostasis

The first priority in the local management of any wound is haemostasis. Normally, applying direct pressure to a wound with a sterile absorbent pad in direct contact with the wound surface will readily stop minor haemorrhage. If a large surface area is involved and the wound is superficial, a haemostatic agent such as Kaltostat (an alginate sheet dressing) may be applied. A secondary absorbent pad can be placed over the wound and held in place with a pressure bandage. Tourniquets should *not* be used.

11.5.2 Cleansing the wound

The aim of wound cleansing is to help to create the optimum local conditions at the wound site for uncomplicated healing, by removing *debris*, such as foreign bodies and devitalised soft tissue, whose continued presence could lead to clinical infection. Failure to remove all dirt and grit from a wound can leave an area of unsightly 'tattooing' (*Colour Plate* **107**), which is often impossible to remove later.

Full-thickness burns or extensive abrasions contaminated by dirt and grit may need to be debrided in theatre under general anaesthetic. Devitalised soft tissue acts as a culture medium, promoting bacterial growth by inhibiting the ability of leucocytes to ingest bacteria and kill them. Unless radical excision of damaged tissue is performed, it will not be possible to remove all gross contaminants (Haury *et al.*, 1980) and the risk of an infection developing is considerable. Larger foreign bodies, such as knives and large pieces of metal, should *not* be disturbed until the patient is in theatre because of the risk of major haemorrhage when the object is removed.

When in contact with traumatic wounds all staff should wear high-quality gloves for their own protection from blood-borne diseases, such as hepatitis B and AIDS. Handling a wound with a gloved hand is also much more gentle and effective than attempting to clean a wound with gauze held in plastic forceps.

Many patients with minor traumatic wounds do not require an anaesthetic for wound cleansing and the removal of trivial foreign bodies such as splinters, superficial grit, and dirt.

The aim is to remove gross contaminants with the minimum of pain to the patient and trauma to the tissues. For a dirty wound, immersing the injured part in water at body temperature eases the pain and helps to loosen debris. It is important to clean the skin surrounding the wound as well as the wound itself. Oil and grease can be removed with a solvent, such as Swarfega, and soap and water can be used to remove dirt. Gauze is more abrasive than cotton wool and is better for removing ingrained dirt. With hand and forearm injuries the patient may be able to do this for himself at a sink with running water, using an abrasive pad. A pad containing an antiseptic, such as povidone–iodine, may be appropriate for a heavily contaminated wound. If clothing needs to be removed, and this is proving difficult, the seams can be carefully cut with a scalpel blade or Lister scissors.

Pieces of glass, grit, and splinters of wood can be picked out using plain McIndoe's forceps or splinter forceps. To remove splinters of wood from beneath a nail it may be necessary to shave carefully down the nail, using a scalpel blade until the splinter can be clearly seen and grasped with forceps.

An embedded fish hook may need to be removed under a local anaesthetic. If barbed, the hook should not be pulled out; it may need to be pushed through the skin, the barb cut off with wire cutters, and the shank then reversed out (*Colour Plates* **108, 109**).

If the presence of foreign bodies is still suspected, radiological or ultrasound examination may be required. If foreign bodies are left *in situ* they can become the focus for an infection (*Colour Plates* **110**).

Once gross contaminants have been removed the wound itself can be cleansed. An antiseptic solution such as Savlodil, containing chlorhexidine and cetrimide, may be appropriate in a dirty wound. Cetrimide has detergent properties and helps to loosen debris. Alternatively, a 3% hydrogen peroxide solution can be used: as oxygen is released the bubbling action loosens dirt. A review of antiseptic cleansing solutions is given in Chapter 4.

Once the wound is rendered free of gross contaminants, reversion to a strict aseptic technique is required for suturing and wound dressing.

11.5.3   *Minor wound management and dressing selection*

Superficial lacerations   Many superficial lacerations merely require cleansing and the application of a simple dressing to protect the wound from contamination. Deeper lacerations require careful exploration, before closure, to exclude the possibility of retained contaminants. After clinical examination, lacerations caused by glass may need to be examined radiologically if retained splinters are suspected.

Clean lacerations, less than 4 hours old, can be closed by suturing or with tapes, such as Steristrips (*Figure 9.6*). The procedure should be explained to the patient who should, ideally, be lying down on a couch or trolley in case of faintness. Children should be accompanied by one sensible parent or guardian. Babies and toddlers can remain seated on the parent's lap, wrapped in a blanket or draw-sheet, with only the injured part exposed.

Skin tapes   For superficial lacerations it is preferable to close the wound with skin tapes, such as Steristrips (*Figure 9.6* and *Colour Plate* **111**), or with non-stitch dumb-bell sutures (*Colour Plate* **112**), rather than with traditional sutures, as this will not require a local anaesthetic and there will be less scarring in the long term. The surrounding skin must be perfectly dry and any hair shaved off close to the skin, otherwise the tapes will not stick. Benzoin tincture can be applied to the skin to aid tape adhesion, but great care must be taken not to allow the fluid to enter the wound itself as this will be painful and can cause inflammation. The edges of the wound are brought together with small gaps left for wound exudate to escape. The aim is to get accurate apposition of the two cut surfaces, under even tension, without inverting (turning under) the skin edges. In a ragged wound such as multiple lacerations to the skin, it may first be necessary to use some strips at fairly wide intervals to approximate the edges of the wound before filling in the gaps. The initial strips may need to be removed as more accurate closure is brought about.

Steristrips alone are not suitable for closing a laceration over a very mobile site, such as the palm of the hand, over a finger joint, or behind the knee. They can be used in conjunction with sutures in some circumstances.

Suturing Deeper lacerations or lacerations over highly mobile sites will require suturing, using an aseptic technique, following initial wound cleansing. In adults, local anaesthesia, using lignocaine (1% or 2% plain), is required both to relieve pain and to prevent the patient from inadvertently moving the injured part during the procedure. Lignocaine with adrenalin may be required in a very vascular area, such as the scalp, but should *never* be used on a finger or toe as the vasoconstrictor effects of the adrenalin can cause tissue necrosis and peripheral gangrene.

Many children dislike needles and may require a short general anaesthetic to allow the doctor to suture even a relatively minor wound. This can be the best course of action for all concerned, saving needless distress to the child and parents, and enabling the doctor to close the wound carefully. Further details on suturing technique are given in Kirk (1989). In the United States, nurse practitioners are trained in wound care and suturing techniques and can become very proficient in this extended role, releasing medical staff time.

Following wound closure by Steristrips or sutures, it may be necessary to place an absorbent pad over the wound temporarily and apply direct pressure for some minutes, to control minor seepage of serosanguineous exudate. If a dressing is required, it should be low-adherent and absorbent (Chapter 3).

Injections for tetanus, if required, should be given after the laceration is closed and seepage of exudate controlled.

Abrasions Superficial abrasions, although not life-threatening, can be very painful, especially if they are extensive. Careful cleansing of the wound and removal of superficial dirt and grit are essential to reduce the risk of infection and to prevent long-term 'tattooing' caused by retained contaminants. Depending on the site of the wound, a simple, fluffed-up tulle gras dressing with an absorbent secondary pad is normally the dressing regimen of choice and can be held in place with a conforming bandage.

Burns Burns vary in severity from simple erythema of a localised area to deep charring of muscle and other extensive tissue damage (*Table 11.3*). Short-term problems for the patient with even a minor burn can include severe pain and fluid loss, and the underlying tissues are very vulnerable to infection. Long-term problems, which are in the minds of many patients when they are brought to the A&E Department, include disfigurement and functional disability.

Although a wide variety of treatment methods are in current use, there is no single method that has clear advantages over the others or is universally applicable. Similar *principles* apply to the management of a minor, superficial burn as are applied to major burns (Section 11.3.4), namely:

- Pain relief.
- Psychological support.
- Wound cleansing.
- Prevention of infection.

A young child will usually require sedation and analgesia before any attempt at treatment is made, and should be accompanied by a parent or guardian whenever possible. An adult should be treated sympathetically and calmly.

The wound should be gently cleansed of gross contaminants and a non-adherent dressing applied to maintain a moist environment and reduce pain (*Figure 3.1*). The doctor may prescribe a topical antimicrobial preparation, such as Flamazine (silver sulphadiazine) to reduce the risk of clinical infection. A secondary absorbent pad will be required to absorb excess exudate, unless a 'bag' dressing is used (*Colour Plates* **113, 114**) (Walsh, 1989), as exudate may continue to leak from the wound for 24 hours or more. Where required, dressings should be held in place with a tubular bandage rather than a conventional conforming bandage, to reduce the risk of tight bands forming and constricting underlying tissue. Levels of exudate can be reduced by elevation of an affected limb (Section 11.5.4). Oral analgesia may be required for up to 24 hours.

Throughout the procedure the nurse should handle the tissues and the patient gently. The patient or his or her carer should be given appropriate written and verbal instructions for managing the wound, including where and when to have the wound re-dressed (Section 11.5.6). The wound should be reinspected by a senior nurse within 24 hours to ensure that the dressing regimen has proved suitable for the patient's needs and there are no signs or symptoms of developing complications.

Bites Bites can be inflicted by domestic animals, particularly dogs, by wild animals and by humans, and have a high risk of becoming infected (Hadfield, 1988). The wounds are not simple lacerations. There is often a significant degree of contusion and there may be tissue loss. The wound is contaminated by saliva containing a mixture of aerobic and anaerobic organisms, many of which are saprophytic in the oral cavity but can cause virulent infection in skin wounds.

The method of treatment will be decided by the casualty officer and will depend on the severity and site of the injury and the age and general physical condition of the patient. Severe injury may require excision of heavily contaminated and devitalised tissue under general anaesthetic, and also delayed primary closure, such as skin grafting, by a plastic surgeon. In less serious cases, in wounds less than 4 hours old, the wounds may be left open and dressed and the patient given a broad-spectrum systemic antibiotic.

Rabies is a rare complication of bites or scratches by animals, unless the animal is infected. Rabies vaccine is not routinely given to patients bitten in the United Kingdom, but a course of injections may be required if the person was bitten while abroad. It is worth checking the current regulations, as these can change.

11.5.4 Supporting the injured part
After cleansing and dressing a wound it may be necessary to elevate or immobilise an injured part. An injured hand should always be supported at shoulder level and not left in the dependent position. The high arm sling (*Colour Plates* **115, 116**) is the traditional way of giving wrist support or elevating an injured hand to reduce oedema. A versatile alternative is to use collar 'n' cuff sling material (*Colour Plates* **117–119**).

11.5.5 Prevention of infection
All traumatic wounds are highly likely to be contaminated with bacteria and other micro-organisms. Whether or not an infection develops depends on several factors (*Table 11.4*), which are explained in more detail in Chapter 5.

The type of wound is certainly a significant factor. Simple lacerations caused by a sharp object are normally clean, with minimal tissue devitalisation, while contused wounds can contain much devitalised tissue, which encourages the growth of micro-organisms. Extensive

Table 11.4 Factors affecting the development of a clinical wound infection following trauma

---

1. Degree of contamination of the wound
   - type of wound
   - nature and extent of contamination
   - time interval between injury and treatment

2. Virulence of the contaminating organism(s)

3. Susceptibility of the host to infection
   - age
   - co-existing chronic infection
   - immune system disorders
   - nutritional status
   - immunisation status

---

superficial abrasions, caused for instance to pedestrians or cyclists involved in a road traffic accident, can be heavily contaminated with dirt and grit and the underlying tissues may be severely bruised, making the development of infection more likely. In wounds contaminated by soil there is always a risk of tetanus and gas gangrene, especially if the wound is deep and there is extensive necrotic tissue present (but tetanus can develop following very minor scratches for which the patient seeks no medical assistance). Bites by animals or humans have a very high risk of developing infection because of the virulence of the contaminating organisms. Thorough *cleansing* of the wound helps to prevent infection by removing gross contaminants.

The casualty officer will decide whether or not it is beneficial to commence the patient on a course of *a broad-spectrum antibiotic*, bearing in mind the factors listed in *Table 11.4*. A rare but very serious complication following traumatic injury is tetanus. The casualty officer will decide whether or not the patient requires active or passive protection from the organism causing this disease (Westaby, 1985b). Policies can change and it is important to be aware of current regulations in this area.

11.5.6 Patient education
Before the patients leave the A&E Department it is very important that they are given simple instructions relating to local management of the injured site, including, where appropriate:

- Limb elevation.
- How to keep the dressing dry and intact.
- How long the dressing should be kept in place.
- When and where to return for a dressing change or suture removal.
- The signs and symptoms of wound complications.
- When and where to obtain further tetanus injections.

Ideally these instructions should be written down, perhaps on a predesigned information leaflet where personalised instructions can be quickly entered. The nurse should ascertain, through simple questioning, that the patient understands the instructions and that all the patient's questions relating to the wound have been answered.

11.6 Medico-legal aspects

People arriving at the A&E Department with injuries may be the victims of accidental injury in the home, at work, or while participating in a recreational activity; they may be the victims of a criminal assault; or they may have mutilated themselves (*Colour Plate* **120**). They may be unable or unwilling to admit to the precise circumstances in which the injury occurred, but the nature and sites of the injuries may speak for themselves (Mant, 1985).

For any traumatic injury *accurate documentation* of the patient's account of the history of the accident and any information supplied by accompanying friends or relatives is very important, as well as full documentation of the assessment and management of the wound (Section 11.4.4). These written records may form part of the evidence in cases of criminal prosecution, industrial compensation, or where patients or their relatives file a complaint against the health authority alleging negligence by medical or nursing staff.

11.7 Non-accidental injury in children

There is a growing body of information on indicators of possible non-accidental injury (NAI) to children, including traumatic sub-arachnoid haemorrhage (Sivaloganathan, 1990), occult eye damage (Levy *et al.*, 1990), and unusual fractures (King *et al.*, 1988). More references to the shaken baby syndrome, the sexually abused battered child and the history of child abuse are given in the Further reading section of this chapter.

When assessing a child with traumatic injuries the nurse needs to be alert to the possibility of NAI:

- Has the accident just occurred, or has there been a considerable delay in reporting it?
- Is there an obvious discrepancy between the nature of the injuries and the parents' account of how the injuries happened?
- Are there finger marks, bite marks, or cigarette burns (*Colour Plates* **121, 122**)?

If NAI is suspected the casualty officer will perform a full physical examination of the child and ask for a second opinion from a paediatrician. It is very important that throughout the procedure both child and parents are dealt with very sympathetically. Things are not always what they seem! A child may be a frequent visitor to the department, may be dirty and covered in bruises but may be very much loved, while an immaculately dressed, polite child with professional parents may be neglected in subtle psychological ways or be physically, possibly sexually, abused. Guidelines on procedures to be followed in the case of suspected NAI will be laid down by the local Health Authority. Normally the Health Visitor and Social Work Department will need to be involved. Action may be required to obtain a place of safety order for the child and a criminal prosecution could result.

Further reading

General

Bradley, D. (ed.) (1988), *Accident and Emergency Nursing* (2nd edn). Bailliere Tindall, London.

Walsh, M. (1989), *Accident and Emergency Nursing: A New Approach*. Heinemann Nursing Books, Oxford.

Westaby, S. and Thorn, A. (1985), Treatment of wounds in the Accident and Emergency Department. In Westaby, S. (ed.), *Wound Care*, pp. 98–109. Heinemann Medical Books, London.

Major traumatic wounds

Beverly, M. and Coombs, R. (1985), The management of compound fractures. In Westaby, S. (ed.), *Wound Care*, pp. 121–130. Heinemann Medical Books, London.

Bradley, D. (1988), Care of major traumatic emergencies. In Bradley, D. (ed.), *Accident and Emergency Nursing* (2nd edn), pp. 53–72. Baillière Tindall, London.

Evans, R.F. (1979), The patient with multiple injuries. *Br. J. Hosp. Med.*, **22**, 329–332.

Muir, I.F.K., Barclay, T.L. and Settle, J.A.D. (1987), *Burns and Their Treatment* (3rd edn). Butterworths, London.

Owen Smith, M. (1985), Wounds caused by the weapons of war. In Westaby, S. (ed.), *Wound Care*, pp. 110–120. Heinemann Medical Books, London.

Westaby, S. (1985), Penetrating wounds of the chest and abdomen. In Westaby, S. (ed.), *Wound Care*, pp. 138–146. Heinemann Medical Books, London.

Non-accidental injury in children

Duhaime, A.C. *et al.* (1987), The shaken baby syndrome. A clinical, pathological and biomechanical study. *J. Neurosurg.*, **66**(3), 409–415.

Hobbs, C.J. and Wynne, J.M. (1990), The sexually abused battered child. *Arch. Dis. Child*, **65**(4), 423–427.

Knight, B. (1986), The history of child abuse. *Forensic Sci. Int.*, **30**(2–3), 135–141.

O'Doherty, N. (1982), *The Battered Child*. Baillière Tindall, London.

References

Bradley, D. (ed.) (1988), Accident and Emergency Nursing (2nd edn). Ballière Tindall, London.

Evans, R.F. (1979), The patient with multiple injuries. *Br. J. Hosp. Med.*, **22**, 329–332.

Hadfield, L. (1988), Putting the bite on. *Nurs. Stand.*, 30 April, 22–24.

Haury, B. *et al.* (1980), Débridement: an essential component of traumatic wound care. In Hunt, T.K. (ed.), *Wound Healing and Wound Infection: Theory and Surgical Practice*, pp. 229–240. Appleton-Century Crofts, New York.

King, J. *et al.* (1988), Analysis of 429 fractures in 189 battered children. *J. Pediatr. Orthop.*, **8**(5), 585–589.

Kirk, R.M. (1989), *Basic Surgical Techniques* (3rd edn). Churchill Livingstone, Edinburgh.

Levy, I. *et al.* (1990), Occult ocular damage as a leading sign in the battered child syndrome. *Metab. Pediatr. Syst. Ophthalmol.*, **13**(1), 20–22.

Mansfield, A.O. and Bradley, J.W.P. (1985), Wounds involving major blood vessels. In Westaby, S. (ed.), *Wound Care*, pp. 131–137. Heinemann Medical Books, London.

Mant, A.K. (1985), Some medico-legal aspects of wounds. In Westaby, S. (ed.), *Wound Care*, pp. 190–200. Heinemann Medical Books, London.

Muir, I.F.K., Barclay, T.L. and Settle, J.A.D. (1987), *Burns and Their Treatment* (3rd edn). Butterworths, London.

Sivaloganathan, S. (1990), Traumatic sub-arachnoid haemorrhage as part of the NAI syndrome. *Med. Sci. Law*, **30**(2), 138–140.

Walsh, M. (1989), *Accident and Emergency Nursing: a New Approach*. Heinemann Nursing, Oxford.

Westaby, S. (1985a), *Wound Care*. Heinemann Medical Books, London.

Westaby, S. (1985b), Tetanus and antibiotic prophylaxis. In Westaby, S. (ed.), *Wound Care*, pp. 91–97. Heinemann Medical Books, London.

12   *Patient Education*

12.1   Why educate patients?

Disease and disability can involve threats not only to physical well-being but also to a person's self-image, social and occupational functioning, and emotional equilibrium (Cohen and Lazarus, 1979; Burns, 1980; Weinman, 1982a).

The consequences of a wound to an individual will depend on many factors, including the site and type of wound, degree of functional disability, visibility of scarring, the availability of social support, the level of economic independence, the person's personality and personal philosophy, and the accuracy of the appraisal by the person of his or her prognosis (*Figure 1.5*). The importance of assessing the potential consequences of a wound for the individual is discussed in Chapter 2.

Counselling a patient with a wound which is likely to have long-term effects, such as a mastectomy wound, an amputation, or a colostomy, requires great sensitivity. It involves assessing the patient's personality and cognitive abilities, deciding on the level and amount of information that the person requires and when and how to impart it, and how to evaluate whether the counselling has been beneficial. Providing information is important: the knowledge gained can be used by patients as a resource in coping with pain (Hayward, 1975) and the stresses associated with hospitalisation (Burns, 1980; Weinman, 1982b). However, accurate information and understanding is not enough. Successful patient education motivates patients to take responsibility for their own health, to the limit of their ability.

It involves encouraging patients to change their behaviour in positive ways, which will promote health and wellbeing. This is no easy task, especially when the behavioural changes required involve giving up long-held strategies aimed at coping with stress, such as overeating, smoking and over-indulgence in alcohol, or long-term compliance with a particular treatment regime.

Because bringing about positive behavioural change is often not easy, the first step is to create a therapeutic environment which

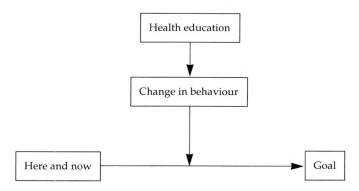

Figure 12.1. Education for change.

encourages the patient to engage in the learning process and which motivates the patient to *want* to change unhelpful behaviour.

12.2 Creating a therapeutic environment for learning

The basis of all effective education is *empathy* between the educator and the patient. Empathy involves understanding patients' feelings about a situation from *their* perspective and communicating this understanding to them in a way which indicates awareness of and respect for them as individuals and acknowledges their specific needs.

In a therapeutic relationship, patients are helped to understand where they are (the here and now) in relation to where they would like to be (the goal) (*Figure 12.1*). Effective, patient-centred communication is a prerequisite for success (*Table 12.1*). Hospitalisation is in itself a stressful experience which produces a less than ideal environment for learning. The learning process is further hindered by non-therapeutic communication (*Table 12.2*).

12.3 Assessment

The first stage in planning an individualised health education pro-gramme is assessment of the patient's existing knowledge, cognitive abilities, and specific problems and needs (Chapter 2).

Empathy encourages:

- More accurate understanding between nurse and patient.
- Greater flow of information.
- Rapid correction of misunderstandings.
- High levels of morale in both parties.

Table 12.1 The basic elements of therapeutic, patient-centred communication

Physical closeness: the nurse indicates to patient that she is willing to become involved.
Active listening: the nurse communicates her interest in the patient non-verbally.
Open-ended comments: the patient is allowed to determine the direction that the interaction should take.
Acknowledgement: of patient's comments as of value.
Restating/seeking clarification: the nurse confirms the accuracy of her own appraisal of the patient's problems, at the same time demonstrating a desire to understand the problem from the patient's perspective.
Focusing/summarising: helps to clarify the most important issues for both parties.
Mutual decision making: deciding on goals and future actions together in a way which emphasises the patient's involvement.

Table 12.2 Indicators of non-therapeutic communication

Maintaining a distance/walking away: the nurse suggests that she is unwilling to interact with the patient, or regards interaction as a low priority.
Failure to listen: the nurse places her needs above those of the patient and demonstrates a lack of interest and concern.
Changing the topic: indicates to patient that the nurse is in control of what can and cannot be discussed, negates concept of mutuality.
Peremptory reassurance: denies validity of patient's fears and feelings.
Being judgmental/giving advice: by imposing her own assessment of the situation the nurse is denying the patient's rights to have opinions and make decisions.

The nurse needs to be able to define the patient's *learning needs* and the patient's *readiness* for health education. The needs of a young paraplegic patient with a large sacral pressure sore are likely to be very different from the needs of an elderly but normally sprightly lady who develops a pressure sore while on bed rest for a pulmonary embolism.

A patient's readiness for health education may be inhibited by physical factors, such as poorly controlled pain or disturbed sleep patterns, or psychosocial factors, such as a recent bereavement.

12.4 Planning

This involves:

- Determining short-, medium-, and long-term learning objectives.
- Selecting the most appropriate teaching strategies for the patient and the subject matter.
- Developing ways of evaluating the effectiveness of the teaching–learning experience.

Teaching strategies might include group discussions, demonstrations, use of video tapes, slides, models, books, and pamphlets. A very readable account of teaching strategies is given by Coutts and Hardy (1985). Examples of patient information leaflets, written for alert patients and/or their carers, are given in Appendices to the chapters on pressure sores (Chapter 6), leg ulcers (Chapter 7), and other chronic wounds (Chapter 8).

12.5   Implementation and evaluation

Implementation involves putting the teaching plan into action, using language the patient can understand, at an appropriate time. Ewles and Simnett (1985) have identified some of the basic principles of effective teaching:

Work from the known to the unknown.
Maximise patient involvement.
Use a variety of teaching methods.
Ensure relevance of material to patient's needs.
Identify realistic goals.
Organise the material into a logical framework.

It is important to try to assess the extent to which the learning objectives have been achieved, by gently probing questions to test the patient's understanding of the subject and by observing whether the patient's behaviour has changed in a way which will promote health.

Further reading

Patient education and counselling

Burnand, P. (1989), *Counselling Skills for Health Professionals*. Chapman and Hall, London.

Claxton, G. (1984), *Live and Learn: An Introduction to the Psychology of Growth and Change in Everyday Life*. Harper and Row, London.

Coutts, L.C. and Hardy, L.K. (1985), *Teaching for Health: the Nurse as Health Educator*. Churchill Livingstone, Edinburgh.

Ewles, L. and Simnett, I. (1985), *Promoting Health: A Practical Guide to Health Education*. Wiley, New York.

Rogers, C.R. (1980), *A Way of Being*. Houghton Mifflin, New York.

Smith, R.E. and Birrell, J. (1990), Encouraging compliance. In *The Staff Nurse's Survival Guide*, pp. 27–29. The Professional Developments Series, Austen Cornish, London.

Psychology and health

Gatchel, R.J. and Baum, A. (1983), *An Introduction to Health Psychology*. Addison Wesley, London.

Rachman, S.J. and Philips, C. (1978). *Psychology and Medicine*. Penguin, London.
Weinman, J. (1982), *An Outline of Psychology as Applied to Medicine*. John Wright, Bristol.

References

Burns, R. B. (1980), Admission to hospital. In *Essential Psychology*, pp. 269–285. MTP Press, Lancaster

Cohen, F. and Lazarus, R.S. (1979), Coping with the stresses of illness. In Stone, G.C. *et al.* (eds), *Health Psychology—a Handbook*. Jossey-Bass, San Francisco.

Coutts, L.C. and Hardy, L.K. (1985), *Teaching for Health: the Nurse as Health Educator*. Churchill Livingstone, Edinburgh.

Ewles L. and Simnett, I. (1985), *Promoting Health: a Practical Guide to Health Education*. Wiley, New York.

Hayward, J. (1975), *Information: a Prescription against Pain*. Royal College of Nursing, London.

Weinman, J. (1982a), Psychological reactions to physical illness and handicap. In *An Outline of Psychology as Applied to Medicine*, pp. 206–221. John Wright, Bristol.

Weinman, J. (1982b), Psychosocial aspects of hospitalisation. In *An Outline of Psychology as Applied to Medicine*, pp. 222–236. John Wright, Bristol.

13 Case Studies

13.1 Introduction

The case studies which follow can be used for individual work, or form the basis of group work, with feedback and general discussion. When deciding on assessment or treatment methods there is *no one correct answer* but it is important for facilitators to identify which assessment methods are essential, which desirable, and which are unnecessary, and to recognise which methods of treatment could be *hazardous*. In all cases the rationale for suggested assessment and treatment methods should be given.

The following framework and questions may help anyone working through the case studies to organise their thoughts in a logical way.

Assessment of the patient

    1a What are the local problems at the wound site?

    1b How do you propose to record these?

    2 What was the immediate cause of the wound?

    3 Is there any evidence of underlying pathology which may:
- Affect wound healing in general?
- Contribute to delayed healing of this particular wound?

    4 Are there any tests/assessments which the nurse could/should do to try to determine the underlying cause of the wound? If yes, what, how, and when?

    5 Should the patient be referred for specialist assessment? If so, to whom, what tests and/or investigations may be performed, and what may be involved for the patient?

    6 Are there any more general patient factors, including psychological and social factors, which could lead to delayed wound healing for this patient?

Planning and implementing care

    1a What are the options for treating the wound itself?

    1b Which would you choose in this case, and why?

2 How might you manage more general factors which could delay wound healing?

3 Would you involve patients or their carers in planning the care? If so, how?

4 Do you need to give the patient any special advice or practical instructions? If so, what and how?

5 Indicate any circumstances in which you would consult the doctor or paramedical colleagues.

Evaluation of care

How and when would you evaluate the effectiveness of the care you propose to give?

Long-term plans

Outline a long-term plan for the patient's care, including:

1 Planned patient education.

2 Any follow-up care that might be required in the community, where the scenario begins in hospital.

13.2   Case studies

Case Study 1

David Jones is a 22-year-old paraplegic living in a local nursing home where he is very happy. He is admitted to hospital for surgery and develops a sacral pressure sore, approximately 3 cm in diameter, which becomes infected with a methicillin-resistant strain of *Staphylococcus aureus*. The wound is malodorous and sloughy. David has had several previous hospital admissions for operative correction of bilateral knee flexion contractures and division of dorsiflexions in his (L) ankle. He blames the doctors for his current infection and has been labelled as a 'difficult and uncooperative patient'. He weighs 35 kg.

Case Study 2

Martin is 6 years old and has grazed both his knees and the palms of his hands after falling from his bicycle on the gravel drive leading into his school. The school secretary has brought him into the Accident and Emergency Department. Martin is rather distressed.

Case Study 3

Mrs Smith is a 65-year-old, rather obese lady, living alone in a first floor flat. She has a superficial sloughy ulcer, approximately 2 cm in diameter, over the medial malleolus. The skin above the ulcer is pigmented and Mrs Smith has some peripheral oedema.

Case Study 4

Mr Green is a 50-year-old former college lecturer who had an abdomi-noperineal excision of rectum to remove a tumour two years ago. He has been re-admitted to a surgical ward with a history of weight loss over the last six months. He is 6ft 3in tall and now weighs 40 kg. He is taken to theatre and found to have extensive metastases. The surgeon closes the laparotomy wound and the patient returns to the ward for terminal care.

It is now 12 days after surgery. Alternate sutures have been removed from the wound. His colostomy is now functioning and is producing large quantities of liquid yellow faecal material and a considerable amount of flatus. After an evening visiting, his colostomy bag becomes detached and his wound dressing is heavily contaminated with faecal material. He expresses to the nurses feelings of disgust and mortification at the mess that he is in and the wound is re-dressed.

On re-dressing the laparotomy wound 3 days later, the nurse notices that it is producing copious quantities of foul-smelling grey/cream coloured exudate. There is marked erythema around the remaining sutures and the edges of the wound have come apart in two places. Results from a wound swab indicate that the wound is infected with *Clostridium welchii*.

Case Study 5

Mr Brown is a 48-year-old newly diagnosed insulin-dependent diabetic who has been admitted to hospital with an ulcer, approximately 4 cm × 2 cm, on the upper aspect of his right foot. There is some black necrotic tissue in the wound and the tendons to two toes are visible. There is dry scaly skin on both legs from ankle to knee. He works in a factory and is divorced. He went to a school for educationally subnormal children but now appears to be coping well, alone at home. His sister visits occasionally. He is very frightened of needles and is, as yet, unable to administer his own insulin.

Case Study 6

Mr Young is a 45-year-old bus driver who has had a chronic pilonidal sinus radically excised 2 days ago. He is anxious to be discharged home and to return to work as soon as possible. The wound bed is clean.

Case Study 7

Sarah is 16. She is brought to the Accident and Emergency Department in her dressing gown, by her mother, with a burn on her forearm. Sarah refuses to say how the burn happened, or to give any other information. The skin over the burn is pale and insensitive to a light pinprick.

Case Study 8
Timothy is 3 years old. He is brought to the Accident and Emergency Department by his grandmother, with a suspected fractured humerus. It transpires that the accident occurred several hours ago. Timothy's parents have remained at home 'because they don't like hospitals'. Timothy himself appears to be rather withdrawn.

Case Study 9
Mrs Fairbairn is a 45-year-old woman with seven children. She has inoperable malodorous, malignant breast carcinoma. The tissue is friable and Mrs Fairbairn is in considerable pain. She refuses to go into hospital and asks her GP if he will arrange for the community nurse to help her to look after the wound at home.

Case Study 10
Mr Roberts is a 30-year-old garage mechanic who arrives alone at the Accident and Emergency Department with a deep laceration to the palm of his hand, having put his hand through a plate glass window. He is anxious to return to his workplace as soon as possible.

Many of these wounds are a manifestation of an underlying pathophysiological problem that may or may not be amenable for treatment. All can be challenging.

Index

Numbers in bold type refer to colour plates.

213